PRAISE FOR PREVIOUS E[...]

D0830326

North Caro[...]

Off the Beaten Path®

"Includes tips on [the] best places to eat and sleep, little-known gems, and how to bypass the tourist traps."

—*The Salisbury Post* (N.C.)

"Fascinating reading . . . a melange of sites, restaurants, lodgings, and directions leading to the author['s] personal choices. Lovingly written . . . enthusiastically testif[ies] to the old notion about seeing America first."

—*Booklist*, American Library Association

"Reveals features [that] will attract even those who had not planned on ever visiting the state. When they do, this will be the handbook to choose."

—*Midwest Book Review*

"The off-the-beaten-path traveler is assured of enjoying these discoveries as much as the author did."

—*Bookpage*

"Ms. Pitzer writes with enthusiasm and knowledge. When she says someplace is worth visiting, you can count on it."

—*The State* (Columbia, S.C.)

"When you're accompanied by *North Carolina: Off the Beaten Path,* it's like having your own personal tour guide."

—*Southern Living*

Help Us Keep This Guide Up to Date

Every effort has been made by the author and editors to make this guide as accurate and useful as possible. However, many changes can occur after a guide is published—establishments close, phone numbers change, hiking trails are rerouted, facilities come under new management, etc.

We would love to hear from you concerning your experiences with this guide and how you feel it could be improved and be kept up to date. While we may not be able to respond to all comments and suggestions, we'll take them to heart, and we'll make certain to share them with the author. Please send your comments and suggestions to the following address:

The Globe Pequot Press
Reader Response/Editorial Department
P.O. Box 480
Guilford, CT 06437

Or you may e-mail us at: editorial@GlobePequot.com

Thanks for your input, and happy travels!

INSIDERS' GUIDE®

OFF THE BEATEN PATH® SERIES

Off the Beaten Path®

SEVENTH EDITION

north carolina

A GUIDE TO UNIQUE PLACES

SARA PITZER

INSIDERS' GUIDE®

GUILFORD, CONNECTICUT

AN IMPRINT OF THE GLOBE PEQUOT PRESS

The prices, rates, and hours listed in this guidebook were confirmed at press time. We recommend, however, that you call establishments to obtain current information before traveling.

INSIDERS' GUIDE®

Text design by Linda Loiewski
Maps created by Equator Graphics © The Globe Pequot Press
Illustrations by Carole Drong
Spot photography throughout © Mike Dobel/Masterfile

ISBN 0-7627-3050-1
ISSN 1539-7769

Manufactured in the United States of America
Seventh Edition/First Printing

Herewith I dedicate this volume to Dr. Jon Crane, esteemed researcher and faithful friend, my north star of the Internet. Please believe me, Sir, I remain your humbly grateful servant.

NORTH CAROLINA

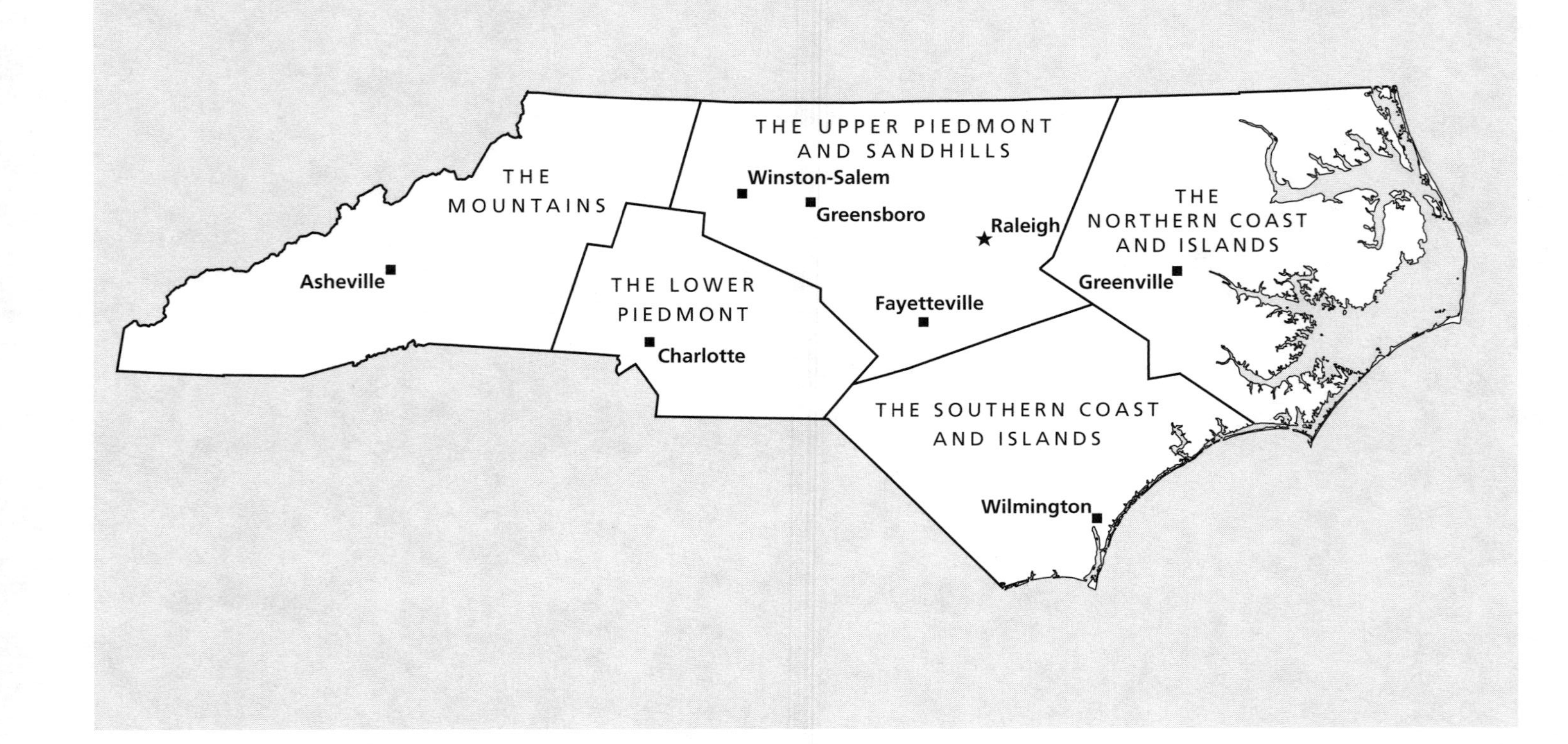

Contents

Acknowledgments

Many of the photographs from which the drawings in this book were made were provided by the North Carolina Division of Travel and Tourism.

Introduction

I was lost—again—somewhere around Raleigh, but nowhere near the place I wanted to be. I'd already pulled into the entrance of a large industrial park, where an executive stopped on his way out to ask if he could help me. I'd already walked along the sidewalk in front of North Carolina State University, where a professor leaving campus gave me detailed instructions on getting out of the city in the direction I wanted to go. And I was pretty sure I was going to get it right, if I could just find the beltway. Seeing that the car in the next lane had both windows down as we waited for a light to turn, I called across to the driver, "Is this road going to take me to the beltway?"

"Where do you want to go?" he yelled back. I told him. "Follow me," he shouted, and when the light changed, took off in a cloud of exhaust. I followed him nearly 10 miles. At the proper entrance onto the beltway, he blinked his turn signal and also pointed emphatically with his left hand, just in case I missed the signal. I turned. He was already gone, leaving me with a grin and a wave.

And that's how people in North Carolina are.

For me, living in North Carolina is no accident of birth or whim of corporate transfer; it's a studied choice. When my husband and I decided that we should both work freelance, it meant that we could live pretty much wherever we wanted to. We spent the better part of a year looking for a place where the topography was appealing, the climate was sunny and temperate, the economy was thriving, and the people were nice. We found North Carolina.

In the years since we moved here in 1983, life has been one joyful discovery about the state after another. Indeed, sometimes it seems too good to believe. Many mornings I wake up thinking: Today's the day I'm going to be disappointed. But I never am.

In 1993 my husband, Croy, died of ALS (Lou Gehrig's Disease). In a way it was the happiest year of his life. Although his body deteriorated, his mind did not, so he knew and understood every day the remarkable friendship and love that our North Carolina friends, neighbors, and business associates showered upon him without restraint. The last photograph ever taken of Croy, a week before he died, shows him sitting by our pool in the sun at the edge of the woods, surrounded by his friends. The sky was Carolina blue, the people were joking, and everybody, including Croy, was laughing. He often said, "This is the most wonderful place on earth." And that day, after sharing a decade of discoveries in North Carolina, we knew it was true more than ever.

I'm making the discoveries on my own now. It tells you a lot about North Carolina that there are still lots of laughing friends around and that the experience continues to delight me. I know you'll enjoy my discoveries, too.

Take the barbecue, for instance. Two authors writing an article on southern barbecue for *Cook's* magazine traveled through several states looking for the best barbecue restaurants, but they were not able to get to North Carolina. They apologized in their article, because, they said, in comparison, nothing else is barbecue at all. (North Carolina barbecue is always pork cooked over a wood fire, never prepared in a sauce, and usually served with slaw and hush puppies.)

Then there's the pottery. This state has scores and scores of potters, working in the historic old production styles and in contemporary studio modes, producing such a variety of work that a collection could easily crowd everything else from a room.

Wineries are catching on too, scores of them, with vineyards thriving in the sunny climate.

As for topography, North Carolina has some of the oldest mountains in the world, the largest natural sand dune on the East Coast, and some of the most unspoiled beaches and islands in the country. The rich soil of the Piedmont and foothills grows apples, vegetables, Christmas trees, cotton, and tobacco, a problematic crop with much historic significance.

Also historically important, North Carolina, one of the thirteen original colonies, played key roles in the Revolutionary War, the Civil War, and World Wars I and II. The area is rich in Indian history; blacks made many early significant advances here; and the Moravians created a historic settlement at Old Salem. The Wright brothers first accomplished powered flight in North Carolina, on a site that is popular today with hang gliders more interested in playing than in setting records.

Each of the three major geographic areas of the state—the coastal plain, the Piedmont, and the mountains—differs radically from the others. It's almost like traveling through three smaller states. The nature of each region influenced the kinds of commerce that flourished historically and that continue to flourish and also left a mark on the people. As you travel you'll hear fascinating changes in the music of the accents of people native to each region.

The coastal plain accounts for almost two-fifths of the state's area. The North Carolina coast has been considered dangerous since the first settlers tried to cope with its ever-changing beaches, currents, and waterways. There was no guarantee that just because you had safely sailed into a particular port once, you would find it safe, or even open, the next time you tried. That's at least one reason why English colonization shifted up toward the Chesapeake and why North Carolina was settled more sparsely and slowly than some other colonies were. Even today you'll find areas that are remarkably sparsely settled compared to most states' coastal regions. For vacationers the main activities and sightseeing highlights are related to the same activities that have long supported the area economically—fishing, boating, and beachgoing.

In the Piedmont, which makes up about another two-fifths of the state, you'll find mostly rolling hills and red clay. Although the clay is harder to work than the sandy soil of the coast, it seems to have held its fertility better against some pretty bad early farming habits. (Wherever they are grown, cotton and tobacco are notorious for wearing out the soil.) Since the Piedmont doesn't have many large stretches of flat land, it didn't invite the huge plantations that had to be worked with many slaves. Smaller family farms were often worked by the people who owned them, perhaps with some hired help. The historians Hugh Talmage Lefler and Albert Ray Newsome point out in their classic *The History of a State: North Carolina* that the narrow, swift streams of the Piedmont, which weren't worth much for transportation, were great for generating power. And that, along with the presence of hardwoods and other resources, accounts for the great number of manufacturing activities that flourish in the Piedmont. Here you find lots of attractions related to manufacturing—tobacco museums, furniture showrooms, and more outlet stores than you can count. Probably because of the past concentration of moneyed manufacturers and merchants, you'll also find rich lodes of cultural attractions and arts here.

The mountains make up the smallest part of the state, but they compensate in interest and beauty for what they lack in area. Some of the highest mountains in the Appalachians are here. As anyone who drives in the mountains knows, transportation is difficult. In earlier times it was nearly impossible; hence the development of small pockets of civilization separated by stretches of wilderness, creating those tough, independent, resourceful, self-sufficient folks—mountain people. This kind of early self-sufficiency and distance from major metropolitan areas made the growth of all kinds of crafts almost inevitable. The mountains are still the richest source of handcrafts in the state.

Although tourism and technology have homogenized somewhat the state's regional populations, you can still find lots of those tall, thin, rangy people. It remains a pretty good joke in the Piedmont for a young woman marrying outside the area to claim she's found herself a mountain man.

As a place to play, the state offers hiking and white-water rafting, waterskiing and snow skiing, freshwater and saltwater fishing and boating, athletics, auto racing, horseback riding, and golf on some of the most famous courses in the country.

Face it, you're not going to be able to do it all or see it all in one trip, or even in ten trips. Don't try to squeeze too much into a single trip, or you'll end up driving a lot and not doing much else. But the driving you do shouldn't be unpleasant if you avoid the interstates around major cities at rush hour and accept the fact that the two-lane roads tend to be well maintained but slow, since there are few good places for passing slow drivers and tractors. To understand the roads and decide when to travel on a major highway and when to get onto secondary roads, you'll definitely need a state map. The best one is the North Carolina transportation map, issued by the North Carolina Department of Transportation and the Division of Travel and Tourism (800–847–4862). You may pick one up free at a welcome center or receive it by writing North Carolina Division of Travel and Tourism, 430 North Salisbury Street, Raleigh 27611.

If you or those traveling with you are in any way physically challenged, you should also request a copy of the book *Access, North Carolina*. This is a remarkably good book published by the North Carolina Department of Human Resources, the Division of Vocational Rehabilitation Services, and the Division of Travel and Tourism. It briefly describes historic sites, state and national parks and forests, and general-interest attractions, focusing on their accessibility of parking, entrance, interior rooms, exterior areas, and restrooms. The book is free. Call the aforementioned tourism number, or check the Web site: www.ncnatural.com/access-nc/.

A state with so many resources inevitably becomes the subject of many books. Depending on your interests, you may find several of them interesting to use along with this guide. The University of North Carolina Press publishes *Turners and Burners: The Folk Potters of North Carolina*, by Charles G. Zug III, the most complete explication of the subject available. The press also publishes many books about North Carolina history. For further information, write University of North Carolina Press, P.O. Box 2288, Chapel Hill 27514.

If you are a devotee of back roads, you may enjoy Earl Thollander's *Back Roads of the Carolinas,* devoted entirely to "nonhighway" drives along roads that often aren't on regular maps. Thollander designed the book, lettered the text in calligraphy, and drew the maps and wash illustrations himself. Often Thollander suggests a dirt road or other obscure route from one historic point to another, which you could use as a much, much slower alternative to the routes I suggest. It is published by Clarkson N. Potter, Inc., 299 Park Avenue, New York, NY 10171. Finally, the North Carolina publisher John F. Blair (1406 Plaza Drive, Winston-Salem 27103-1485) offers several books about the history and ecology of the North Carolina coast, plus an appealing book of photographs and native comment, *Ocracoke Portrait*, by Ann Ehringhaus. It's especially fun to read such books ahead of time and then carry them with you to consult, because the material comes alive as you see the subject matter firsthand.

With or without the books, though, North Carolina comes alive when you travel here because of its people. Significant history, appealing countryside, even good food can be part of any well-planned trip. Adding helpful, friendly, almost uniformly cheerful people changes the mix from plain cake to an angel food celebration. In the years I've been traveling almost continuously about the state, I've not had a single unpleasant experience with a North Carolinian. Unless you carry a chip the size of one of Mount Mitchell's ancient trees on your shoulder, you won't either. And if you're in that bad a mood, don't come. If you can't have fun in North Carolina, you can't enjoy yourself anywhere. Might as well stay home.

Maybe I shouldn't have talked so loud. Maybe I shouldn't have been so enthusiastic. Maybe I shot myself in the foot, big time, because North Carolina has been discovered. It happened fast. Not long ago the state was pretty much all off the beaten path, except for development around Raleigh and Durham, Greensboro, and more recently, Charlotte. But within the past few years, the population has soared; housing developments and shopping malls circle not only the major cities but many of the smaller towns as well. Suddenly there's a Wendy's and a car wash at every intersection. Ever-widening highways cover great expanses that used to be woods or farmland or fishing holes with concrete and macadam. Let's face it, we're talking about sprawl here, just as it's happened, for instance, in places like parts of California; around Atlanta, Georgia; and in the Pocono Mountains of Pennsylvania. That's the bad news.

But it's the good news, too, because with the rush of growth, some people are getting worried about losing what makes this place special, and they're acting decisively to preserve some of it. Two examples come to mind at once— the little town of Hillsborough, up near the Virginia border, and the city of

NORTH CAROLINA GENERAL WEB SITES

North Carolina Division of Tourism
www.visitnc.com

Bed-and-Breakfasts and Inns
www.bbonline.com/nc/ncbbi

African-American Heritage
www.ncculturetour.org

Golf in North Carolina
www.visitnc.com/golf

Sports in North Carolina
www.nccommerce.com/sports

North Carolina Crafts
www.discovercraftnc.org

Native American Culture
www.cherokeeheritagetrails.org

Salisbury at the center of the state. In places like this and in other communities, residents are emphasizing historic preservation and working to keep their downtowns vital.

Along with this development, another new dimension has changed North Carolina—the immigration of Hispanic and Asian people as well as people from European countries, a result of the evolving global economy. Many Hispanics have come to find jobs better than those at home. They've often started out in the jobs nobody else seemed willing to do, like the hot, heavy work of making bricks and quarrying granite and cleaning shopping malls. But as their hard work pays off and the children move up in school, the Hispanic population is becoming a force in the state. Mexican restaurants and stores selling the kinds of ingredients with which Hispanics cook dot most communities, while supermarkets try to keep up with the new customers too. Similarly, Asian immigrants have brought their influence, reflected in Thai, Vietnamese, Korean, and Chinese restaurants, even in smaller towns. Add to that the influence of transplanted Yankees with their demands for bagels and Philadelphia cheese steaks, Italians who like their prosciutto and salami, and vegetarian Muslims, and you've got the core of a surprisingly sophisticated population in an area that once consisted almost entirely of down-home Southerners. Their shops

NORTH CAROLINA WELCOME CENTERS

North Carolina Welcome Centers
4324 Mail Service Center
Raleigh 27699-4324
(919) 733–7552
www.commerce.state.nc.us/tourism/welcome

Interstate 26
Columbus
(828) 894–2120

Interstate 40 West
Clyde
(828) 627–6206

Interstate 77 North
Dobson
(336) 320–2181

Interstate 77 South
Charlotte
(704) 588–2660

Interstate 85 North
Norlina
(252) 456–3236

Interstate 85 South
Kings Mountain
(704) 937–7861

Interstate 95 North
Roanoke Rapids
(252) 537–9836

Interstate 95 South
Rowland
(910) 422–8314

and restaurants have become part of the state and worthy of off-the-beaten-path status.

What it means is that even if you've been here before, visiting North Carolina now is a whole new experience.

North Carolina has state parks and recreation areas that are visited by twelve million visitors every year. Many have camping, fishing, and hiking. Some offer special educational programs. Some are developed, while others remain wild. For full details check the Web site: www.ncparks.net.

North Carolina State Parks

IN THE MOUNTAINS

Burnsville
Mount Mitchell
(828) 675–4611

Connelly Springs
South Mountains
(828) 433–4772

Jefferson
Mount Jefferson State Natural Area
(336) 246–9653

Jefferson
New River
(336) 982–2587

Nebo
Lake James
(828) 652–5047

Roaring Gap
Stone Mountain
(336) 957–8185

Sapphire
Gorges
(828) 966–9099

IN THE PIEDMONT AND SANDHILLS

Albemarle
Morrow Mountain
(704) 982–4402

Apex
Jordan Lake State Recreation Area
(919) 362–0586

Danbury
Hanging Rock
(336) 593–8480

Durham
Eno River
(919) 383–1686

Henderson
Kerr Lake State Recreation Area
(252) 438–7791

Hillsborough
Occoneechee Mountain
(919) 383–1686

Hollister
Medoc Mountain
(252) 586–6588

Kings Mountain
Crowders Mountain
(704) 853–5375

Lillington
Raven Rock
(910) 893–4888

Orrum
Lumber River
(910) 628–9844

Pinnacle
Pilot Mountain
(336) 325–2355

Raleigh
William B. Umstead–Crabtree
(919) 571–4170

Raleigh
William B. Umstead–Reedy Creek
(919) 571–4170

Seven Springs
Cliffs of the Neuse
(919) 778–6234

Southern Pines
Weymouth Woods
(910) 692–2167

Troutman
Lake Norman
(704) 528–6350

Wake Forest
Falls Lake State Recreational Area
(919) 676–1027

AT THE COAST

Atlantic Beach
Fort Macon
(252) 726–3775

Carolina Beach
Carolina Beach
(910) 458–8206

Creswell
Pettigrew
(252) 797–4475

Elizabethtown
Jones Lake
(910) 588–4550

Gatesville
Merchants Millpond
(252) 357–1191

Kelly
Singletary Lake
(910) 669–2928

Kure Beach
Fort Fisher State Recreational Area
(910) 458–5798

Lake Waccamaw
Lake Waccamaw
(910) 646–4748

Nags Head
Jockey's Ridge
(252) 441–7132

Pine Knoll Shores
Theodore Roosevelt Natural Area
(252) 726–3775

Swansboro
Hammocks Beach
(910) 326–4881

Washington
Goose Creek
(252) 923–2191

Wineries and Vineyards in North Carolina

www.ncwine.org

THE MOUNTAINS

Asheville
Biltmore Estate Winery
(800) 543–2961

Boomer
Cerminaro Vineyard and Winery
(828) 754–9306

Candler
Ritler Ridge Vineyards
(826) 665–7405

Laurel Springs
Thistle Meadow Winery
(800) 233–1505

Ronda
Windy Gap Vineyards
(336) 984–3926

Sparta
Chateau Laurinda
(800) 650–3236

Tryon
Rockhouse Vineyards and Winery
(828) 863–2784

Union Mills
The Teensy Winery
(828) 287–7763

Valdese
Waldensian Heritage Wines
(828) 879–3202

HEARTLAND

Albemarle
Dennis Vineyards Winery
(800) 230–1743

Stony Mountain Vineyard
(704) 982–4402

Boonville
Rag Apple Lassi Winery
(336) 367–6000

Black Wolf Vineyards
(336) 374–2532

Dobson
Shelton Vineyards
(336) 366–4724

Germanton
Germanton Vineyard and Winery
(336) 962–2075

Hamptonville
Laurel Gray Vineyards
(336) 468–8463

Lewisville
Westbend Vineyards
(336) 945–5023

Mocksville
RayLen Vineyards and Winery
(336) 988–3100

Morrisville
Chatham Hill Winery
(919) 380–7135 or
(800) 808–6768

Mount Airy
Old North State Winery
(336) 789–9463

Round Rock Winery
(336) 352–5595

Pine Level
Hennant Family Vineyards
(919) 965–3350

Pittsboro
Silk Hope Winery
(919) 742–4601 or
(800) 316–3829

Salisbury
Old Stone Vineyard and Winery
(704) 279–0939

Yadkinville
Hanover Park Vineyard
(336) 463–2875

COAST

Edward
Bennett Vineyards
(252) 322–7154 or
(877) 762–9463

Knotts Island
Martin Vineyards
(252) 429–3542 or
(252) 429–3564

Moonrise Bay Vineyard
(252) 429–9463 or
(252) 429–9056

Ocean Isle Beach
Silver Coast Winery
(910) 287–2800

Rose Hill
Duplin Winery
(800) 774–9634

The Southern Coast and Islands

Along the Grand Strand

Like most of this country's coastal areas, the beaches of North Carolina attract plenty of tourists, but some have so far managed to avoid the near honky-tonk atmosphere of the better-known places such as Myrtle Beach, just below the North Carolina—South Carolina border.

Close enough to that border to confuse anyone who misses the North Carolina welcome center on U.S. Highway 17, the little community of ***Calabash*** comes as a surprise to all but the people who visit beaches in the area regularly. The sign proclaiming Calabash the "seafood capital of the world" seems bigger than the town, which covers only a couple of miles and has only a few hundred permanent residents. But you'll find more than thirty restaurants, all specializing in seafood. Mostly they're owned and run by local fishing families, are casual, and feature fresh "Calabash-style" deep-fried seafood.

The Coleman family claims to have started the original Calabash restaurant. At first they held outdoor oyster roasts in the 1930s. When they moved indoors, they added fried seafood, which is what most people think of now when they think of Calabash, although the oyster roast is still popular with diners who don't mind a little mess.

THE SOUTHERN COAST AND ISLANDS

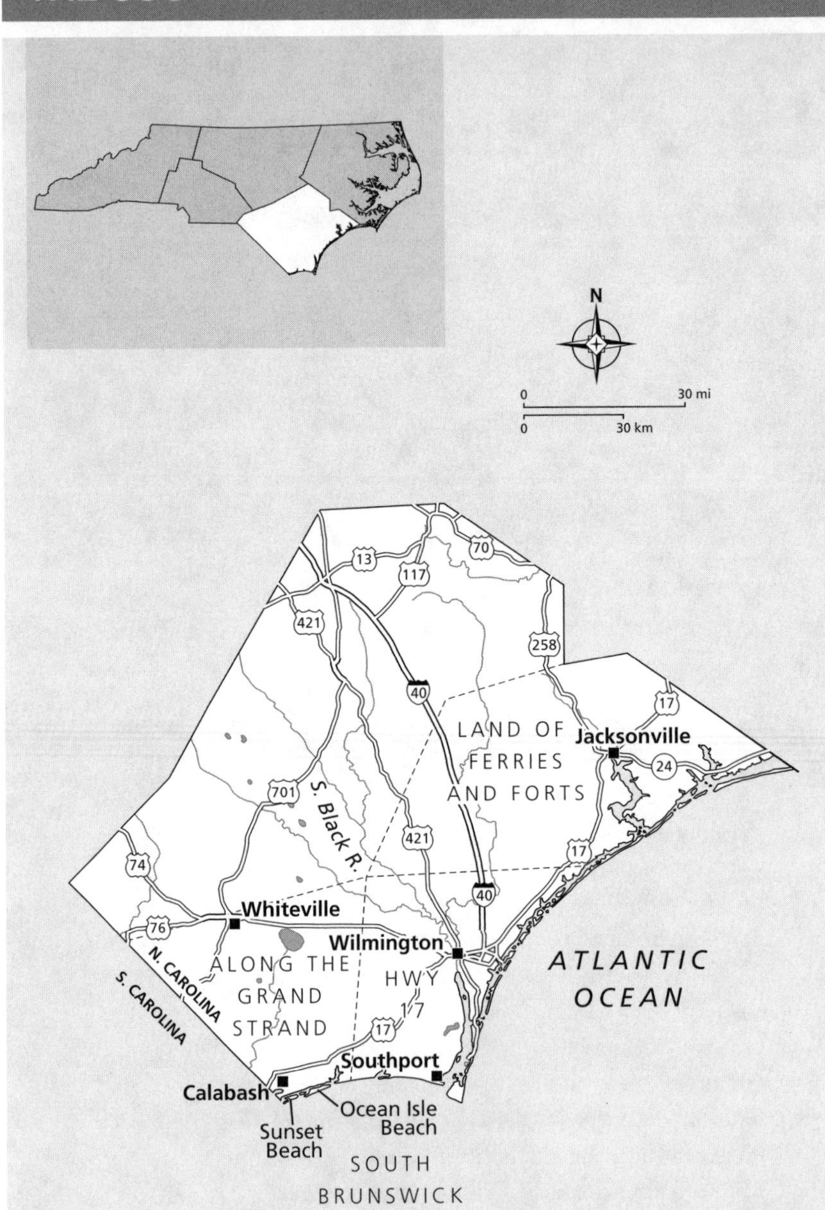

Talkin' the Talk

In North Carolina what we say is sometimes just the opposite of what we mean, but other North Carolinians get the point. For instance, when a comment begins, "Bless his heart" or "Bless her heart" it sounds as if you're about to say something nice, but it's actually a signal that what's coming next is critical: "Bless his heart, his elevator doesn't go all the way to the top." Or "Bless her heart, she can't even boil water in a microwave." On the other hand, we show affection with the seemingly negative statement, "She's a mess." Or, even more affectionately, "She's a real mess."

And when someone says something with which we agree, we don't say so. Instead we say, "You got that right."

It all makes perfect sense. You just have to know the code.

"Calabash-style" means the seafood has a light, almost tempuralike, coating. Of course it's always served with hush puppies; it's easier to separate income and tax than it is to get seafood in Calabash without hush puppies.

When you order an oyster roast, you're presented with a huge kettle full of oysters steamed just until they opened, a shucking knife to prod the oysters out of their shells, a dish of melted butter, a roll of paper towels, and a wastebasket to catch the oyster shells as you open them.

Don't expect the kind of oyster you get when you order oysters on the half shell—neatly arranged on a bed of ice, usually a dozen to a plate. Rock oysters come in big stuck-together clumps, large, medium, and small.

ANNUAL EVENTS IN THE SOUTHERN COAST AND ISLANDS

Holden Beach
Day at the Docks
(late March)
(910) 842–6888

Nags Head
Nags Head Independence Day Fireworks
(252) 441–5508

Shallotte
Annual N.C. Oyster Festival
(mid-October)
(800) 426–6644

Wilmington
Riverfest
(early October)
(910) 452–6862
www.wilmingtonriverfest.com

Chili Cook-Off
(last Saturday in October)
(910) 763–6216

N.C. Azalea Festival
(early March)
(910) 754–7177

Heads Up! Heads On!

If you've never seen shrimp with their heads and legs on, you're in for a surprise, because they look like squirmy, swimming critters, not the neat, pink C-shaped bits surrounding a cup of cocktail sauce.

Local shrimpers sell some of their catch by the sides of most of the roads in the coastal area. They may set up in a crude shelter or off the back of a truck or simply sit there in lawn chairs. They keep the shrimp iced down in coolers.

When you buy shrimp this way, the price per pound is lower than in markets because the shrimp still have their heads on. They seem so loosely attached you can't help but marvel that they haven't come off during some underwater activity! You can pop the heads off easily.

If you have any worries about the freshness of the shrimp, just ask to smell them. If they smell briny, they're fine. If you catch a whiff of ammonia (which has never happened to me at a roadside stand), don't buy them.

The restaurants in Calabash sit along both sides of State Route 179, just off US 17. They also run down a couple of side streets toward the water. Only a few years ago, the restaurants were the only thing there, but as the area continues to develop, such unlikely businesses as a New York—style deli and bakery and several clusters of specialty shops have sprung up. Somehow the restaurants just keep on serving fish and don't seem to pay much attention to the other establishments. And lots of local people from the Myrtle Beach area still drive to Calabash for a weekly outing.

One of the largest restaurants is ***Captain Nance's Seafood Restaurant,*** 9939 Nance Street, on the Calabash River (which is still full of shrimp, crabs, and flounder). The restaurant is open from 11:00 A.M. to 9:00 P.M. seven days a week, year-round (910–579–2574).

Coleman's Original Calabash Restaurant, 9931 Nance Street, may vary hours seasonally. Call (910) 579–6875.

Ella's of Calabash, at 1148 River Road, is another small restaurant, with a Southern, family feel, that is popular with local folks looking for a low-key atmosphere in which to enjoy seafood and a beer or soft drink. This place has been around since the 1950s and has a comfortable, well-established feel. Ella's presumably has fed its full share of rainy-day customers, judging by the following legend displayed near the front: COIL UP YOUR ROPES AND ANCHOR HERE/TILL BETTER WEATHER DOTH APPEAR. You can seek food or shelter here from 11:00 A.M. to 9:00 P.M., seven days a week, year-round except Thanksgiving and Christmas. Phone (910) 579–6728.

AUTHOR'S FAVORITE PLACES IN THE SOUTHERN COAST AND ISLANDS

- Sunset Beach
- Southport
- Orton Plantation Gardens
- Historic Wilmington District
- North Carolina Aquarium
- Poplar Grove Plantation
- Cedar Point

In summer Calabash is busy, attracting tourists from Myrtle Beach as well as from the beaches to the north, so the best time to visit is in the slower seasons.

Nearby, also on the Calabash River, leaving from the marina, boats in the ***Hurricane Fishing Fleet*** are available to charter for fishing trips and scenic cruises. Their schedule is affected by weather and season, so you definitely need to call ahead (910–579–3660) to arrange your trip.

The South Brunswick Islands

Driving north on US 17 just over 10 miles takes you to the beginning of the South Brunswick Islands. Sunset Beach, Ocean Isle Beach, and Holden Beach differ from one another as much as the siblings in most families. Part of the chain of barrier islands off the coast that stretches both north and south, the South Brunswick Islands have no boardwalks and relatively little commercial development except for beach houses and a few small grocery stores.

In the fall of 1989, Hurricane Hugo accentuated an interesting phenomenon along Holden Beach, Ocean Isle, and Sunset Beach. The hurricane didn't do any more damage than any good storm does, breaking up some docks, flooding some first-floor rooms in cabins, and lifting off a piece of roof here and there. But it changed the beaches, hastening an erosion process that was already obvious, moving sand and dunes from the east and depositing them farther west. This means that beachfront at Holden Beach grows noticeably more narrow with each storm, as does the east end of Ocean Isle's beachfront, leading to such black-humor jokes as the one suggesting that the way to get cheap oceanfront property here is to buy third row and wait. Meanwhile the beaches on the west end of Ocean Isle and those on Sunset Beach are growing visibly broader. It takes regular dredging to keep the waterway between Ocean Isle and Sunset Beach open because the currents continue to dump sand there. Beaches have broadened so much at Sunset Beach that when you

Spanish Moss

Not Spanish. Not moss. This gray-green epiphite thrives almost anywhere in the South where warm air and high humidity are present.

Legend has it that an Indian princess cut her hair on her wedding day, as was traditional, and hung it over an oak tree. But the newlyweds were killed the day they married and buried under the same oak. The princess' hair turned gray, started to grow, and has been spreading among the trees ever since.

Southerners have been trying to figure out a use for Spanish moss for generations. In Louisiana it was used to stuff mattresses in the 1800s. Those that survive are decidedly stiff and crinkly. More recently it's been bagged as a decorative item for florists, but it's only pretty as long as it's exposed to moisture in the air. Take it inland and it turns gray and brittle and crumbles.

My college roommate, back in my Pennsylvania days, kept a bunch, tied with pink ribbon, hanging on a nozzle in the shower room. It did very well there until somebody stole it.

If you want to take Spanish moss home with you, keep it damp as you travel. At home, hang it in a steamy place, such as a shower stall.

stand at water's edge, you can't see the first-row cottages behind the dunes. It sounds like good, forward-thinking planning; actually, it's nature.

This shifting creates some problems for developers and homeowners but does not in any way spoil the pleasure of visiting any of the islands. Indeed, if you're interested in the ecology of coastlines, try to find a copy of *The Beaches are Moving,* by Wallace Kaufman and Orrin H. Pilkey Jr., published by Duke University Press in 1979. The book describes, explains, and predicts such activity, though it focuses on beaches along both the east and west coasts and doesn't talk specifically about the South Brunswick Islands. Browsing through the book, which is rich in historical data and information about how tides, storms, and so on work, while you stay in the South Brunswick Islands it is like having your very own little nature model to study as you read. It's great fun and genuinely instructive.

Access to ***Sunset Beach*** still depends on a one-lane swing bridge across the Intracoastal Waterway. A swing bridge differs from a drawbridge in that the movable part of the bridge swings to the side rather than lifting up to allow tall ships to pass under. It's rare in these times. It's also threatened. Developers have plans to replace it with a higher, modern bridge that would accommodate more and faster traffic. At the moment, people who like the sleepy, undeveloped atmosphere of Sunset Beach are fighting to stop the new bridge. They'll probably lose. But at least for the immediate future, this is a place with only a few paved roads and sidewalks, no high-rise condos, and no pink giraffes, water slides, or beachfront grills. What the island does have is glorious, wide, flat beaches and clean white sand. From most of the beach area, you can't see any buildings at all. The beach homes, most of which are available for rent, sit hidden behind the dunes. The best way to enjoy Sunset Beach is to rent one of these houses. They are handled by three rental agents. The newest of these, which may therefore be trying harder, is the Odom Company, which does everything from letting you go directly to your rental home instead of stopping to check in at the office to lending you crab traps and charcoal grills. The office (910–579–3515 or 800–446–3435) is open seven days a week, year-round, from 9:00 A.M. to 5:00 P.M. but closes at 2:00 P.M. Sundays. During the summer season cottage rentals are usually by the week, Saturday to Saturday. At other times terms are more flexible. Other agencies are Sunset Vacations (910–579–5400 or 800–331–6428) and Sunset Properties (910–579–9900 or 800–525–0182).

Also, near where the bridge comes onto the island, you can rent rooms at Sunset Beach Motel on Main Street (910–579–7093). Web site: www.northst.com/sunsetbe.htm.

Whether you stay awhile or just pass through, a nice place to stop for dinner is the ***Sunset Grille and Waterfront Tavern,*** on the mainland right next

Beach Memory

When we first visited Ocean Isle Beach, my husband and I stayed in one of the units of the Pirates' Den, an inexpensive beachfront accommodation with one bedroom, a pretty decent kitchen, a toilet that rocked a little on its base, a slightly musty smell, and an outstanding view of the ocean. It remained a favorite place for a long time. Once I spent a couple of weeks there finishing a manuscript while Himself went back to work. Being without a car, I walked across the causeway to Williamson Realty to mail the manuscript. This was scary because the sides of the bridge came only about to my knees. To get away from the feeling of falling over the edge, I crossed the causeway by walking on the yellow line.

When the people at Williamson heard my story, they mailed my manuscript and then drove me back across the causeway. In later years, when we had a little more money and wanted to include kids and friends in our vacations, we stayed in larger, nicer homes on the canals. But recently, in the off-season, when I wanted to go back alone for a week to read and listen to jazz, I returned to the Pirates' Den. It stands as stable as ever, one of the sturdiest buildings on the beach. The toilet still rocks a little on its base, the place still smells musty, and it still has an outstanding view of the ocean.

I'll go again.

to the bridge that crosses the waterway to the island. The restaurant is one of the thoroughly established operations in the area that attracts customers year-round. For years its name was the Italian Fisherman, and the menu leaned heavily toward Italian seasonings. Recently the head chef, Garry Fields, bought the restaurant and added more entrees such as steaks and ribs to the menu. Not that the Italian influence is gone. One of the most popular dishes is linguini with white clam and shrimp sauce. This is the kind of place where the same people work year after year and remember those visitors who return. Although there is a complete bar, and drinks are served in the dining rooms as well, the atmosphere is holiday casual, and entire families, including babies in high chairs, can eat comfortably here. The guests tend to be as friendly as the staff, often striking up conversations from one table to another. One summer evening an eighteen-month-old in a high chair was doing a standard smear job on her face, head, and hair with spaghetti. A diner at the next table snapped a picture of the scene and later sent it to the child's parents. The Sunset Grille and Waterfront Tavern (111 Causeway Drive; 910–579–2929) is open seven days a week during the summer season, from 5:00 to 9:00 P.M. In the off-season the restaurant is open fewer days and shorter hours. They are usually busy, so reservations are a very good idea.

Just south of Sunset Beach, by water, not by road, lies ***Bird Island.*** It is one of the last undeveloped, privately owned barrier islands on the East Coast. It is a popular place for birding and just spending time in a spot that people have not managed to change. The only sure way to get there is by boat. If you don't own one, try visiting a marina. Some people wade across from Sunset Beach at low tide, but a few of them have come close to having to spend the night there when the tide came in faster than they realized.

The next island north is ***Ocean Isle Beach.*** To get there, drive north on US 17 about 5 miles and turn right onto Route 179 South, which takes you directly to the Odell Williamson Bridge, across the Intracoastal Waterway. The fact that the island was originally settled in 1954 by Odell and his family, who rowed across the waterway after Hurricane Hazel to get to the island, tells you something about the island. The Williamson family still runs a lively rental, sales, and building business on the island. Although there is a water slide, you'll find little other commercial development here. A few convenience shops and gift shops sell beachwear, suntan lotion, and other items tourists buy. This island is more settled, with sidewalks, all-paved roads, some cluster homes and condos on the west end, and more traditional beach homes on the east end. Also on the east end, a series of paved and natural canals, where the homes have docks, can accommodate boats or just provide pleasant off-ocean outdoor lounging space. A few hundred permanent residents live on the island.

A Birdie at the Beach

Sand makes great beaches. It also makes devilish sand traps. It takes another golfing enthusiast to understand why you'd go to the beach and spend the time playing golf, but if you do, you'll be in good company. New golf courses spring up faster than dandelions.

North Carolina has more than 600 golf courses dotted across the state, designed by such masters as Donald Ross, Tom Fazio, Arnold Palmer, Rees Jones, and Jack Nicklaus.

North Carolina golf courses have hosted the Ryder Cup, the US Open, the US Senior Open, the US Women's Open, and regular PGA tour events.

For a free copy of the *North Carolina Golf Guide*, a comprehensive listing of courses in the state, call (800) VISIT–NC or check the Web site: www.visitncgolf.com.

Their homes are mingled among those used strictly for vacation and rental. It's a nice mix, and especially if you do not stay in beachfront properties, you can learn a lot about the island from these people and form friendships that continue past your visit. In recent years the relatively new ***Museum of Coastal Carolina,*** 21 East Second Street (910–579–1016; www.ncbrunswick.com), has attracted vacationing children and school groups. The museum of natural history concentrates on the Carolina coast, with dioramas and Civil War artifacts, as well as Native American artifacts and a fine collection of seashells and fossils. The museum is open from 9:00 A.M. to 5:00 P.M. Friday and Saturday, 1:00 to 5:00 P.M. Sunday. The hours are shorter in the off-season. ***Williamson Realty,*** one of several realtors that handle island homes, is pleasant to deal with if you want to rent a cottage or condo. Their Saturday-to-Saturday rental schedule during the season, with more flexibility at other times, operates much the same as rentals on Sunset Beach. The office (910–579–2373 or 800–727–9222) is open from 9:00 A.M. to 5:00 P.M., Monday through Saturday, and Sunday from noon to 4:00 P.M. (closed on Sundays during December, January, and February). Web site: www.williamsonrealty.com. ***Sloane Realty*** (910–579–6216 or 800–843–6044) is another well-established, friendly rental agency. Their offices are open six days a week from 9:00 A.M. to 5:00 P.M., Sundays from 10:00 A.M. to 4:00 P.M. Web site: www.sloanerealty.com.

Ocean Isle Inn, 37 West First Street (800–352–5988) has seventy rooms on the waterfront. Facilities include an outdoor swimming pool and sundeck, an indoor heated pool and hot tub, and the use of boats, rafts, and canoes. The inn serves a complimentary continental breakfast. Web site: www.oceanisleinn.com.

Try the ***Islander Inn*** at 57 West First Street (888–325–4753). Web site: www.islanderinn.com.

Standing on the west end of Ocean Isle Beach, you can see Sunset Beach. It looks close enough to wade to, which old-timers remember doing before erosion and currents changed the shape of the islands. Standing on the east end of Ocean Isle Beach, you see ***Holden Beach,*** also seeming almost close enough to wade to. Without a boat, though, getting to Holden Beach requires a drive of about fifteen minutes. Richard Mubel, the news editor for the *State Port Pilot,* once wrote for the *Brunswick Magazine* that Holden is a place where "old meets new, where tradition bisects progress and where history intersects the path of the future." He's talking about the contrasts between the back side of the island, along the Atlantic Intracoastal Waterway and the Lockwood Folly River Inlet, and the oceanfront. Shrimpers and anglers descended from families who settled the area still work along the waterway and inlet, as well as in the open sea, but the oceanfront is strictly a vacationland of white beaches and summer cottages. You'll find more shopping in this area, but compared to major coastal resort areas, it's still quiet and appeals to people who like a little more activity than can be found at Sunset or Ocean Isle without getting into plastic, chrome, and glass. Half a dozen rental agents renting cottages and condos, a campground, and a motel serve the area. ***Alan Holden Realty*** (800–720–2200) has the most properties and friendly people to answer the phone. They're open from 9:00 A.M. to 5:00 P.M., seven days a week, year-round. Web site: www.holden-beach.com. ***Coastal Vacation Resorts*** rents nearly 200 cottages and a few condos. Call (800) 252–7000. Web site: www.atlanticvacation.com. The ***Gray Gull Motel*** (910–842–6775), an older but

Let's Pedal!

Ocean Isle Beach is a great place to take your bicycle. The streets are paved, which makes for easy riding, and traffic is heavy only during the standard coming and leaving day, Saturday. The island is about 12 miles long, end-to-end, a nice ride on nearly flat planes. It's also fun to ride up and down the canal streets, looking at the houses and their kitschy names. My favorite for years was, "The stoned crab." The house had a picture of an out-of-kilter crab with a silly grin. New owners, with a less 1970s sense of humor, painted out the letter "d" and now the house is just the stone crab.

You'll find several places where you can take a bike down onto the beach, too. Riding there is good at low tide, when the sand is damp and hard. Sand that the water doesn't reach, even at high tide, is soft and hard to manage, better for walking. For a perfect early-morning workout, you can ride on the beach, then park the bike and walk for a while.

BETTER-KNOWN ATTRACTIONS IN THE SOUTHERN COAST AND ISLANDS

Wilmington
Battleship *North Carolina*
(910) 251–5797

Cape Fear Museum
(910) 341–4350

Cape Fear Coastal Beaches
Wrightsville, Carolina, Kure
(800) 222–4757;
Web site: www.capefear.nc.us

clean establishment, rents individual rooms. They, too, operate year-round. This small motel is located between the light and the bridge where you first drive onto the island.

If you enjoy local festivals and if you lo-o-o-o-ve seafood, try to schedule your Brunswick Island trip for the third weekend in October, during the annual ***North Carolina Oyster Festival.*** This festival began as a small oyster roast in the late 1970s. Every year the party got a little better and in three years got itself proclaimed the official oyster festival of North Carolina. It takes a couple hundred community volunteers to run the event, which now includes a beach run, a bullshooting (tall-tale-telling) contest, and the North Carolina Oyster Shucking Championship. This contest is no small potatoes. It has produced not only a national oyster shucking champion but also the top female oyster shucker in the world. With all that shucking going on, it stands to reason somebody's got to be doing some eating. That's where you come in. Steamed oysters, fried oysters, oysters on the half shell, boiled shrimp, fried flounder, and of course the ubiquitous hush puppies are available in abundance. In addition to the food and contests, the festival features two days of live music that include beach music (shag), top forty, country and western, and gospel. Also artists and craftspeople display their wares for sale. For fuller details and firm dates in any year, call (800) 426–6644. Web site: www.ncbrunswick.com.

Highway 17

The Brunswick Isles are served by businesses in the town of ***Shallotte,*** a few miles inland on US 17. This is the place to stop when you need to do laundry or pick up a bicycle pump from the hardware store or get a prescription filled in a good-sized pharmacy. From Shallotte, driving north on US 17 brings you to ***Southport,*** on the western bank of the Cape Fear River where the river joins the Atlantic Ocean. The harbor accommodates yachts, charter boats, and fishing

Some Kinder, Gentler Prose

The author Robert Ruark was born in Southport. He wrote novels that made people angry, especially *Something of Value,* about Africa. (After it was published, the government of Kenya wouldn't let him back in the country.)

He was rough, tough, rude, and crude, and he died in London from internal bleeding before he was fifty. But he had a softer side, too. Ruark wrote *The Old Man and the Boy,* a memoir about spending time as a boy with his grandfather, E. H. Adkins, a Southport river pilot. He often stayed in his grandfather's house at 119 North Lord Street. The house, still a private residence, is now 110 years old. It is not open to visitors, but the book is easy to find because of its local interest.

piers. The town, rich in military and maritime history, was first called Smithville after Benjamin Smith, who became governor of North Carolina, but in 1887 the name was changed to Southport. To get into town from US 17, turn right onto State Highway 211. Shortly you'll be driving into what is obviously still a real fishing village with stores and gas stations and marinas, although growing numbers of tourist-oriented shops are opening. Many of the homes in Southport are listed on the National Register of Historic Places. The old twelve-bed ***Fort Johnston Hospital,*** dating back to about 1852, has been moved and turned into a private residence; the ***Old Brunswick Jail,*** dating back to the early 1900s, now houses the Southport Historical Society. In the ***Keziah Memorial Park*** you find a tree that the Cape Fear Indians bent over as a marker when it was just a sapling. It may be more than 800 years old. Half a century ago children could crawl under its arch. And the ***A. E. Stevens House,*** circa 1894, is noted as the home built for Mr. Stevens and his betrothed. She changed her mind and married his best friend. They built a house across from Mr. Stevens, who remained a bachelor the rest of his life. There's lots more, equally human and interesting, all mapped out on a 1-mile, self-guided walking tour called ***Southport Trail.*** You'll find a nice assortment of restaurants, antiques shops, and specialty stores in the area, too. Their names and sometimes their proprietors may change from year to year, but they're always fun. A shopping guide with a map as well as the free self-guided walking-tour brochure of Southport's historic sites is available at the visitors center, 113 West Moore Street, open from 8:30 A.M. to 5:00 P.M., Monday through Friday, 9:00 A.M. to 4:00 P.M., Saturday. Call (800) 388–9635. Web site: www.cityofsouthport.com.

Southport used to be the special province of people with boats and people who fish. Even those who docked their boats in Southport and lived inland didn't expect much in the way of elaborate accommodations or shopping. This is all changing—that's the good news *and* the bad news. As specialty shops and antiques shops open, more tourists come in, making the place not quite so off-the-beaten-path as it used to be. But the good news is that you can find more places to stay and eat.

Lois Jane's Riverview Inn (106 West Bay Street; 800–457–1152) is a small bed-and-breakfast in a 1891 home that is owned and operated by fourth-generation direct descendants of the builder. Although it was carefully restored in 1995, the house retains much of its original character and furniture. One of the guest rooms, called "Lois Jane's Room," is furnished and decorated exactly as she kept it in her lifetime, right down to a collection of Wedgewood plates on the wall. Guests gather around a table in the crimson dining room to share breakfast and conversation. The inn is directly across from the river.

For less intimate and less expensive accommodations, ***Sea Captain Motor Lodge*** (608 West West Street; 910–457–5263) a complex of two-story brick motel buildings, clustered around an Olympic-sized swimming pool and a gazebo, across from the South Port Marina, manages to avoid the blandness of chain motels while providing comfortable, clean rooms with refrigerators, phones, and cable TV. Web site: www.seacaptainmotorlodge.com.

And for a special occasion, you can book a ***"Boat and Breakfast"*** stay aboard the ***Stephania*** sailboat. You don't actually have to sail anywhere. The boat is docked while you sleep, and breakfast prepared at a local restaurant is delivered to you in the morning. When the 37-foot, twin-cabin boat isn't being used for an overnight interlude, you can book it for morning, afternoon, sunset, and moonlight sails. No morning cruise is scheduled for the day after a B&B booking. When you do sail, you'll be encouraged to take the helm for a picture of yourself in position. Jay Harvey is captain and his wife, Jackie, is admiral, but she says that's just another word for gopher. Check the *Stephania*'s Web site: www.windsofcarolina.com. To make reservations or book a sail, call (910) 457–1162, (910) 278–7249, or (910) 232–3003.

The Hunter 375 sloop, ***Endless Summer,*** also takes cruises from Southport. Call (910) 253–0531 to make arrangements.

Another popular excursion from Southport takes you to ***Bald Head Island*** by private ferry. Only a couple hundred people live here, and future plans for the island call for tightly limited new construction. The first lighthouse in North Carolina was built on this island. ***Old Baldy Light House and Smith House Museum*** (910–457–5003) commemorate the island's history. The most notable aspect of the island now is that no motor vehicles are allowed, which means you move about in golf carts, or on bicycles, or you walk. Overnight accommodations on the island include ***Marsh Harbour Inn*** (Keelson Row; 866–454–0488) with fifteen rooms, and ***Theodosia's Bed and Breakfast*** (2 Keelson Row; 800–656–1812; Web site: www.theodosias.com), of similar size.

Tours of the island and its museum, complete with lunch, originate at Southport. For details call (910) 457–5003.

North of Southport via State Highway 133, ***Brunswick Town State Historic Site*** marks the first settlement in the Cape Fear area. Here you can study the remains of the colonial port town of Brunswick and the earth mounds of Fort Anderson that the Confederate Army built about one hundred years later. Some of the old foundations have been excavated and are uncovered as archaeological exhibits. The mounds have survived pretty much intact since the Civil War and actually make a good spot from which to see the older ruins. A visitors center on the site has slide presentations and exhibits about the colonial town and the artifacts excavated from the ruins. This is one of those well-managed sites where you can learn about both colonial life and the Civil War and get a sense of the continuity from the one time to the other. Brunswick Town is open Tuesday through Saturday from 1:00 to 4:00 P.M. These hours may vary, so it's a good idea to call ahead, (910) 371–6613. Admission is free.

About 10 miles north of Southport, still on Highway 133, you come to ***Orton Plantation Gardens,*** a delight for anyone who loves flowers and grand old trees. The first owners were James and Luola Sprunk, who built terraces and ornamental gardens with live oaks lining the walkways. Later, with the help of a landscape architect, additional gardens and water features were added, and the gardens were opened to the public. Blooms extend over a long season, beginning with camellias in late winter; azaleas in spring; oleander, crape myrtle, and magnolias in summer and fall. Plantings of annuals add extra splashes of color. Orton House, a good example of Southern antebellum architecture, is an impressive feature on the property too, but it is a private residence, so you must content yourself with admiring the exterior and visiting the small family chapel that is open to the public. The gardens are open daily March through August from 8:00 A.M. to 6:00 P.M., September and November from 10:00 A.M. to 5:00 P.M. Admission is $9.00 for adults, $8.00 for seniors, and $3.00 for children. Phone (910) 371–6851.

After this, the easiest thing to do is return to US 17 to drive on up to ***Wilmington.*** People who live here call Wilmington the best-kept secret in North Carolina. They're of two minds as to whether that's good or bad. The thriving, historic community has a full share of entrepreneurial types who've done much to revitalize waterfront areas and old downtown buildings. They welcome tourists and new business. Some of the old-timers would rather the community's cultural and historical attractions not become too well known, lest all the new traffic spoil the ambience.

In 1989 Wilmington, which was settled before the Revolutionary War and was the last Atlantic port open to blockade runners during the Civil War, celebrated its 250th anniversary.

Historic restoration and preservation in the official ***Historic Wilmington District*** have produced an appealing neighborhood that deserves more attention. One interesting approach is the ***Wilmington Adventure Walking Tour,*** by Bob Jenkins (910–763–1785). He's been doing this for years, answers the phone himself, and says he is grateful to be able to keep on. The tour takes about two hours. Jenkins calls it a "casual stroll on the original survey of the 1734 city." It takes in town houses, gardens, commercial buildings, churches, and fountains. The tour concludes with an 1858 theater and an 1892 courthouse and includes a twelve-minute video showing more sightseeing possibilities in the entire Cape Fear region. Tours run from April 1 to November 1. They leave daily at 10:00 A.M. and 2:00 P.M. from the foot of Market Street on the Cape Fear River. Look for a guide with a straw hat and a walking stick. Reservations are not necessary. Tickets are $10.00 for adults, $5.00 for children ages six to twelve. Jenkins will conduct tours for groups of five or more from November through March if you call ahead to arrange it and he's not off somewhere else.

There are two buildings in the area worth seeing inside. The beautifully restored ***1770 Burgwin-Wright House*** (910–762–0570) stands at the corner of Third and Market Streets. It was built in 1770 on the foundation of the abandoned Wilmington City Jail. One reason the owner chose this site and kept the foundation was because it had a tunnel running down to the water, so he could get to the boats without going outside. Open Tuesday through Saturday 10:00 A.M. to 4:00 P.M. Closed on major holidays. Admission is $6.00 for adults, $3.00 for full-time students. The ***Zebulon Latimer House*** (910–762–0492) at 126 South Third Street is one of the few remaining examples of a town house of the time. The same family inhabited it from its completion in 1852 until the historical society took it over in the 1960s. About 60 percent of the furnishings are the family's original belongings. Three of the four floors are open, so you can see everything from beds to china. The house also has archives and a library for those who want to study further, with a researcher available on Tuesday and Thursday. The house is open Monday through Friday from 10:00 A.M. to 4:00 P.M., Saturday and Sunday from noon to 5:00 P.M. Closed on major holidays. If a tour is in progress when you arrive, you may join it, be taken separately by a docent, or wait for the next group to gather. Admission is $6.00 for adults, $3.00 for full-time students.

Another pleasant way to see the Wilmington District is to take a ***Springbrook Farms*** sightseeing tour (910–251–8889) by horse-drawn carriage, with a driver who narrates as you pass the historic sites. At Christmas a nice touch is that you ride in a closed reindeer-drawn carriage, snuggled in a lap rug, for a tour narrated by Santa. Owner-operator John Pucci says this appeals especially to children and romantics. Tours leave from the corner of Water and Market Streets. Hours vary with the season, weather, and day of the week. To plan a tour, call ahead. If no one is there, you can still learn current tour hours by listening to a recording. Sometimes tours may be arranged for different times by appointment. Rates are $9.00 for adults, $4.00 for children.

The Daughters of the Confederacy are responsible for creating the oldest history museum in the state. In 1898 they announced their intention to establish a "creditable museum of confederate relics." The ***Cape Fear Museum*** was the result. For years it was moved from place to place, looking for a home. Since 1992, it's been housed in a large structure built just for the museum at 814 Market Street.

Not all the exhibits are about the Civil War. One comes from a tad before the Civil War—the reproduction of the 20-foot-long Wilmington ground sloth, believed to have lived one-and-a-half million years ago. The creature had fur and hand-shaped appendages with claws, and it stood 15 feet tall. The original was found during construction on a dam basin at Randall Parkway, Wilmington, in 1991. The state gave the original to the North Carolina State Museum of Natural Sciences in Raleigh, which in turn created the reproduction of urethane foam and steel for the Cape Fear Museum. Experts say the creature was not a dinosaur, but an ice age mammal.

The Michael Jordan Discovery Gallery features natural history of the upland forests, bottom land, and maritime forest in interactive exhibits for children and includes also some artifacts from Jordan's years growing up in Wilmington.

Yet another part of the museum shows one-third scale wood carvings of bride figures by Frank Haines, with costumes researched and sewed by Elizabeth Haines. The brides range from Pocohantas to Queen Nefertiti.

But all that doesn't mean the museum has abandoned the Civil War. Along with military artifacts and representations of the Wilmington waterfront as it was in 1863, you'll find a diorama of the second battle of Fort Fisher in 1865.

The museum is open Tuesday through Saturday 9:00 A.M. to 5:00 P.M., Sunday 1:00 to 5:00 P.M. Admission is $5.00 for adults, $4.00 for senior citizens and college students with valid ID, and $1.00 for children three to seventeen. Children under three are free. Phone (910) 341–4350. Web site: www.capefearmuseum.com.

If you are traveling with children, or with grown-up model railroad nuts, go to the ***Wilmington Railroad Museum,*** 501 Nutt Street, which spells out a major part of the town's history. Although Wilmington is known now for being the state's main deepwater port, railroading used to be Wilmington's major industry. In 1840 the Wilmington and Weldon Railroad, with 161 miles of continuous track, was the longest in the world. About 1900 it merged with several other rail lines to become the Atlantic Coast Line Railroad, with headquarters in Wilmington. But in 1960 the company moved the whole shebang to Jacksonville, Florida. Unlike enterprises that move away these days, though, Atlantic Coast Line did not leave its employees in the lurch but took all 1,000 of them, along with their families, to Florida.

The museum depicts the history not just of the Atlantic Coast Line but also of railroading in the Southeast, through a variety of exhibits. The red caboose in the children's corner is a draw for kids and can be booked for birthday parties. For more historical viewing, the museum also has a 1910 Baldwin steam engine; a Seaboard Coastline Railroad caboose; and a Richmond, Fredericksburg, and Potomac Railroad box car. Other displays include everything from railroaders' gear going back more than a hundred years to illustrations of ghost stories about train disasters. For the hobbyist, large layouts of Lionel and HO-gauge model layouts are enough to send you to the nearest model railroad store. The museum is open March 15 to October 14, Monday through Saturday 10:00 A.M. to 5:00 P.M., Sunday from 1:00 to 5:00 P.M. From October 15 to March 14 the museum is open Monday through Saturday, 10:00 A.M. to 4:00 P.M. Phone (910) 763–2634. Admission is $3.00 for adults, $2.50 for senior citizens and military, $1.50 for children ages three to twelve. Children under two are free. Web site: www.wilmingtonrailroadmuseum.org.

One attraction locals know well and tourists often miss is the ***Louise Wells Cameron Art Museum,*** (910–763–0281) at the intersection of Independence Boulevard and the Seventeenth Street Extension, remarkable especially for an important collection of the original color prints of Mary Cassatt, the nineteenth-century American artist who worked with the Impressionists in France. Until recently the museum housing the collection, St. John's Museum of Art, comprised three historic buildings on Orange Street. But while the museum collections grew, the buildings wouldn't stretch any farther, and only about 11 percent of the museum's holdings could be displayed at once, so supporters raised funds for a new building, with a new name, in a new location. St. John's Museum of Art closed the last day of December 2001. The new Louise Wells Cameron Art Museum, designed by architect Charles Gwathmey, has 42,000 square feet, about triple the earlier space, and it sits on a campus of almost ten acres.

Like St. John's, it is the only accredited art museum in the region and has, in addition to the Cassatt work, a permanent collection featuring 200 years of North Carolina art and temporary exhibitions that change regularly. The facilities include an extensive gift shop, a cafe, and a sculpture garden. A series of Confederate defensive mounds that were built near the end of the Civil War on the property provide a new dimension the old museum didn't have. The museum galleries are open Tuesday through Saturday 10:00 A.M. to 5:00 P.M., Sunday 10:30 A.M. to 4:00 P.M. Admission is $5.00 for adults, $8.00 for a family. Web site: www.cameronartmuseum.com.

You can walk to ***Chandler's Wharf*** and the ***Cotton Exchange*** on the Cape Fear River. These two complexes of restored historical warehouses and buildings now house a variety of specialty shops and restaurants rather than maritime activities. They are near where the River Walk meets the Cape Fear Bridge. Among the restaurants in this area, ***Roy's Riverboat Landing,*** at the corner of Water and Market Streets (910–763-7227), ***Elijah's Oyster Bar*** on Ann Street at the waterfront (910–343–1448), and the ***Pilot House,*** also on the Ann Street waterfront (910–343–0200) serve lunch and dinner. A more recent addition, ***Le Catalan,*** a wine bar, wine shop, and cafe at 224 South Water Street, across from the Chandler's Wharf shops (910–815–0200), features a wine bar, light meals, and desserts with a French accent.

From all these points along the river, you can see the ***Battleship* North Carolina,** a memorial to the 10,000 North Carolinians in the armed services who died during World War II. The ship, which was in service from 1941 to 1947, has been moored directly across the Cape Fear River from historic downtown Wilmington as a memorial since 1961. A self-guided tour through the crew's quarters, galley, sick bay, engine room, pilothouse, and other areas takes about two hours. Admission is $9.00 for adults, $4.50 for children, $8.00 for seniors and active or retired military people. The entrance, with parking, a visitors center, a gift shop, and a snack bar, is at the intersection of U.S. Highways 17/74/76/421. The ship is open mid-May to mid-September 8:00 A.M. to 8:00 P.M., and closes at 5:00 P.M. other times. Web site: www.battleshipnc.com.

During the summer an alternative to parking at the battleship site is to take the ***Riverboat Taxi*** over from Chandler's Wharf. Originally it was a World War II U.S. Navy launch. It leaves every half hour for the battleship from 10:00 A.M. to 5:00 P.M. daily. Modest rates.

You can't get seasick on the battleship unless you have a wildly vivid imagination. If you'd like to test your sea legs a bit more realistically, you could try a riverboat cruise on the **Henrietta III,** which leaves from the foot of Dock Street on the Cape Fear River. These cruises range from sightseeing cruises to themed party cruises to dinner cruises. It's all planned and public, but if you're

Battleship *North Carolina*

in the mood for it, the gaiety can be a lot of fun. The original *Henrietta* was the first steam paddleboat built in North Carolina, and it ran the river between Wilmington and Fayetteville for forty years. James Seawell (no joke), the builder, named it for his daughter. The *Henrietta III* includes a dance floor and an air-conditioned dining room, in addition to the outdoor deck space you'd expect. If she can see this modern version, poor Henrietta is probably wishing herself back to the future. Sightseeing cruises leave at noon and 2:30 P.M. April through October, rain or shine. Admission is $11.00 for adults, $5.00 for children two to twelve. Phone (910) 343–1611 or (800) 676–0162. Web site: www.cfrboats.com.

To shift from history to contemporary attractions: If you're interested in the entertainment business, you can tour the ***Screen Gems Studios,*** 1223 North Twenty-third Street. Even people who live here don't seem to realize it, but North Carolina has become a big moviemaking state, and North Carolina Screen Gems Studios is the largest working studio facility in the country outside of California. Unlike the Florida attractions, it is a real, working studio, not a space gussied up for tourists. The walking tour takes about an hour and includes real works in process. As a tour guest, you must not get in the way of production, the actors, or the crew, and you may take pictures only in certain, designated areas. The guides are local production people who tell stories about their own experiences in the business. They've shot not only such movies as

Ready on the Set—Take One

North Carolina has become the third busiest filmmaking state in the United States and is actively recruiting Hollywood studios as well as independent filmmakers and production companies to the state. One of the state's attractions is that its diverse topography and development offer settings that can look like anything from a resort in the Catskills to barren beaches to bustling cities. In 2000, eighty-one major productions were shot in North Carolina, including nineteen features, six movies-of-the-week, and fifty-seven television episodes. Movie production included regions of the state from the coast to the mountains. Producers shot *Domestic Disturbance,* with John Travolta, in Wilmington; Spike Lee's *The Original Kings of Comedy* in Charlotte; and MGM's *Hannibal,* with Sir Anthony Hopkins, in Asheville. Viagra commercials were shot in North Carolina, as were commercials for Miller Lite, Coca-Cola, and Visa. The state has seven studio complexes, thirty sound stages with more than a million square feet of production space, and 400 production and support service companies.

Day of the Jackal, and *Teenage Mutant Ninja Turtles* here, but also television series including *Matlock* and *Dawson's Creek,* as well as many television commercials. The tour schedule varies depending on the weather and whatever else is going on, so it's a good idea to call ahead (910–343–3433) if you plan to include the studios in your activities. Admission is $12.00 for adults, $5.00 for children under twelve. Web site: www.screengemsstudios.com.

The people of Wilmington love a party, and there's no better one than ***Riverfest,*** which celebrates the city's history and its location between the Cape Fear River and the Intracoastal Waterway. Riverfest always happens the first weekend each October along Front Street and in the historic downtown district. The first Riverfest, in 1979, was the scheme of a group of Wilmingtonians looking for a way to revive Front Street and the downtown after retailers moved to a mall and shopping centers. That first party comprised a few concessions, trolley rides, and fireworks. People liked it so much the town did it again the following year and has continued ever since, adding new entertainment each year. You can expect to find more than 150 craft vendors, three stages of entertainment, a variety of races and contests, and exhibits, all set in the mood that comes with longtime, ongoing success. Web site: www.wilmingtonriverfest.com.

When it comes to places to stay, Wilmington has a healthy number of hotels and motels, as well as about twenty bed-and-breakfast facilities. Two of these stand out as special places, each with easy access to the historic district. ***Catherine's Inn,*** 410 Front Street, offers five guest rooms in an 1875 Italianate Victorian home. The inn sits on a shaded lot, in a residential area on the waterfront. It has a swimming pool, gardens, and sitting areas in the backyard, and inside the rooms are furnished with period antiques, many of them from Catherine Ackiss's own family. Pride of place goes to the family's baby grand piano, which she refinished herself. But the real draw here is Catherine, who announced years ago to her husband, Walter, that she wanted to be "a hostess." And she's done it, earning a reputation as an innkeeper who treats guests as she would special family. She expects guests to make themselves fully at home in the dining and living rooms as well as on the porch and in the garden, and she keeps a refrigerator stocked with soft drinks and beer for guests to help themselves. Phone (800) 476–0723 or (910) 251–0863. Web site: www.catherinesinn.com.

At 114 South Third Street, ***Rosehill Inn Bed and Breakfast*** is the kind of place other innkeepers visit for a night out. The decor and furnishings reflect the dash of Dennis Fietsch and his partner Laurel Jones. They did much of the renovating themselves, and she made all the bed and window treatments. Built in 1848, the neoclassical revival house has a fireplace of Italian marble and rosewood and a beautifully refinished pulpit staircase. Throughout the house, especially in the six guest rooms, roses and the color rose figure prominently in the decor. Dennis's breakfasts include specialties such as gourmet omelets. Phone (910) 815–0250 or (800) 815–0250. Web site: www.rosehill.com.

Land of Ferries and Forts

Just a few miles away from the historic port of Wilmington, you come to a series of beaches: Wrightsville, Carolina, Wilmington, and Kure. For folks seeking out-of-the-way places, the beaches don't offer the same secluded charm as the Brunswick Islands, but they can be fun, with enough amusement and entertainment to please the kids without doing in Mom and Dad, especially if you avoid the peak summer season. A number of historical and marine attractions are especially important and interesting.

Hootie Hooo

It's a sound like no other—the Annual National Hollerin' Contest at Midway High School in Spivey's Corner. The contest began in 1969 as part of a radio broadcast and has grown to attract more than 10,000 people to the little town on US 412, just south of Dunn. The event has grown to include whistling, fox-horn blowing, and conch blowing, and, of course, the ubiquitous North Carolina barbecue. The contest is always the third Saturday in June. For details call (910) 567–2600.

Wrightsville Beach is 12 miles east of Wilmington. It operates as a year-round island resort and has plenty of motels and some nice, casual, moderately priced seafood restaurants.

The ***Wrightsville Beach Museum of History,*** 303 West Salisbury Street, is one of those grassroots enterprises that reflects its own small area in unique detail and just makes you feel good with its honesty. The museum is in the fourth-oldest cottage on the island and does two things. First, it provides a good example of what beach cottages in the area used to be like, furnished just with odds and ends left over from permanent homes. And it houses a variety of permanent and changing exhibits that tell you about the history, geography, and culture of Wrightsville Beach.

For instance the kitchen remains pretty much intact, with white ceramic tile, a white porcelain kitchen sink, and an assortment of cooking utensils typical of the early twentieth century. Photographs show how other rooms might have been furnished with stuff collected here and there. A 12-foot model of Wrightsville Beach in about 1910 shows the Lumina Pavilion, where couples danced to the music of Benny Goodman, a bathhouse for changing into beachwear, and a trolley, as well as sections of beach and the boardwalk. The model is still a work in process, and the museum solicits additions and contributions to it.

Changing exhibits may include anything from the history of surfing to a retrospective on lifeguards to photographs from the collection of a local news photographer. The museum gives attention to the history of the barrier islands, the beach, the Civil War, and Hurricane Hazel. An oral history video shows area residents recalling life as it used to be in Wrightsville Beach.

The museum is open from 10:00 A.M. to 4:00 P.M. Tuesday through Friday, noon to 5:00 P.M. Saturday, and 1:00 to 5:00 P.M. Sunday. Admission $3.00. Phone (910) 256–2569. Web site: www.wbmuseum.com.

Driving south from Wilmington on U.S. Highway 421 for a little less than 20 miles takes you to the beaches on ***Pleasure Island.*** This area is highly commercial and built up, but if you stick it out to Kure Beach, you'll find two attractions worth taking time to see if you're interested in the naval aspects of Civil War history and in marine life.

On US 421, 3 miles south of Kure Beach, is ***Fort Fisher National Historic Site.*** The fort stood up under heavy naval attack during the Civil War, and some of the 25-foot earthwork fortifications that protected the Cape Fear River and the port of Wilmington from Union forces remain. Reading about such parapets is one thing; looking at them and musing on how they must have been built before the days of bulldozers is a more vivid experience, intensified by such touches as a reconstruction of the gun emplacement and a history trail. There's also a museum that displays Civil War artifacts and offers an audio-visual show, models, and dioramas on the history of the fort. If you travel with a picnic cooler, you'll enjoy the picnic area on the site. Admission is free but donations are appreciated (910–458–5538). Open April through October, 9:00 A.M. to 5:00 P.M. Monday through Saturday, 1:00 to 5:00 P.M. Sunday; November through March 10, 10:00 A.M. to 4:00 P.M. Tuesday through Saturday, 1:00 to 4:00 P.M. Sunday. closed on major holidays.

One of North Carolina's three aquariums, ***North Carolina Aquarium at Fort Fisher,*** across from Fort Fisher National Historic Site, has been expanded to a 93,000-square-foot aquarium at the mouth of the Cape Fear River. The expansion emphasizes waters of the Cape Fear River system, with exhibits moving from life in the freshwater rivers and swamps to saltwater marshes to reefs and, finally, the open ocean. In the atrium, cypress and hardwood trees represent the freshwater rivers and swamps habitat, filled with frogs, indigenous snakes, turtles, and fish. Other features include a wave tank that simulates the surf on the shore, and a touch pool offers the opportunity to get familiar with sea urchins, horseshoe crabs, and other sea dwellers. But the main feature of the aquarium is a 200,000-gallon ocean habitat, housing everything from large sharks to loggerhead turtles. Open 9:00 A.M. to 5:00 P.M. every day but Thanksgiving, Christmas, and New Year's Day. Admission $6.00 for adults, $5.00 for active military and senior citizens, $4.00 for children ages six to seventeen, children under five free. Phone (910) 458–8257. Web site: www.ncaquariums.com.

When you get this far south on the island, you will have two choices. You can take the Fort Fisher Ferry to Southport, which brings you close to the Brunswick Islands, whence you began driving, or you can backtrack up the island and take the bridge across to Wilmington, also whence you began driving. At first glance the obvious way to avoid those whences and the dilemma of decision would be to begin by taking the ferry from Southport to Fort Fisher, then drive north on the island and finally cross over to the delights of Wilmington. You may indeed decide to do it that way, especially if you're not traveling during the peak summer months. But you need to know that the ferry crossing takes an hour. For current schedule information when it's time to decide, phone (800) BY–FERRY or check the Web site: www.ncferry.org.

Should you decide to backtrack to Wilmington, you can give the kids a pleasant break by stopping at the ***Tote-em-in Zoo,*** about 10 miles south of Wilmington on US 421. The zoo, which has been in business more than thirty-five years, features more than 130 different animals, a museum of exotic mounted specimens, and another museum of varied artifacts from around the world, including arrowheads and World War II items. Open from spring thaw until the first hard freeze, roughly March through November, from 9:00 A.M. to 5:00 P.M. daily; the rest of the year, 9:00 A.M. to 4:00 P.M. Call ahead because hours vary seasonally and according to weather (910–791–0472). Admission is $6.00 for adults, $4.00 for children two to eleven.

If you're interested in North Carolina wineries, you may want to schedule a side trip while you're in the Wilmington area to ***Duplin Wine Cellars,*** about an hour's drive from the coast. The winery is in Rose Hill, on U.S. Highway 117, about halfway between Wilmington and Goldsboro. The winery conducts tours and tastings and, of course, sells its wines. Tours are preceded by an audiovisual presentation on the history of Southern winemaking. Duplin Wine Cellars (910–289–3888) is especially well known for its Magnolia, a soft dry table wine, its Hatteras Red, and its scuppernong dessert wine. The word *scuppernong* is an Indian word meaning "sweet tree." Scuppernong is the oldest grape in America.

The winery has added a bistro to its offerings, serving lunches such as prime rib and French dip and dinners with entrees like chicken stuffed with shrimp and crab. The winery is open Monday through Saturday, 9:00 A.M. to 6:00 P.M., Friday 9:00 A.M. to 9:00 P.M. Lunch is available from 11:30 A.M. to 2:00 P.M. Monday through Saturday, and dinner from 6:00 to 10:00 P.M. Friday. Web site: duplinwinery.com.

From Wilmington the best way to head north is to drive on US 17 for a while. Stretches of it are annoyingly full of strip-city areas where traffic is heavy and slow. Taking some of the little side roads seems like a good idea, and you can if you wish without fear of getting lost, because most of them eventually loop back to US 17 anyway. But the loops are disappointing. You won't find much but scrubland, little clusters of homes or mobile homes, and perhaps some tobacco fields. It's OK for a break but quickly becomes about as boring as the more direct approach on US 17.

One interesting stop, right on the highway shortly after you leave Wilmington, is the ***Poplar Grove Plantation*** (910–686–9518; Web site: www.poplargrove.com). This is a nonprofit operation supported by the Popular Grove Foundation. It has an unusual history in that it not only survived the Civil War, but also became economically successful again by growing peanuts. The original plantation operated in the tradition of the times, as a self-supporting agricultural community with more than sixty slaves. The manor house burned down in 1849 and was rebuilt the following year where it now stands. When you visit the plantation, guides in period costume lead you on a tour of the manor house—a three-floor Greek Revival building—and the outbuildings, describing what daily life on the plantation was like.

Now that the plantation's restaurant, which serves lunch and dinner, has been moved from the manor house into a new building built just for the restaurant, the size and variety of exhibits in the manor house have been increased to make a complete plantation museum. The top floor displays bedrooms. On the main floor a parlor, dining room, and library are filled with appropriate period pieces. On the lower floor you'll find displays of handmade textiles, old quilts and coverlets, a floor loom, spinning wheels, and other textile-related artifacts such as an early Singer sewing machine, a clock reel, and a mother-in-law. The mother-in-law isn't going to ask to go home with you or anything; it's a device for winding yarn without an extra person to hold it.

In another room a series of displays depicts agricultural activities from 1860 to 1960, especially peanut production. This was a peanut plantation, remember. The equipment includes a horse-drawn peanut planter and an assortment of hand tools, many found buried on the site. Photographs add detail to the exhibit.

When you visit you'll probably have an opportunity to watch some crafts demonstrations. The plantation has three resident craftspeople: a blacksmith, a weaver, and a basket maker. At least one of them is always demonstrating. Some of what they make—rag rugs for instance—is for sale.

The outbuildings include a tenant house, smokehouse, herb cellar, kitchen (plantation kitchens were always in separate buildings), blacksmith shop, and turpentine and saltworks display. With or without a guide, looking at these buildings dramatically brings home some realities of history. A visitor looking at the small, roughly finished, uninsulated tenant house said, "It's hard to imagine that a whole family actually lived in here." Another visitor, seeing the mock hams, sausages, and bacons hanging in the smokehouse, wondered what the real thing would have been like in such hot weather and said, "It's a wonder everybody didn't die of food poisoning."

For children Poplar Grove Plantation has lots of open spaces—shaded with live oaks, sycamores, and magnolias—for running, a playground, and some farm animals they can see and maybe even touch. Open Monday through Saturday 9:00 A.M. to 5:00 P.M., Sunday noon to 5:00 P.M. Admission is $7.00 for adults, $6.00 for senior citizens, $3.00 for children six to fifteen. Last tour begins at 4:00 P.M. Closed Easter Sunday and Thanksgiving Day. Closed Christmas week and remains closed until first Monday in February.

Continuing north on US 17 takes you through some very local, untouristy areas, such as Holly Ridge, where the mayor's office is also the office of Ocean Aire Realty. If you want more of a sense of the area, shortly after you pass Holly Ridge turn left on Verona Road, and following the signs, head toward

Haws Run. You'll go by some pretty little houses with lovingly tended gardens, then an abandoned trailer park, and finally many occupied mobile homes on the way back out to US 17. This detour of only a few miles gives a view of what many small North Carolina communities near the coast are like.

Then you're into the area around Jacksonville, which is shaped and colored by ***Camp Lejeune Marine Base.*** Traffic is fairly heavy, and the area bulges with the kind of commercial development that surrounds military bases: motels, restaurants, arcades, shopping centers, and the like. But even though driving through such a section isn't as relaxing as spinning along a country road, it's tremendously instructive and sometimes funny. Most of the people you see in the vehicles are heartbreakingly young men with perfect posture and haircuts so short you can almost see their scalps from the next automobile. Often they're in pairs or groups, and often they're towing boats or hauling bikes. The progression of the establishments and signs you pass along the road tells a story: Foxy Lady, New Ink Tattoo Shop, Luigi's (where you can get a remarkably good Italian meal), a motel sign WELCOME MR. NUNNERY, Real Value Diamond Outlet, an assortment of churches, and the Maternity and Newborn Store.

Here's information of a more dignified nature. Camp Lejeune is one of the most complete training centers in the world and covers 110,000 acres. You may wish to stop at the Beirut Memorial, honoring those killed in Beirut and Grenada. It is outside the gate of Camp Johnson on State Highway 24. You can't get onto the base without a pass, and you can't get a pass without a driver's license and registration certificate. The information center at the main gate on Highway 24 is open twenty-four hours a day (910–451–2197).

From Jacksonville you could logically continue up US 17 to New Bern, or you could travel east on Highway 24 toward the ocean to check out the Bogue Banks and then go on to Morehead City, Beaufort, and Atlantic, and ferry across to the Outer Banks. Better yet, if you're not hurrying, avoid this section of Highway 24, which runs along another edge of the Marine base, and continue north about 15 miles more on US 17, where you pick up State Highway 58, which runs southeast along the side of the Croatan National Forest and is a much more pleasant drive to the coast. ***Cedar Point*** is a nice place to stop for a picnic or a rest and perhaps a hike along the Cedar Point Tideland Trail. You'll find camping areas and picnic tables in the shade along the water. Nearby is Cape Carteret, a little town that's probably completely solved its crime problem by locating its ABC (liquor) store right next to the police station and town hall.

Places to Stay in the Southern Coast and Islands

HOLDEN BEACH

Gray Gull Motel
At the bridge
Holden Beach 28462
(910) 842–6775

OCEAN ISLE BEACH

Ocean Isle Inn
37 West First Street
Ocean Isle Beach 28469
(800) 352–5988

The Winds
310 East First Street
Ocean Isle Beach 28469
(910) 579–6275
(800) 334–3581

SOUTHPORT

Lois Jane's Riverview Inn
106 West Bay Street
Southport 28461
(800) 457–1152

Riverside Motel
103 West Bay Street
Southport 28461
(910) 457–6986

Sea Captain Motor Lodge
608 West West Street
Southport 28461
(910) 457–5263

SUNSET BEACH

Sunset Vacations
401 South Sunset Boulevard
Sunset Beach 28468
(910) 579–5400
(800) 331–6428

WILMINGTON

Best Western Carolinian
2916 Market Street
Wilmington 28403
(910) 763–4653
(800) 528–1234

Catherine's Inn
410 South Front Street
Wilmington 28401
(800) 476–0723
(910) 251–0863

Comfort Inn
Executive Center
151 South College Road
Wilmington 28403
(910) 791–4841

Days Inn
5040 Market Street
Wilmington 28405
(910) 799–6300
(800) 329–7466

Rosehill Inn
114 South Third Street
Wilmington 28401
(910) 815–0250
(800) 815–0250

WRIGHTSVILLE BEACH

Harbor Inn
701 Causeway Drive
Wrightsville Beach 28480
(910) 256–9402
(888) 507–9402

Places to Eat in the Southern Coast and Islands

CALABASH

Captain Nance's Seafood Restaurant
Riverfront
Calabash 28467
(910) 579–2574

SOUTHPORT

Sandfiddler Seafood Restaurant
1643 North Howe Street
Southport 28461
(910) 457–6588

Thai Peppers Restaurant
115 East Moore Street
Southport 28461
(910) 457–0095

SUNSET BEACH

Sunset Grille
Causeway
Sunset Beach 28468
(910) 579–2929

WILMINGTON

Elijah's
2 Ann Street
Chandler's Wharf
Wilmington 28401
(910) 343–1448

Roy's Riverboat Landing
2 Ann Street
Chandler's Wharf
Wilmington 28401
(910) 763–7227

THE SOUTHERN COAST AND ISLANDS WEB SITE

North Carolina Ferry Systems
Web site: www.ncferry.org

The Northern Coast and Islands

Peaceful Places

Your next major stop as you head north along the coast is ***Morehead City,*** a deep port where the Intracoastal Waterway joins the Atlantic Ocean. It is both a commercial fishing town and a summer resort area, appealing especially to sport fishers. The waterfront is more devoted to commerce than tourism, has more than 5,000 square feet of continuous wharf, and includes a lot of shipping storage space. That means the waterfront isn't really pretty; it's too commercial and busy, but the activity is authentic and interesting. As a traveler, if you aren't here to fish, you're probably here to eat fish. The area has plenty of moderately priced motels and more seafood restaurants than you could patronize in two weeks' hard eating. If you ask people where to go, they'll most often make the unlikely sounding recommendation of the ***Sanitary Fish Market Restaurant*** (252–247–3111). It's just a block from U.S. Highway 70, on Bogue Sound. This is a big, casual, family-oriented place that seats more than 600 people and serves all kinds of seafood. It has been owned and operated by the same family since 1938. Ted Garner, who has since passed on, opened the restaurant with a partner. Today his son, Ted Jr., along with his own children, Jeff

THE NORTHERN COAST AND ISLANDS

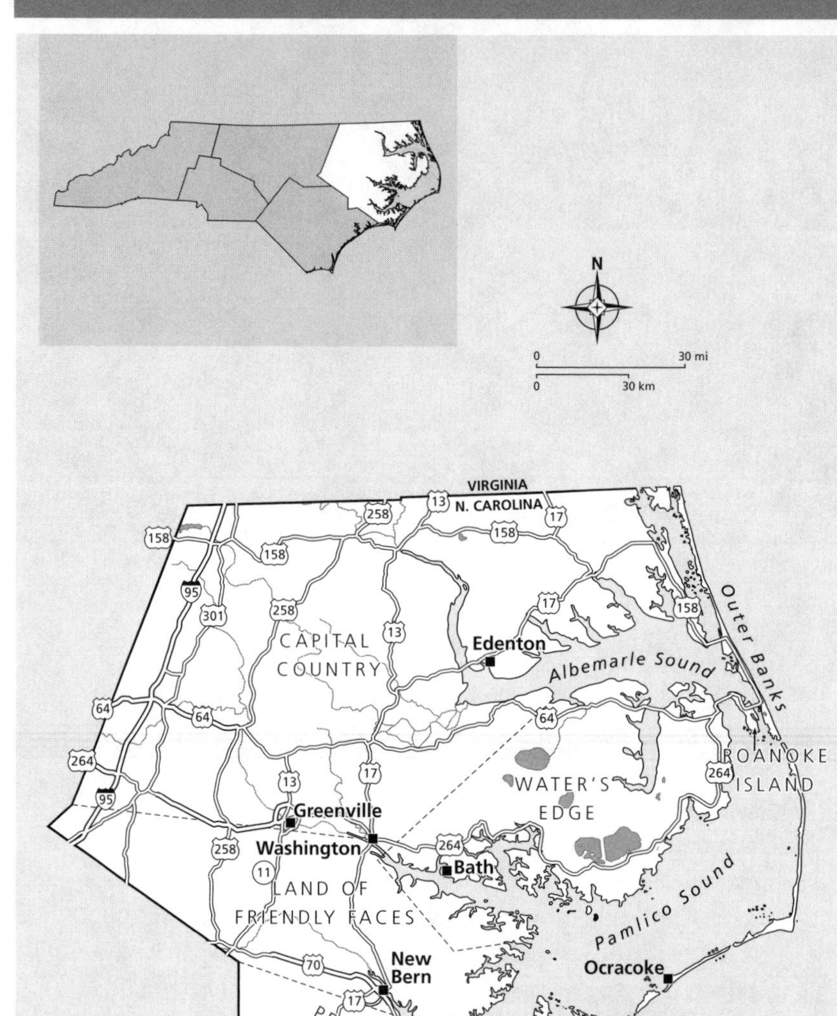

and Lisa, continue to run the business. "It's unusual to find a family in the business this long," Ted says. "It's hard work and a lot of people burn out." He says he thinks he has been able to keep going because he enjoys the work and has a core of good staff people, many of whom have been with the restaurant for years. Open from 11:00 A.M. to 8:30 P.M. daily during the peak (summer) season. May close earlier at other times. Closed in December and January.

The ***Carteret County Museum of History and Art,*** 1008 Arendell Street, is the kind of place that makes you feel good about people, just regular folks, and what they can accomplish when they set their minds to it. The Carteret County Historical and Genealogical Society owns and operates the museum almost entirely on volunteer help and donated funds. Cindi Hamilton, the only paid staff person, says, "The community built this museum. They gave their time and labor and money." They opened the museum in 1988 in a building that had served at various times as a school and a church, but in 2001, the museum moved to its new, greatly expanded space on Arendell Street. For tourists the displays of county artifacts, including Native American items, pieces from the Civil War and World War II, a fully furnished Victorian parlor, and clothing from the 1800s, are probably the most interesting aspect of the museum. But the facilities for historical research and genealogical study are also widely used and richly detailed. Cindi Hamilton says a staff of seventy-five volunteers do everything from guiding visitors through the museum to helping them with research. The museum is open Tuesday through Saturday, 10:00 A.M. to 4:00 P.M. Admission free. Phone (252) 247–7533. Web site: www.rootsweb.com.

ANNUAL EVENTS IN THE NORTHERN COAST AND ISLANDS

Kill Devil Hills
National Aviation Day–Orville Wright Birthday
August 19
(252) 441–7430

Annual Artful Gala
late February
(252) 473–5558

Manteo
Virginia Dare's Birthday Celebration
August 18
(252) 473–2127

Morehead City
Annual N.C. Seafood Festival
Waterfront
(mid-October)
(252) 726–6273

Outer Banks
Annual Outer Banks Stunt Kite Competition
Jockey's Ridge State Park
(mid-October)
(252) 441–4124
or (800) 334–4777

oddburials

People in Beaufort like to tell stories. Unquestionably their favorites are those about the Old Burying Ground. The oldest date you can make out on a grave marker is 1756, but the cemetery was deeded to the town in 1731. One story is about the English soldier who was buried standing up because he swore he would never lie down on foreign soil.

And then there's the little girl buried in a barrel of rum. Seems that before her father took her off to England on a ship, he promised her mother that he would bring the child back again. Unfortunately, she died aboard the ship, and embalming her in rum was the only way he could think of to keep his promise.

From Morehead City it's just a short drive over the Paul Graydon Bridge to ***Beaufort.*** The first step to having fun in Beaufort is learning to say it properly—*BOW-ford.* This separates it from that place in South Carolina spelled the same way but pronounced to rhyme with "phew." People in Beaufort, North Carolina, care and respond accordingly.

This was once a fishing village, settled by French Huguenots and English sailors more than 275 years ago. The port was active during three wars: the American Revolution, the War of 1812, and the Civil War. Today, Beaufort is a laid-back vacation area in which historic preservation and restoration have been impressive. Much of the downtown has been designated a National Historic Landmark, and the Beaufort Historical Association has restored a number of early buildings that are open to the public.

Local art is offered in the ***Mattie King Davis Art Gallery*** on the grounds of the Old Town Beaufort Restoration Complex, where local artists and craftspeople display their pottery, weaving, oil painting, watercolors, and other original art. It's open April 1 through October, Monday through Saturday from 10:00 A.M. to 4:00 P.M. No admission fee.

The ***North Carolina Maritime Museum,*** 315 Front Street, contains artifacts ranging from fish and fossils to ships, including a model-ship collection and a collection of 5,000 seashells from all over the world. Serious boat people visit here to watch wooden boats being built and restored. Open Monday through Friday from 9:00 A.M. to 5:00 P.M., Saturday from 10:00 A.M. to 5:00 P.M., Sunday from 1:00 to 5:00 P.M. (252–728–7317). For a schedule of special events, write the museum at 315 Front Street, Beaufort 28516. Web site: www.ah.dcr.state.nc.us. No admission fee.

One way to see the sights and learn a lot about local lore is by taking one of the ***Beaufort Historic Site Tours*** operated by the historical association. All tours leave from the welcome center at 130 Turner Street. Call ahead for all tour arrangements (252–728–5225 or 800–575–7483), Monday through Saturday from 9:30 A.M. to 5:00 P.M. March through November, 10:00 A.M. to 4:00 P.M. in winter. Web site: www.historicbeaufort.com.

The home tour includes not only old homes but also the jail, courthouse, and apothecary shop. Admission is $6.00 for adults, $4.00 for children.

From April 11 through October, the narrated English double-decker bus tours cover the downtown district and go out past a house that is reputed to have been a hangout for Blackbeard and his pirates in the late 1600s. The tour narrator gives a lively mix of fact and folklore. These tours run Monday, Wednesday, Friday, and Saturday at 11:00 A.M. and cost $6.00 per seat.

Narrated tours of the Old Burying Ground at Ann Street, where stones date back to 1709 and possibly earlier, are offered Tuesday through Thursday in summer and fall. The narrator tells colorful stories about unusual circumstances through which people came to be buried here. Admission is $6.00 for adults, $4.00 for children. You may walk around the grounds anytime free.

Of the several bed-and-breakfast establishments you might choose, ***Langdon House,*** at 123 Craven Street (252–728–5499), is especially congenial. This colonial home, built in 1732, is the oldest building in Beaufort operated as a bed-and-breakfast. A recently added luxury suite has a side-by-side whirlpool with hydro massage. All four rooms have private baths and queen-size beds. Two porches, one on the first and another on the second floor, invite people-watching, stargazing, and woolgathering. Breakfast is a full show—no soggy doughnuts in a box with coffee in Styrofoam cups here. Some mornings, for instance, it's orange-pecan waffles with orange butter. Some mornings you can have an authentic Mexican breakfast if you mention ahead of time that you'd like it.

Part of the establishment's charm comes from the antiques, including paintings and musical instruments that earlier residents of the building have donated

AUTHOR'S FAVORITE PLACES IN THE NORTHERN COAST AND ISLANDS

- Beaufort
- North Carolina Maritime Museum
- Langdon House
- T & W Oyster Bar
- Portsmouth Island
- Aurora Fossil Museum
- Mattamuskeet National Wildlife Refuge
- Weeping Radish
- Wanchese
- Hope Plantation
- Somerset Place

in the interests of the restoration's authenticity. A bigger attraction yet is the congeniality of the people. Jimm Prest knows the area intimately and likes to talk about it.

Langdon House is a small operation. Jimm, his Latina wife Lizzet, and a little extra help usually run the show, which means personal attention that is pretty much one-on-one with guests. Want to sleep till noon and have breakfast late? Jimm's willing. He says he wishes more people understood that if you want that kind of small-town, individualized situation, you can't expect chain-motel desk service at the same time. You may call for a reservation, for instance, and get a message on the answering machine saying that Jimm's gone for groceries, a haircut, or a couple days' vacation, telling you when he'll return, and asking you to call back then—just as you'd do if you were phoning a friend.

Because he's been in the area so long, Jimm knows all the Beaufort restaurants well. For a simple meal he suggests the ***Net House*** (252–728–2468), a short walk away at 133 Turner Street, where you can get broiled or lightly battered-and-fried seafood. You'll recognize it when you get there, because of the big red crab out front.

For a more upscale menu, ***Front Street Grill*** (300 Front Street; 252–723–3118) has out-of-the-ordinary entrees beautifully presented with delicate sauces and garnishes. The menu changes frequently and often reflects an ethnic influence—Thai or Mexican or Greek, for instance—without actually copying any other cuisine. Reservations are strongly suggested here.

A more recently established lodging alternative in Beaufort is the ***Pecan Tree*** (252–728–6733), a five-room, two-suite inn at 116 Queen Street that emphasizes the luxuries, with elaborately dressed beds, a Jacuzzi/sauna/exercise room, and a lounge. It has well-tended perennial gardens and has been popular with honeymooners. Web site: www.pecantree.com.

Shiver Me Timbers!

Most of the coastal towns and islands in the area lay some claim to Blackbeard, the notorious pirate who built a fleet of captured ships and terrorized the seas in the 1700s. He captured a French Guinea ship in 1717, renamed it *Queen Anne's Revenge,* and put forty huge guns, called blunderbusses, aboard. Later, he deliberately ran the sailing vessel aground near Beaufort, which was known as Fishtown in those early days, as part of a plan to dump his fleet and crew, while escaping with his loot and getting a pardon from England. In 1997, salvage crews found what they believe to be the remains of *Queen Anne's Revenge* in about 20 feet of water at Beaufort Inlet. They found a blunderbuss barrel, a ship's bell, and a cannon ball. All these items now belong to the state of North Carolina.

Wet Adventure

I paddled my first sea kayak in Beaufort. This is not something you start out doing gracefully. Getting into a life vest and wet suit takes some squirming. Crawling into the small open area of the kayak becomes an exercise in humility. And sitting with your legs stretched straight out in front of you seems an impossibility.

But then somebody gives you a shove off the sloped ramp and into the water, and after a few tentative strokes, paddling this thing across the waterway to an island seems doable.

It takes a while to remember which rudder to push and even longer to get really proficient at paddling so the boat goes where you want it to. Then it all comes together, and the kayak moves silently and efficiently across the water, and except for avoiding other boats and catching glimpses of the wild ponies and the birds on the islands, nothing else matters.

Be warned: Sea kayaking is addictive.

Langdon House cooperates in handling overflow and referring extra guests with the ***Captain's Quarters,*** a bed-and-breakfast in a Victorian house at 315 Ann Street (252–728–7711 or 800–659–7111). Captain Dick and Ruby Collins like to chat. Captain Dick's title comes not from the sea, as you might suppose, but from his days as an airline pilot. When you appear for your continental breakfast, he says, "Top o' the mornin' to ya!"

One could stay in Beaufort a long time just wandering around, eating seafood, and sitting on the porch reading trashy novels. But you can find more adventure if you want it, too. On the waterfront, near the North Carolina Maritime Museum on Front Street, you'll find ***Outer Banks Ferry Service*** (252–728–4129), which will take you to ***Shackleford Banks,*** an island populated only with wild horses; ***Carrot Island,*** a good place for shelling as well as Bird Shoals and Sand Dollar Islands; and on ***Cape Lookout,*** tours to visit the lighthouse and keepers' quarters and ride a jeep to the cape point. These are great activities in good weather but miserable places on cold, stormy days—assuming you could even get a ferry to take you over then—so it's better to arrange a trip once you see how the weather is going to be. Captain Perry is a good, reliable operator who started the service because during the time he worked in real estate people kept asking him how to get to the islands. "I wanted to provide that service in a safe, businesslike way," he says. Even if you are not particularly agile, you won't have trouble getting into the boat because he instructs you to "sit and spin": sit on the wide edge of the boat, spin around, and land your feet on the floor. He provides a sturdy ladder for easy descent onto the island beaches.

While you're in the area, take a half-hour drive some evening to the ***T & W Oyster Bar*** in Swansboro (252–393–8838). This is a local restaurant not too many tourists find. It specializes in oysters. You can get them steamed or raw. T & W serves oysters in such volume that they move them into the steamers with shovels. People who know about the place sometimes show up with their pickups to get a load of shells for their driveways. Raw oysters are served on the half shell, but you'll have more fun if you sit at the bar and order the steamed oysters, starting with maybe a half peck, although you'll probably want more. You can order them "well, medium, or rare." Rare comes to you just barely heated through. Shuckers stand behind the bar, open your oysters, and put them on your plate—dropping the shells onto a conveyor belt that moves them away somewhere. "Where are those shells going?" isn't a question that enters your mind as you're eating because, for one thing, the oysters are very good. But also, the shuckers, usually high school boys, keep up a steady stream of conversation about local goings on: who's doing what to whom, how late they stayed out last night, how long it took them to learn to shuck with any speed, how much it cost to get a tattoo. You name it, these guys have an opinion. You may get a shucker working on a case of teenage angst or a professional charmer. No matter which, it's fun.

cockadoodledoo

While you're eating oysters, you'll probably be invited to save one for a rooster. The shuckers make these. Each claims to have his own special version, but generally a rooster is a saltine cracker spread with horseradish; layered with Tabasco, black pepper, and an oyster; and topped with a slice of jalapeño pepper. Big men break out in a sweat eating a rooster. It's a macho thing, but any woman who wanted to try one would certainly be encouraged.

People who don't like oysters can order steamed shrimp or even burgers or fried fish, but the fun is at the bar. And don't expect any fancy booze here. The chardonnay comes in a big plastic jug labeled "use this first," and the beers are your basic Bud, Bud Light choices, served in pitchers. The only proper way to end the meal is with a piece of Key lime pie, which, when it arrives, is an unlikely shade of green never intended by the Maker—but it tastes pretty good.

They'll tell you oysters are available during all the months with "R" in their names, but the more accurate description is "during the cool months." Oysters aren't good when it's hot.

T & W is open 5:00 to 9:00 P.M. daily except Sunday, when the hours are noon to 9:00 P.M. Located on Highway 58 about 5 miles south of its intersection with Highway 24.

Assuming you are ready, eventually, to leave Beaufort, you should push on north almost to the end of US 70 East, to the little town of ***Atlantic*** (not to be confused with Atlantic Beach), where you can catch the ferry to the Outer Banks. Looking at your map, you will see that the Outer Banks is a long series of islands off the North Carolina coast. Some of them are fully developed resort areas; others have no concessions or services at all.

In particular, visit ***Portsmouth Island.*** It's uninhabited now, but 635 people once lived on the 30-mile-long island in the village of Portsmouth. Ultimately, they couldn't survive the weather, especially hurricanes. A particularly bad one in 1846 opened Hatteras and Oregon Inlets and changed shipping patterns, which cut off future economic development for the village. Gradually the people left, first the young and then the old. According to Joel Arrington, writing in the magazine *Wildlife in North Carolina,* only fourteen people remained on the island in 1950; the last male resident died in 1971, after which the remaining two women gave up and moved to the mainland. The buildings of the village remain a little beat-up but intact, maintained by the U.S. Park Service.

Your difficulty in seeing the village will be that, even after you've ferried across to the island, you need a four-wheel-drive vehicle to travel the 18 miles up the beach from the ferry landing to the village, because there are no roads. But getting a ride in a four-wheel-drive vehicle in North Carolina isn't as hard as it sounds. They are ubiquitous, especially among sportsmen (and it's not sexist to leave out women here, for there are few). Enough such people like to visit the village that you should be able to arrange a ride if you don't have a four-wheel-drive vehicle of your own. Indeed, the sight of half a dozen or so men in fishing clothes, sitting quietly on the benches inside the old, weathered, and abandoned Portsmouth Village Methodist Church when they're supposed to be at water's edge fishing, may be as special an experience as visiting the village. This isn't a likely place to lodge. A few cabins, locally known as "hooches," are rented, but during peak fishing seasons they're reserved as much as two years in advance. Still, if you'd like to try some truly primitive conditions on the island, it doesn't hurt to ask. For information about ferry hours and renting hooches, write Morris Marina at Star Route Box 761, Atlantic 28511; or phone (252) 225–4261.

A simpler way to visit the village, though less colorful and a bit more on the beaten (or should it be rowed, in this case?) path, is to take a skiff from Ocracoke Island that brings you directly to the spot. You need to arrange this in advance. Phone Rudi Austin (252–928–4361) to charter a ferry. The more people you can round up to make the trip with you, the less it costs per person. Figure about $40 for two, round-trip, but only about $15 per person when you have three or more.

If you're not sure how to manage the trip and would like more information and advice, call the Ranger Station (252–728–2250) for enthusiastic, knowledgeable help. They have a list of all the ferrying services and can put you in touch with the one that will work best for you.

Harkers Island doesn't attract a lot of traffic. It's a people place, not yet a tourist place, where a few people still remember when hunting waterfowl for food was a natural part of daily existence, not a recreational sport. They remember carving decoys because they needed them to attract ducks, not to set up on the mantel as decorator items. The ***Core Sound Waterfowl Museum*** honors that Down East heritage and provides a place for carvers to practice the old art and younger people to learn it or at least see it in action. The museum attracts visitors from all over the world.

Most days you'll find two or three local wood-carvers at work on the porch, telling stories about the days when waterfowl were so plentiful their clusters looked like islands out in the sound. When decoys got lost or drifted away, it wasn't a big deal. They just carved more as part of the daily routine. Nothing fancy about it. The early decoys didn't have to fool anybody but the flocks of birds high overhead.

A new, much larger museum is in the works—on sixteen acres at Shell Point, next to the National Park Service's Cape Lookout National Seashore headquarters near the tip of the island. It's a community effort, the money being raised by local people, with such attractions as a viewing platform on Willow Pond built by volunteers with donated materials. Whatever state the place is in when you get to Harkers, it's a heartwarming stop. The museum is open year-round 10:00 A.M. to 5:00 P.M. Monday through Saturday and 2:00 to 5:00 P.M. Sunday. Admission is free. For more information call (252) 728–1500. Web site: www.coresound.com.

Portsmouth Island and Harkers Island are part of the 56-mile-long ***Cape Lookout National Seashore*** (252–728–2250), which comprises North Core Banks, South Core Banks, and Shackleford Banks. A good place to sort out all the possibilities is at the visitor center at the end of Harkers Island, in a house that used to be the keepers' quarters near the Cape Lookout Lighthouse, at the end of the island. The lighthouse itself is not open for visitors, but it's a great subject for photographs and sketching. The center is open 8:30 A.M. to 4:30 P.M. seven days a week. Closed Christmas and New Year's Days. A variety of tours and camping arrangements are available, but before you sign up for anything, remember that the undeveloped islands don't have roads, bathrooms, or water, so you must be able to climb in and out of boats and walk a reasonable distance to spend time on them. You also need to carry in your own drinking water. As one park ranger says, "It's really a backcountry experience." It doesn't hurt to take along a good insect repellent, either. Two concessionaires affiliated with the National Park Service providing ferry, tour, and camping options are Alger Willis Fishing Camps, Inc. (252–729–2791) on South Core, and Morris Marina Kabin Kamps Ferry Service, Inc. (252–225–4261) on North Core.

Land of Friendly Faces

The entire area along the northern coast, the barrier islands, and the Outer Banks is a maze of toll ferries, free ferries, private ferries, and bridges. The way you organize your trips here depends on everything from the weather to how much time you want to spend driving or being ferried. Remember that a ferry is not a fast way to travel. In planning trips in this area, it sometimes works better to find a pleasant base to which you return after each foray in a new direction. Try ***New Bern*** as a slightly inland base from which, one way or another, you can get to a wonderful variety of places to spend a day or so. Everyone in New Bern will have ideas for you, which will certainly include ***Oriental.***

Oriental is about 25 miles east of New Bern on State Highway 55. It has won a reputation as the sailing capital of the East Coast and almost always has a sailing school or camp in progress. Except for some antiques shops, a modest motel or two, and some restaurants, there's not much here except nice people. If you want to spend a night at a bed-and-breakfast here, the ***Inn at Oriental,*** at 508 Church Street (252–249–1078), has eight rooms with private baths, king- and queen-size beds, and facilities for the handicapped. The inn was built at the turn of the twentieth century and has been restored to duplicate the feel of an English country inn—with contemporary amenities. The innkeepers serve a big breakfast. Web site: www.innatoriental.com.

Then again, once you're in New Bern, you may not want to go anywhere else at all—not just because there's so much to see and do but also because this is one of the friendliest towns anywhere. To give you an idea, a couple staying

crossing the water

The North Carolina ferry system links many coastal and island communities that would otherwise take hours to reach by road or be completely inaccessible except by private boat. The system, which has been running since the mid-1940s, is operated by the North Carolina Department of Transportation. It is one of the largest ferry systems in the nation.

Crossing times range from twenty minutes to get from Cherry Branch to Minnesot to two and a half hours for the trip from Ocracoke to Swan Quarter. Schedules vary with the seasons. For full details call (800) BY–FERRY or check the Web site: www.ncferry.org.

at a bed-and-breakfast inn in the historic district was walking to a nearby restaurant where they had dinner reservations when they stopped to admire an especially nicely restored house. The owners, who happened to be on the porch, invited the couple in for a drink and showed them around. They spent so much time chatting that the couple never did make it to the restaurant.

On the outside chance that you might not be so generously befriended by strangers, stop in the tourist center at the Chamber of Commerce about 2 blocks from US 70, near the Trent River at the end of Middle Street, when you get to town. Signs point the way from all major entrances. Everyone here is extraordinarily friendly, too. One middle-aged travel writer who stopped in for maps and directions struck up a conversation with a teenage summer assistant. They've been corresponding ever since.

If you're an antiquer, be sure to get a copy of the brochure "Antiques Shops of New Bern," which gives particulars on more than a dozen antiques shops, complete with a map and an explanation of American furniture styles from Queen Anne (1725–1750) through the arts and crafts and mission styles of the early 1900s.

You'll also be able to pick up full details on ***Tryon Palace*** Restorations and Garden Complex, where first a royal government and then an independent state government were housed. In colonial times Tryon Palace, at 610 Pollack Street, was known as the most beautiful building in America. The elaborate formal gardens as well as the elegant buildings and furnishings have been restored.

Tours conducted by guides in costume lead you through the rooms; give you a look at demonstrations of candle making, cloth making, cooking, and other period activities; and fill you in on specific facts about the buildings and their earlier, illustrious occupants. If you just want to walk around in the gardens, you can take a self-guided tour. The complex (252–514–4900 or 800–767–1560) is open year-round, Monday through Saturday from 9:00 A.M. to 4:00 P.M., and Sunday from 1:00 to 5:00 P.M. Closed Thanksgiving Day, December 24–26, and January 1. Admission is $15.00 for adults, $6.00 for students with identification. Write Tryon Palace, Box 1007, New Bern 28560. Web site: www.tryonpalace.org.

Much less well known than the Tryon Palace are these three small museums, each within walking distance of the other.

The ***Attmore–Oliver House Museum,*** built in 1790, at 511 Broad Street (parking at 510 Pollock Street), belonged at one time to Samuel Chapman, who had earlier been a first lieutenant under General George Washington. It features eighteenth- and nineteenth-century antiques, artifacts related to New Bern's history, and a Civil War museum room. There's also a collection of eighteenth-century dolls. Open Tuesday through Saturday from 1:00 to 4:30 P.M. (252–638–8558). Closed mid-December to the first weekend in April. Admission is $2.50 for ages twelve and up.

The ***New Bern Fireman's Museum,*** across the corner at 408 Hancock Street houses a collection of memorabilia of North Carolina's earliest fire company, from 1845, and of the Button Company, a rival volunteer company. The New Bern Fireman's Museum claims the title of "oldest volunteer fire company in North Carolina." The museum guide himself has been a volunteer fireman for many years. The displays include early steamers and pump wagons, large photographs, and the mounted head of an old fire horse named Fred, who, at least according to publicists, died in harness answering a false alarm in 1925. No information is offered about what happened to the rest of the horse. Open Monday through Saturday from 10:00 A.M. to 4:00 P.M. Closed Thanksgiving, Christmas, and New Year's Day. Admission is $2.00 for adults, $1.00 for children. Phone (252) 636–4087. Web site: www.newbernmuseums.com.

At ***Bank of the Arts,*** 317 Middle Street (252–638–2577), about a block away, you'll find artists' exhibits in sculpture, oil, watercolor, pottery, and photography. The exhibits change every month. Originally a neoclassical bank building, it is now home to the Craven Arts Council and Gallery. The gallery has 30-foot-high ceilings with ornate colored plaster in the Beaux Arts style. Sometimes afternoon concerts, storytellers, and folksingers are featured. Open Monday through Friday noon to 4:00 P.M.

Tryon Palace, New Bern

The ***New Bern Trolley Cars*** (252–637–7316 or 800–849–7316) combine the fun of motion with the expertise of tour guides who know the history of New Bern and tell it well. The trolley tours, which run through the historic downtown district, last ninety minutes. Tour hours vary with the seasons, so you'll do better by calling to find out what's happening during your visit to the area. Tickets are available where the trolley begins its route, next to Tryon Palace: $12.00 for adults, $6.00 for children.

In a town as historically significant as New Bern, you could easily get overwhelmed by more historical data than you really want on a vacation, but to enjoy the area you should know at least a few basic facts. The community was first settled in 1710 by Swiss and German immigrants, who named it for Bern, Switzerland. It was capital of the colonies from 1766 to 1776 and then state capital. Economically, the area flourished mostly because of its port at the time of the Revolution, slumped during the Civil War, then recovered fairly quickly. From about the time of World War II, it has gradually restored its historical spots and become a comfortably established, low-key attraction. Irrelevant but fun to know: Pepsi-Cola was invented here, but the inventor went bankrupt during a sugar scarcity. Caleb Bradham created a drink in 1898 at his pharmacy that he said did not contain the "impurities" found in bottled health tonics and other drinks, referring to the alcohol and narcotics some of them contained. People liked it and started calling it, "Brad's drink." Bradham's photograph shows a good-looking man with dark hair, a long face, high arching eyebrows, and a quirky smile under a narrow mustache. He looks like the drink made him happy. He made the stuff in the cramped basement of his store, bottling the syrup for his fountain and other pharmacies in the area. In a few years he was doing enough business to realize he was on to something and incorporated as Pepsi-Cola on December 24, 1902. Today the ***Birthplace of Pepsi-Cola,*** 256 Middle Street, is a memorabilia gift shop in the same location, owned by the Pepsi-Cola Bottling Company. For 64 cents you can buy a fountain Pepsi and drink it sitting at a table surrounded by Pepsi memorabilia—signs and shirts and lamps and key rings and magnets and limited edition displays. A video narrated by Walter Cronkite telling the Pepsi-Cola story is available to watch while you're in the store. The store is open Monday through Saturday, 10:00 A.M. to 6:00 P.M. Phone (252) 636–5898. Web site: www.pepsistore.com.

An interesting and historical, yet cheery and comfortable place to stay in New Bern, is ***Harmony House Inn,*** 215 Pollock Street (252–636–3810 or 800–636–3113). Sooki and Ed Kirkpatrick, the proprietors, bring to innkeeping the kind of personable warmth that makes business travelers who stay there regularly feel free to stop in unannounced, use the phone in the inn's office,

Showing the Colors

During the summer and into autumn in New Bern, you'll notice the streets are lined with trees blooming in a range of colors from palest pink to bright red to dark purple. *Lagerstroemia indicia,* commonly known as crape myrtle, is the official shrub of New Bern. Originally native to China and tropical and subtropical countries, crape myrtle is popular throughout the South and not hardy north of Baltimore. Hybridizers have created dwarf versions of the plant for smaller gardens. The bark on *Lagerstroemia* flakes away from the wood in patches, showing a lighter color underneath that attracts the eye in winter after the tree has shed its leaves and branches.

and then hurry out to the car, saying they'll be back to spend the night on the way through tomorrow. Web site: www.harmonyhouseinn.com.

The story of the house is complex. It began as a four-room, two-story home with Greek Revival styling. As the family grew, the house was enlarged. Around the turn of the twentieth century, as the children grew older, two sons wanted the house, so it was sawed in half, and one side was moved 9 feet away from the other. A huge hallway and another set of stairs were put in to join the building yet divide it into two separate dwellings. Now the two hallways, front doors, and sitting areas are all part of the inn. It's furnished with antiques and reproductions created by local craftspeople, and in the parlor is an 1875 organ in perfect working order. Breakfast is always an extravaganza, including eggs, cheese, meat, cereal, and fruit. You are invited to participate in an evening social hour with white wine; sherry is put out later in case you'd like a nightcap.

After a day of touring, you can rest awhile and then walk to dinner. ***Henderson House,*** right across the street at 216 Pollock (252–637–4784), has been serving fine meals for nearly twenty years. The atmosphere is elegant. Dining specialties include a hot soup and a cold fruit soup, as well as a seafood casserole, scallops, lobster, and chicken entrees. All spirits are available. As you'd expect, all the desserts are homemade. Everything is delicious, the kind of dining that guests at the bed-and-breakfasts talk about over breakfast the next morning. Dinner is served from 6:00 to 9:00 P.M. Tuesday through Saturday.

Water's Edge

One interesting trip from New Bern is the drive north on US 17 to Washington, where you pick up U.S. Highway 264 to Bath, Belhaven, and Swan Quarter. The trip winds through mostly rural areas.

You'll find a lot of local color just before you come to Washington, at ***Chocowinity,*** billed as "Home of the Indians," where the high school boasts having won a series of state and regional girls' basketball titles and cheerleading championships, beginning in 1980. Chocowinity is a crossroads community, not set up to lure or serve tourists, so don't count on it as a place to stop, fuel up, eat, and so on. Look at it as an absolutely honest glimpse of small-town coastal North Carolina.

From here you can drive on through Washington to Bath or get to Bath by crossing the Pamlico River on the ferry, which you approach by following State Highway 33 East from Chocowinity through corn and tobacco country, past a brick house with a stonework chimney that's bigger than the house, past Possum Track Road, and on to Aurora—a drive of about 33 miles. This route actually backtracks some, and you could get to Aurora faster by taking State Road 1003 from US 17 just outside New Bern, but then you'd miss Chocowinity. It all depends on how much exploring you want to do.

Twin Lakes Resort, 1618 Memory Lane (252) 946–5700, offers swanky camping. You have a choice of trailer sites (some shaded), tent sites, and pull-throughs, supplying water and electricity. Also on the grounds are hot showers, campfires, laundry facilities, pay phones, ice, firewood, church services, a boat ramp, a fishing pier, waterskiing, a playground, recreational facilities, a camp store, and a picnic area.

According to a chatty soul named Dianne, people sometimes bring big tents, refrigerators, and small television sets—everything they need to stay for a long time. Camping on this scale is $30 a night weekends, $25 weekdays. Primitive camping (though Linda can't imagine who'd want it) is $25 a night

BETTER-KNOWN ATTRACTIONS IN THE NORTHERN COAST AND ISLANDS

New Bern
Tryon Palace
(800) 767–1560

Manteo
Lost Colony Outdoor Drama
(252) 473–2127
(800) 488–5012

Roanoke Island
North Carolina Aquarium
(252) 473–3493

Nags Head
Jocky Ridge State Park
(252) 441–7132

Kill Devil Hills
Wright Brothers National Memorial
(252) 441–7430

weekends, $20 weekdays. Ask for directions when you call. Web site: www.twinlakesnc.com.

Close to the juncture of State Highways 33 and 306, the little town of Aurora—population about 500—is home to the ***Aurora Fossil Museum,*** on Main Street. This museum is great for kids who are turned on by hunting for artifacts and equally rewarding for anyone looking for a better understanding of the geological history of eastern North Carolina from the birth of the Atlantic Ocean to the present.

Millions of years ago this part of the state lay under the ocean. Fossils anywhere from five to twenty-two million years old are on display in the museum, along with a variety of murals and an eighteen-minute video explaining the history of the region. The fossils include giant teeth from 40-foot sharks, bones from extinct birds, and skeletons of dolphins that had necks. Some scientists speculate that the existence of the neck proves dolphins once lived on land and evolved to adapt to the sea.

The museum gets its artifacts from a large phosphate mine a few miles north of town. An exhibit in the museum shows a mock phosphate pit to illustrate how phosphate is mined and where the fossils come from. And outside the museum stands a huge pile of coarse phosphate materials through which visitors may sift for fossils. What you're most likely to find here are prehistoric shark's teeth.

The museum is about more than fossils and prehistoric times and now includes such exhibits as a collection of Native American artifacts. The museum is open 9:00 A.M. to 4:30 P.M. Monday through Saturday. Closed on holidays. Phone (252) 322–4238. Web site: www.pamlico.com/aurora/fossils.

From Aurora, Highway 306 North runs to the Pamlico River Ferry. The ferry is free. The crossing takes about twenty-five minutes. From the ferry landing, go left on State Highway 92 into historic ***Bath,*** where you come first to the visitor center.

Bath is the kind of place you fantasize about when you dream of leaving the rat race for a simpler way of life. The town, with a population not much over 200, only 3 blocks long and 2 blocks wide, is friendly and without guile; people cutting their grass or working in their gardens wave as you walk or drive by. They're proud of their history but see it with enough humor to name the state liquor store "Ye Olde ABC Package Store."

The folks in the ***Historic Bath Visitors Center*** at 207 Carteret Street encourage you to see the twenty-five-minute orientation film, "A Town Called Bath," before you begin a self-guided walking tour or take one of the guided tours. These tours are given on the hour, with the last tour leaving an hour before closing time. Hours are 9:00 A.M. to 5:00 P.M. Monday through Saturday

Whitfield's Curse

Bath opened the first public library in the American colonies in the early 1700s, started the first shipyard in the state in 1701, and was the state's first capital in 1744. So why did such a forward-looking town never grow the way some other seaport towns did?

Local legend has it that the townspeople rejected Methodist evangelist George Whitfield when he came in 1774 to save their souls. They didn't want to hear his preaching, and they wouldn't give him a place to stay in town. Whitfield got back at them by placing a curse on the village: ". . . you shall remain, now and forever, forgotten by men and nations. . . . "

After that the town burned three times, and even today the population stays at about 200 souls, which may or may not be saved.

and from 1:00 to 5:00 P.M. Sunday, from April through October 31. Winter hours are 10:00 A.M. to 4:00 P.M. Tuesday through Saturday, 1:00 to 4:00 P.M. Sunday. Tours take about an hour and a half. Modest admission is charged (252–923–3971). Web site: www.pamlico.com/bath.

You can approach the history a couple of different ways. Bath was the home of Blackbeard, the pirate, and some of his loot is still supposed to be buried somewhere in the area. It's also the oldest incorporated town in North Carolina. The Palmer–Marsh House, from the colonial period, dates back to about 1740. The St. Thomas Church, which was begun in 1734, is the oldest church in the state. It has been restored and is still used by the Episcopal Diocese as an active place of worship, although visitors are allowed to come in anytime for a self-guided tour. The St. Thomas parish had a collection in the early 1700s of more than 1,000 books and pamphlets from England, and that collection became the first public library in North Carolina.

From Bath, it's a pretty drive of 11 miles on State Highway 99 to Belhaven. Here you can visit ***Belhaven Memorial Museum,*** in Old City Hall on East Main Street. The collection represents the idiosyncratic personal interests of Eva Blount Way in collections she began about 1900, when she would have been about thirty years old. She began with buttons, ending up with about 30,000 of them. This won't make much sense if you're so young you've seen only standard plastic buttons found on most clothing today. But before plastic, buttons were made from all kinds of materials: precious metals, gemstones, wood, shells. They were often highly ornate, hand produced, and beautiful. In Eva's day, practically all women had jars full of buttons or kept buttons on long strings. Eva's collection just got a little out of hand. She also got interested in old coins, early American kitchenware, coffee grinders, antique dolls, and toys. The displays now include Civil War items, military memorabilia from two world wars, farming tools, and so on. One quirky addition is an X-ray machine from the 1920s that looks like something from a Flash Gordon serial. The museum advertises itself, "It's like spending a day in your grandmother's attic." Belhaven Memorial Museum is open every day but Wednesday 1:00 to 5:00 P.M. Admission free; donations appreciated. Phone (252) 943–6817. Web site: www.beaufort-county.com/belhavenmuseum.

At Belhaven pick up US 264 East, crossing the Intracoastal Waterway to Swan Quarter—a nature lover's paradise, filled with water, woods, and wildlife, where people so far have made only the lightest noticeable mark. Most of this distance is lovely, although you'll probably see a lot of heavy equipment in some areas. In early summer hibiscus bushes bloom along the road, red and yellow cannas adorn the lawns of farmhouses and mobile homes, and apple trees bear so heavily that the fruit seems to be dripping from the laden and drooping branches.

At Swan Quarter you can either take the ferry to Ocracoke, probably the best known of the barrier islands, or you can continue driving up the coast along US 264 to Manns Harbor, where you cross the bridge to Roanoke Island and continue on over the ***Outer Banks*** islands. If you plan to take the ferry, a two-and-one-half-hour ride, call the Ocracoke Visitors Center (252–928–6711) ahead of time to check on current schedules and weather conditions.

"ibegtodiffer . . ."

Another North Carolina travel writer who was on a panel with me told the audience that she was "underwhelmed" by Ocracoke and advised them not to bother going there. For sure, she said, there was nothing for her twelve-year-old son to do there. The moral is that if you or the people traveling with you want specifically organized "things to do," skip Ocracoke. The fact that the writer quoted is still alive and in good health says a lot for my self-control and restraint.

Ocracoke, an old fishing village, is fun if you're willing to take a couple of days and just hang out; if all you do is drive through, you'll miss most of what it has to offer. Of course there's history. As early as 1715 Ocracoke was a port of the North Carolina colony, where Blackbeard, the pirate, buried his treasure and lost his head. The head got carried off to Bath; presumably the treasure's still somewhere on the island. These days, fishing, bicycling (you can rent bicycles here), and bird hunting are bigger attractions than treasure hunting. But mostly Ocracoke is a place to escape the chrome-and-plastic world of commercial tourism. You can enjoy the remnants of Old English lilting in the speech of some of the old-timers as you walk around the village, read up on local history and nature, and visit the famous pony pens where the remaining descendants of the famous Spanish mustangs are protected. For full information about the island, ferries, and marina, contact the Ocracoke Visitors Center (252–928–6711). ***Ocracoke Island Lighthouse*** (888–493–3826), on Point Road, is the oldest lighthouse still in use in North Carolina. It was built in 1823. The tower is 75 feet tall, built of brick and concrete, with 5-foot-thick base walls. The white tower serves as an entrance beacon to Ocracoke Inlet. The tower is not open to the public, but you may tour the grounds. Admission is free. Web site: www.ocracoke-nc.com/light.

Fair warning here—Ocracoke gains in popularity as a tourist destination every year, and to enjoy it as a slower-paced place, you need to plan a trip that doesn't land you on the island at the peak of the summer season in July and August. Although you can still enjoy the island's 16 miles of clean, unspoiled beaches without crowding or concessions then, you'll find the area around the harbor full of people wandering about, gaping, and filling the restaurants. Not that there's anything wrong with that. Ocracoke, after all, has set itself up to serve tourists. But you'll get a much better sense of the place and its people during the slower times.

A good example of this is ***Edwards of Ocracoke,*** 226 Back Road, a place to stay in the village. This is one of the long-established lodgings, with motel rooms and efficiencies, cottage apartments, and a couple of private cottages all clustered around a tree-shaded yard with lawn chairs, grills, and a place to clean fish. The accommodations are relatively inexpensive and quite plain, but comfortable. It's a place with no affectations, run by Wayne, Trudy, and Bert Clark, all of whom came to the place after leaving more high-powered jobs and education. It's friendly and homey. But in the busiest times, such as mid-July, it's also full of people, so you definitely won't have any sense of privacy and silence on a tiny island. Phone (800) 254–1359. Web site: www.edwardsofocracoke.com.

Listening for the Lilt

As the older residents of Ocracoke leave this world, to be replaced by younger, more mobile generations, and as television standardizes speech accents, the unique speech patterns with Old English inflections become harder to find. It's easier to hear if you know what you're listening for, and a project at North Carolina State University can help you. The N.C. Language and Life Project Web site (www.ncsu.edu/linguistics/ocracoke.htm) offers the opportunity to hear the brogue and see a video about the speech patterns of earlier Ocracoke natives.

In the bed-and-breakfast category, ***Berkley Manor*** at 60 Water Plant Road, sits on several acres on the waterfront at the south end of the island. The rooms, with gleaming cedar paneling, might be described as "luxuriously rustic." Some of them have fireplaces and some have Jacuzzis. Guests have the use of nicely appointed sitting rooms and a tower from which they can look out over the ocean. This kind of accommodation costs considerably more than places like Edwards. Phone (800) 832–1223. Web site: www.berkleymanor.com.

Virtually everyone who visits the island ends up having at least one meal at ***Howard's Pub and Raw Bar Restaurant,*** on State Highway 12 at the north end of the village. This is a big, clattering place with a menu that has everything from thick, hand-shaped burgers to oysters on the half-shell. Portions are generous, service is friendly, and the atmosphere is casual. People seem to be having a good time, especially those seated on the screened porch. In addition to a wine list, Howard's has a huge line-up of beers, more than 200 of them, from domestic Coors and Rolling Rock to microbrewery organic beers such as Butte Creek Pale Ale to regional microbrewery specialties. Also, Howard's has a line of T-shirts, hats, sweatshirts, mugs, magnets, and the like emblazoned with its logo. For all the commotion, you don't get the feeling of being churned through a corporate eating place here, and especially in the off-season, it's fun. The restaurant is open every day of the year from 11:00 A.M. to 2:00 A.M. Phone (252) 928–4441.

Another popular restaurant on the island is ***Captain Ben's Restaurant,*** on Highway 12, just north of the ferry terminal. The restaurant specializes in seafood; its signature dishes are shrimp scampi and Maryland crab cakes. You can enjoy wine or beer here, in a casual atmosphere. The restaurant is open April through October, from 11:30 A.M. to 9:00 P.M., serving lunch and dinner. Phone (252) 928–4741 for reservations.

No matter how much you like it, sooner or later you'll have to leave Ocracoke. A free ferry will take you from Ocracoke to Cape Hatteras. Hatteras is pretty well built up and can have heavy traffic on its main highway, but you should plan on a visit to the ***Pea Island National Wildlife Refuge,*** south of the Oregon Inlet, where you can see more birds than you even knew existed—more than 250 different species. Serious bird-watchers spend days here. You need a good insect repellent, a shirt with long sleeves, a hat with a brim, suntan lotion, and drinking water to make the experience comfortable. Binoculars help, too. Some observation decks let you see not only the ocean and wildlife but also shipwrecks on the shore. The refuge is open every day from dawn to dusk. The information office is open Monday through Friday, 9:00 A.M. to 4:00 P.M. from April through October. Admission free. Phone (252) 987–2394 or (252) 473–1131.

Next, still along the Outer Banks, at Frisco, you'll find the ***Native American Museum and Natural History Center*** (252–995–4440) on Highway 12. The museum has a nationally recognized but too-seldom-seen collection of Native American artifacts and exhibits. In the natural history center, you'll find educational displays, special films, live exhibits, and a nature trail winding through the maritime forest. The people who work here say it's impossible to tell what the most popular exhibits are because favorites vary with each individual, but the stone artifacts attract a lot of attention, the Hopi wishing drum really does work, and people who commune with nature in the maritime forest claim some unusual experiences. The gift shop is popular, too, because it sells genuine Native American crafts. The museum is open Tuesday through Sunday, 11:00 A.M. to 5:00 P.M. To request information by mail, write the museum at Box 399, Frisco 27936. Modest admission is charged. Web site: www.nativeamerican museum.org.

duediligence

People at the Native American Museum are pretty pumped up after being visited by an anthropologist and archaeologist husband-and-wife team. She, curator at a large museum in Cleveland, Ohio, said that she saw better specimens here than they had in Cleveland. She and her husband spent almost two hours looking at everything.

It's possible to drive on up the Outer Banks, but it's monotonous in some undeveloped areas, full of traffic elsewhere, and generally just not as interesting as you'd expect it to be. You might do better to ferry back across to Swan Quarter and from there drive north on US 264, toward Manns Harbor, where the bridge takes you across to Manteo on Roanoke Island. This trip takes you into the ***Mattamuskeet National Wildlife Refuge,*** a breathtaking wilderness of 50,000 acres comprising Lake Mattamuskeet, marshland, timber, and cropland. The lake is 18 miles long and about 6 miles wide, the largest natural lake in North Carolina.

In parts of the acreage, water levels are controlled mechanically to allow local farmers to plant corn and soybeans and to allow for overseeding some acres to provide food for the wildlife. The wooded areas along the boundaries of the refuge contain pine and mixed hardwoods. Some commercial logging and controlled burning are used to keep the woodlands healthy.

Headquarters for the refuge (252–926–4021) is off State Highway 94, 1½ miles north of US 264, between Swan Quarter and Englehard. Stopping in is a good way to learn all the possibilities of the place. At various points you can crab, fish in fresh- or saltwater, and hunt. The area begs for bird-watching, photographing, and painting. Depending on the time of year, you might spot swans, Canada geese, song- and marsh birds, and even bald eagles, as well as deer, bobcats, and river otter. Some hunting of swans, ducks, coots, and occasionally deer is allowed.

But this is a refuge administered by the U.S. Fish and Wildlife Service of the Department of the Interior and operates by its rules. You can't camp, swim, or collect exotic plants here. There are restrictions on firearms. The refuge is open from for daylight use daily. For full details on how to enjoy the place and lists of lodgings available nearby, write Refuge Manager, Mattamuskeet National Wildlife Refuge, Route 1, Box N-2, Swan Quarter 27885. Web site: www.albemarle-nc.com/mattamuskeet/refuge.

Mattamuskeet Lodge on the property is no longer open for visitors inside because of structural problems, but it's still an interesting place to take pictures from the outside, and the story of the lodge stands as proof that people have been messing with the environment to make money for a long time. Beginning in 1911, three different investors tried to drain Lake Mattamuskeet to build a community they wanted to call New Holland and farm what would be rich soil once the water was gone. They built a pumping station in 1915, where four coal-fueled steam pumps moved 2,000 gallons of water per second. This was the largest pumping station in the world. But the whole enterprise was so expensive that each of the investors ultimately gave up on the idea and the U.S. government took over the land in 1934, establishing a waterfowl sanctuary. The Civilian Conservation Corps turned the pumping plant into a lodge, with an observation deck in the tower that had been a smokestack. The lodge has been empty since 1974, but local volunteer groups, the nonprofit group Partnership for the Sounds, and the U.S. Fish and Wildlife Service are raising money to restore the lodge so it can be used for research and education about migratory waterfowl. The first weekend in December, the ***Swan Days Festival,*** with local craft and food vendors, guided tours of the refuge areas, and workshops, focuses attention on the lodge and the refuge. The refuge office and lodge Web site (www.albemarle-nc.com/mattamuskeet/refuge/) provide details.

When you're in the area, it's fun to gas up at the ***Mattamuskeet Sportsman's Center*** on US 264, where the proprietor will dispense information, advice, directions, and such necessities as fishing and hunting equipment, bait shrimp, worms, ice, candy, beer, and soda. Oh, yes, and food.

From Mattamuskeet Lake, US 264 continues through lonely marsh and woodland up to Manns Harbor and across to Roanoke Island. The main community here, Manteo, used to be a small resort area. It's growing now, not excessively, but too much to suit the longtime residents who remember when the road through town didn't turn into bumper-to-bumper ribbons of automobiles during rush hour.

Roanoke Island

You'll remember from your grade-school history lessons that ***Roanoke Island*** is where the English first tried to establish a colony in the New World in 1585, encouraged by Queen Elizabeth I and led by Sir Walter Raleigh. They named it for Raleigh but couldn't keep it going. A year later those who had survived returned to England. In 1587 Raleigh tried again, this time including women and children in the group led by John White. Virginia Dare was born here. Then Sir Walter went sailing away for supplies. By the time he got back, three years later, the colony had vanished, leaving no signs of what might have happened to it. The ***Fort Raleigh National Historic Site*** memorializes the lost colony with a restoration of the old fort and a granite marker commemorating Virginia Dare's birth as the first English child born here. From June through August, the drama *The Lost Colony,* performed outdoors at the Waterford Theatre on the site, tells the story. One of Andy Griffith's acting roles in his pre-Mayberry years was as Sir Walter Raleigh in this show. Everything about this outdoor drama happens on a grand scale, on a stage in front of the bay so the water almost seems to be a backdrop. Many of the effects are marvels of engineering. For instance, three ships "sail" in front of the stage, moved by a combination of ropes and human energy. Moderate admission charged. Phone (800) 488–5012 for exact schedules. Be sure to ask what the current policy is regarding bad weather. Web site: www.thelostcolony.org.

Rain Time

The weather was cold and blustery the first time I saw a performance of *The Lost Colony*. As I was getting ready to sit down, a young man's hat blew off and landed at my feet. I retrieved it and ended up sitting next to him.

Shortly into the performance, I realized he was saying every performer's lines along with the actors—and he had it all down perfectly. He saw me notice and explained that he used to be in the show. It was common for the actors to learn each other's lines, he said, in case one of them couldn't perform and needed a stand-in.

By this time the rain was coming down pretty hard. The young man said the Indian dancers had two dance tempos—regular time and rain time. When the weather was bad, they danced faster to get the whole show finished so they wouldn't have to give back money to a rained-out audience.

This night, although the crowd sat willingly under umbrellas watching the show, the dancers just couldn't go fast enough. Pouring rain brought everything to a halt, and as we left, theater staff handed us tickets for another performance.

Elizabeth II

Next to the theater, the ***Elizabethan Gardens*** (252–473–3234) created by the Garden Club of North Carolina as a memorial to the lost colonists, bloom from spring until fall, with roses, crape myrtle, lilies, hydrangeas, and summer annuals. The garden features an extensive collection of old garden ornaments, some dating back to the time of the first Queen Elizabeth, as well as a sunken garden, a wildflower garden, an herb garden, and camellias and azaleas in season. Open April and May 9:00 A.M. to 6:00 P.M.; June, July, and August to 7:00 P.M.; September and October to 6:00 P.M.; November to 5:00 P.M.; December, January, and February to 4:00 P.M.; March to 5:00 P.M. Admission is $6.00 for adults, $5.00 seniors, $4.00 for children ages six to eighteen; children under five are admitted free.

Complete your history lesson by visiting the **Elizabeth II *State Historic Site,*** across the bridge and opposite the Manteo waterfront. The museum (252–473–1144) contains exhibits depicting life in the sixteenth century, including a reproduction of a sailing vessel similar to what would have been used to bring the first colonists to Roanoke in 1585. A twenty-minute multimedia program gives you the feel of those early voyages and what it would have been like to live on the ship. In the summer costumed actors portray early marines and colonists. After seeing the film, you may tour the ship. Operating hours vary seasonally. Moderate admission is charged. Web site: www.roanokeisland.com.

In downtown ***Manteo*** (named for an Indian of Roanoke who went back to England with the early sailors) on US 64/264, you can pick up a bit of local family history by staying at ***Scarborough Inn*** (524 US 64; 252–473–3979), run by longtime residents of the island. Six rooms in the inn and four in the annex are furnished with comfortable old furniture that has been in the family, or at least in the community, for generations. It's not fancy stuff but the kind of things you remember from visiting old Aunt Lizzie or Great-grandma. Nearly every piece has a story that Rebecca and Fields Scarborough, who love to talk, will tell you gladly. The rooms are simple but comfortable. Two units over the barn are outfitted with king-size beds. Each room has a private bath, a small refrigerator, and a coffeemaker with coffee provided. No breakfast is served, but Rebecca leaves a couple of packs of doughnuts by the coffeemaker. Rates include the use of bicycles for exploring the island. Web site: www.scarbor ough-inn.com.

Across the road from Scarborough Inn, the ***Weeping Radish*** specializes in authentic German food served by waitresses in Bavarian costume and accompanied by a variety of dark and light beers from the Weeping Radish microbrewery, all to the tune of Bavarian folk music. The pub and restaurant operate on varying schedules depending on the season. Tours of the brewery are available on a varying schedule. Phone (252–473–1157) for details.

For more elegant accommodations and dining, try ***Clara's Seafood Grill.*** According to the Scarboroughs, Clara's, in the waterfront condos overlooking rows of sailboats and yachts, makes the best crab cakes in town. Advertised on the menu as "more crab than cake," these hefty crab cakes are coated with a tempuralike batter that barely contains the large lumps of crab bursting from the cake. The catch of the day comes with cornbread, hushpuppies and a house

All the Town's a Stage

If you strike up a conversation about *The Lost Colony* with some of the local people in Manteo, you'll quickly discover that the show is a town industry. It has had its share of famous people, like Andy Griffith, on the stage, but at one time or another, many of the townspeople also have appeared in the show, treating it as their summer job. Others have worked as crew and stagehands, helped maintain the costumes, answered telephones, made reservations in the office, and taken tickets at the gates.

I stood with three women ranging in age from about thirty to early sixties as they compared notes. They'd all played one of the same female parts at different times. They mentioned the character's name, but I didn't recognize it from having seen the show, so you probably have to know the script to remember it. I could tell that being in the show had been a magical experience, if a strenuous one, for each of them, and while they didn't really want to work that hard again, they still missed it.

Drink Up

Before Prohibition, North Carolina produced more wine than any other state in the country. The state is gradually rebuilding its wine production, with more than 250 vineyards and twenty-one wineries. The state's most local grape is the scuppernong, which settlers cultivated 400 years ago in the settlement of Sir Walter Raleigh, known now as the "Lost Colony." See the listing of Wineries and Vineyards in North Carolina on page xvi.

salad. Beer and wine are available. The atmosphere is upscale, but casual dress is appropriate. Clara's (252–473–1727) is in the condo division at the corner of Sir Walter Raleigh and Queen Elizabeth Avenues. Open daily for dinner.

You might put what you don't spend at Clara's toward a special night at the ***Tranquil House Inn.*** The inn, on the Shallowbag Bay waterfront in downtown Manteo, whispers "luxury" when you enter—clearly a fine-wine-and-cheese kind of place. The building is a reproduction of a typical nineteenth-century Outer Banks inn, with added contemporary conveniences a nineteenth-century traveler wouldn't even have dreamed about. Because of the pale cypress woodwork, glass, and stained glass throughout, the inn's interior seems almost as bright and sunny as the docks outside. The inn has an upscale gourmet restaurant with a fine wine list. In the guest rooms you'll find not only the expected amenities such as television and telephone but also Oriental carpets, fine furnishings, and hand-tiled bathrooms. Rates, commensurate with the luxurious atmosphere, vary seasonally and include a buffet breakfast (405 Queen Elizabeth Avenue; 252–473–1404 or 800–458–7069). Web site: www.tranquilinn.com.

A simpler, thoroughly pleasant place to stay, ***Scarborough House Inn,*** run by Phil and Sally Scarborough, stands on a quieter residential street at 323 Fernando Street. Phil and Sally kept Scarborough Inn for years before they decided to sell it to their son and his wife and build this smaller place. The five-room bed-and-breakfast is furnished with antiques, and each guest room has a small refrigerator, a coffeemaker, and a microwave oven. Phil and Sally provide a light continental breakfast in the room. They say they are "as local as they come." They know the history of everybody and everything on the island and can tell you how things have changed there over the years. Sally and practically everybody in her family performed at some time or another in ***The Lost Colony*** and can tell wonderful stories about things that have happened related to the show over the years. Phone (252) 473–3849.

The distinctly local ***Endless Possibilities,*** 105 Budleigh Street (252–473–5121), a charity-based organization to raise funds for the Outer Banks

Hotline Crisis Intervention and Prevention Center, is also a source of inspiration, education, and woven pieces for visitors. Endless Possibilities opened in 2002, selling fiber art to raise money for the hotline and also teaching volunteers to weave. Many of the weavers have come from difficult relationships and homes and find their work here part of rebuilding their lives. Visitors are invited to sit at a loom and try it themselves. For a donation of $35 you can take home what you weave. A volunteer will help take the weaving off the loom and tie the knots to finish it. Other woven pieces, handbags, rugs, wall hangings, and scarves are for sale as well.

The other community on Roanoke Island, ***Wanchese*** (named for another Indian who took off for England), doesn't seem to know it is surrounded by tourists. Most of the people of Wanchese fish for a living. Driving on State Highway 345 South to the village, you pass modest homes—many with a boat in the yard—battered vans, worn pickups, and lots of churches, flowers, and pets. Signs in some of the yards invite you to buy handcarved duck decoys, driftwood, wood crafts, and nursery plants. All the people you see in the community will talk to you pleasantly and seem to enjoy your watching them work on the docks. At least one family maintains a "shedder" operation for harvesting soft-shell crabs as they shed their shells.

Fisherman's Wharf Restaurant (252–473–5205), a large, unpretentious restaurant on the wharf, surrounded by pilings, wild stands of Queen Anne's lace, and rolls of chicken wire, specializes in broiled and fried seafood and Wanchese crab cakes at modest prices. From your table you can watch the same fishing fleets that probably caught what you're eating. Sometimes broadcasts from a religious radio station drift through a speaker at the door. Open from noon to 9:00 P.M. Monday through Saturday, from mid-April through October or later, depending on the weather.

Before you leave Roanoke Island, take time to visit this branch of the ***North Carolina Aquarium,*** about a mile north of Manteo, off U.S. 64. Here you get a close-up view of live marine life, including sharks, eels, and sea tur-

They Saw the Light

The saga of saving the Cape Hatteras Lighthouse captured the imaginations of many North Carolinians. Photographer Mike Booher and writer Lin Ezell worked together to publish a coffee-table-sized book, *Out of Harm's Way: The Move of the Millennium*, detailing the move of the 200-foot-high tower in words and pictures. They felt so strongly about the importance of the project that they donated their work, and the publication was supported by other donations as well.

Cape Hatteras Lighthouse

tles. A touch tank, as the name implies, lets you feel live crabs and starfish. The aquarium maintains a full calendar of special events, from seafood-cooking workshops to field trips and cruises. The aquarium has been greatly expanded recently and includes a 285,000-gallon "Graveyard of the Atlantic" tank where marine life mingles with scuba divers and a replica of a sunken ship. Open daily 9:00 A.M. to 5:00 P.M. Admission is $6.00 for adults; children six to seventeen are $4.00. Phone (252) 473–3493 or (800) 832–3474. Web site: www.aquariums.state.nc.us.

From Manteo, a short drive across the bridge on US 64/264 takes you to Bodie Island (which isn't really an island anymore but a location along the northern section of the Outer Banks), where it's worth stopping to see the Bodie Island Lighthouse, operating since 1872. Aside from Coquina Beach, a good beach for swimming and fishing, you won't find many attractions here. A turn to the south, however, takes you to Hatteras Island, home of the tallest lighthouse in America, the ***Cape Hatteras Lighthouse.*** When the Cape Hatteras Lighthouse was built in 1870, it stood thousands of feet from the Atlantic Ocean. But erosion gradually brought the sea closer and closer. In the last decade, experts said the lighthouse would soon fall into the ocean if it were not somehow protected. After lengthy controversy about what to do and how to do it, Congress authorized nearly $12 million to move the lighthouse away from the shoreline, preserving it as a historic structure.

In June 1999 the old lighthouse was moved 1,300 feet inland, barely an inch at a time, while North Carolinians watched reports of the progress on the Internet and on nightly television news.

Now the lighthouse stands 3,000 feet from the ocean at high tide, about the same distance as when it was first built, and is open for visitors. If you're up for climbing more than 260 steps, you can stand on a balcony at the top to survey the area.

What used to be the lighthouse keeper's home is now a visitor center where you can check out exhibits about local history and pick up a map for a self-guiding nature trail that begins nearby.

In the summer season the lighthouse is open every day from 10:00 A.M. to 4:00 P.M. In the off-season it closes earlier. The visitor center is open from 9:00 A.M. to 5:00 P.M. daily. Admission is free. Call (252) 995–4474 for details. This area is undeveloped because the protected Cape Hatteras National Seashore comprises Hatteras, some of the southern end of Bodie, and Ocracoke. Here you can see natural beaches and their attendant wildlife, seashells as they wash ashore and accumulate, and vegetation dwarfed and gnarled by salt and wind but not threatened by macadam, all without water slides. For more information on the area, write the Superintendent, Cape Hatteras National Seashore, Route 1, Box 675, Manteo 27954, or call (252) 473–2111.

It's a different story turning north from Bodie Island. You drive through the kind of beach-strip conglomeration of motels, restaurants, gas stations, fast-food chains, and beach shops that typifies most popular beach areas. As a follower of unbeaten paths, you might choose to skip it, unless you're interested in seeing the ***Wright Brothers National Memorial*** at ***Kill Devil Hills,*** which marks the spot where Wilbur and Orville Wright first got off the ground in powered flight on December 7, 1903. The visitor center here has full-sized copies of the brothers' glider and their first plane. The brothers' workshop and living quarters have been re-created too. Open daily from 9:00 A.M. to 5:00 P.M. Admission is $2.00 per person or $4.00 per car (252–441–7430).

Just south of Kill Devil Hills, on the U.S. Highway 158 Bypass in Nag's Head, ***Jockey's Ridge State Park*** (252–441–7132) makes a good place to stop, play in the sand, and get some exercise. This is the highest sand dune on the East Coast, where prevailing winds generally range from 10 to 15 miles an hour. Kite flying here is just about perfect. Hang gliding is popular, too. The park has a picnic area and a shelter, as well as swimming and fishing on the sound.

Enjoy a more rural setting at ***Nags Head Woods Preserve*** (252–441–2525), 701 West Ocean Acres Drive. This is a 1,400-acre maritime forest with more than 5 miles of hiking trails. It also has a visitor center and a gift shop, and you can arrange kayak field trips in the summer. The preserve is open from 10:00 A.M. to 3:00 P.M. Monday through Friday. Closed on major holidays.

Kill Devil Hills is a destination resort area, probably the kind of thing you're trying to avoid. But if it seems appropriate to spend the night, try ***Cypress House,*** at 500 North Virginia Dare Trail, a big, square, blue-green beach house run by Karen and Leon Faso. It was originally a sea captain's hunting and fishing lodge. The six guest rooms are done in cypress, with white ruffled curtains and ceiling fans. It might surprise the sea captain that the rooms have private baths and color television. The inn is open April through October. Rates include a full breakfast. Call (252) 441–6127 or (800) 554–2764. Web site: www.cypresshouseinn.com.

Once you get this far north on the Outer Banks, it makes more sense to keep driving north on US 158 across the bridge onto the mainland than it does to backtrack. Following US 158, you can pick up US 17 South at ***Elizabeth City.*** Elizabeth City merits at least a brief stop, if only because it is at the site of a canal dug in 1790 with the unlikely name of Dismal Swamp Canal. A Coast Guard installation nearby and the local shipyard make this clearly a working, rather than a vacationing, area. The town, however, has a number of interesting historical buildings that are easy to check by taking a walking tour. For a map write the Chamber of Commerce, 502 East Ehringhaus Street, P.O. Box 426, Elizabeth City 27907, or call (252) 335–4365. Web site: ecacc@interpath.com.

The ***Museum of the Albemarle*** (252–335–1453), about 3 miles south of town on US 17, provides information on the area, known as the Historic Albemarle Area, along with displays of artifacts and exhibits related to local history. (Colonists first revolted openly against the English monarchy here.) The exhibits tell the story of the area's people from the time of its Native Americans. Open Tuesday through Saturday from 9:00 A.M. to 5:00 P.M. and Sunday from 2:00 to 5:00 P.M. Closed Monday and major holidays. Admission is free. Web site: www.albemarle-nc.com/MOA.

Another interesting spot in Elizabeth City is the ***Historic Main Street District,*** one of four National Register Historic Districts in Elizabeth City. It has the largest number of brick antebellum commercial buildings in the state. The early nineteenth- and twentieth-century storefronts are now home to specialty shops, restaurants, art galleries, and antiques shops. Free brochures for a self-guided tour of the district are available at the Museum of the Albemarle. Phone (252) 335–4365.

And you don't have to have a boat to enjoy the ***Mariner's Wharf*** (252–335–4365) on the Intracoastal Waterway waterfront where boats are offered free dockage for forty-eight hours. The "Rose Buddies" greet each boat with a rose and a welcome to Elizabeth City.

returninghome

Dorothy Spruill Redford, a descendant of the Somerset slave families, published a book entitled *Somerset Homecoming: Recovering a Lost Heritage* (Doubleday, 1988). In it she details the research it took to identify and find descendants of the Somerset families; describes contacting them; and tells about the huge, emotional reunion or, more accurately, first union, they held on the plantation. Redford includes much plantation history in her book as well.

The next community along US 17, Hertford, the Perquimans County seat (population only about 2,000) is on the Perquimans River, which feeds into Albemarle Sound. It's worth a stop to visit the ***Newbold-White House,*** believed to be the oldest house in North Carolina, probably built sometime between the early 1660s and 1685. The house has been restored, preserving much of the original handwork of the brick chimneys and walls and some of the woodwork. Though not the original, the furnishings are authentic pieces dating from the seventeenth century. Open from March to the week before Christmas, Tuesday through Saturday, 10:00 A.M. to 4:30 P.M. Sunday 2:00 to 5:00 P.M. Other times by appointment, 151 Newbold White Road; (252–426–7567). Admission $3.00; students with ID $1.00. Web site: www.newbold whitehouse.com.

You can learn a lot about the character of the area by taking two tours here, the ***Historic Hertford Walking Tour*** (252–426–5657), Hall of Fame Square, Church Street, and a self-guided driving tour of the ***Old Neck Rural Historic District*** (252–426–7567). Web site: www.perquimans.com.

The walking tour takes you by old waterfront homes and the 1828 Perquimans County Courthouse and into a district of antiques stores and cafes. The Historic Hertford District is listed on the National Register of Historic Places. A free tour booklet is available by writing to the Perquimans County Chamber of Commerce, P.O. Box 27, Hertford 27944; you can also get a free map for the driving tour of Old Neck Rural Historic District, New Hope Road, and Old Neck Road. The driving tour runs through a National Register Historic District and into the countryside, past old plantation homes.

As an alternative plan if you are pressed for time, you may decide to skip the northern Outer Banks and go back from Roanoke Island on US 64, which takes you across the Alligator River and through the ***Alligator River Refuge*** (it's not clear whether the refuge protects people from alligators or the other way around), where you'll find lots of wildlife, picnic areas, and boating access. Either way, make your next stop Edenton, the first capital of colonial North Carolina. From US 64, take State Highway 32 North. On US 17, keep going about 15 miles west from Hertford.

Capital Country

Although ***Edenton*** is in no way backward, it has managed to retain the calm and slower pace that we associate with earlier times and has done an outstanding job of preserving its historical sites and promulgating the facts.

Blackbeard lived here, even though he hung out in Bath and maybe left his treasure there. This would have been good pirate country. It was a busy port town in the eighteenth and early nineteenth centuries. During the Revolutionary War supplies were shipped from here to Washington's army farther north.

Edenton had some of the earliest female political activists, too. In 1774 fifty-one women gathered in the courthouse square to sign a declaration vowing not to drink English tea or wear English clothing.

To steep yourself in colonial and Revolutionary War history, you have a choice of a guided or self-guided walking tour or a trolley tour. Pick up a walking-tour map for a quarter, or join a guided tour for a modest fee at the ***Historic Edenton Visitors Center,*** 108 North Broad Street (252–482–2637; Web site: www.edenton.com). A free audiovisual presentation gives you some orientation in the area's history. The Barker House (ca. 1782) was the home of Thomas Barker, a colonial agent in England, and his wife, Penelope, one of those ladies who boycotted English tea and clothing.

Call the visitor center also to arrange a guided walking tour of Historic Edenton. It takes a couple of hours. The tour includes four interesting buildings: Chowan County Courthouse, one of the oldest in the country, built in 1767; the Cupola House, noted for its elaborate Georgian woodwork inside; the James Iredell House State Historic Site, built in 1773, home of the first attorney general of North Carolina; and St. Paul's Episcopal Church, built in 1736. You may also purchase tickets to go into individual buildings apart from the tours.

In addition to the walking tours, you can take a guided trolley tour, which goes into the outskirts of town as well as through the downtown. Walking tours leave several times a day. They include time inside some of the homes. The cost of tours is moderate and varies according to their length and the number of homes visited. The visitor center is open from 9:00 A.M. to 5:00 P.M. Monday through Saturday, 1:00 to 5:00 P.M. Sunday. Shorter hours in winter. You'll know you're at the visitor center when you see the flag with a teapot flying in the doorway.

Because it's so pleasant, full of flowers, friendly people, and lovely waterfront vistas, spending the night in Edenton rests and relaxes you.

The ***Lords Proprietors' Inn*** (252–482–3641; Web site: www.lordspropedenton.com), at 300 North Broad Street, has earned a reputation as one of the most elegant and gracious inns in the state. The inn comprises three separate restored homes in the historic district, grouped around a lawn and gardens and the Whedbee House, on a brick patio, where continental breakfast is served. Each of the twenty rooms has private bath, cable television, videocassette player, and telephone.

All the guest rooms are light and airy. The common rooms have lots of open space, beautifully refinished old floors, and many whimsical decorating touches.

A few steps away, at 304 North Broad Street, you'll find you have an entirely different lodging alternative. The ***Governor Eden Inn*** (252–482–2072), four rooms with private bath and television in an old neoclassical family home, gives you the feeling of stopping in to spend the night with a friendly relative. Joy and Barry Caron, proprietors, offer complimentary afternoon refreshments and serve a full breakfast. Web site: www.governoredeninn.com.

As for places to eat when you're in town, you're in for a true off-the-beaten-path experience at ***Lane's Bar-B-Que*** on Highway 32 south of town. For the most fun, sit at one of the five tables in the front rather than in the larger dining room in back. Up front you can enjoy the company and comments of the local workers, such as the men from nearby Edenton Utilities, as they have lunch and swap wisecracks. Call (252) 482–4008.

"Boy, did it rain or did it rain?"

"It was so bad I had to get up in the trees and swing to the truck."

The restaurant serves burgers and a variety of home-cooked platters, but the barbecue deserves first place on your list of choices. Open from 11:00 A.M. to 8:30 P.M. every day.

When you study North Carolina history, much of it seems to be about war campaigns, documents, and declarations. Two plantation tours in the area give you a more personal look at history on the day-to-day level.

Hope Plantation, about 20 miles west, in Windsor on State Highway 308, 4 miles west of the highway bypass, re-creates rural domestic life in northeastern North Carolina during the colonial and Federal periods. The plantation belonged to Governor David Stone, who also served in the state House of Commons and later as a U.S. senator. Stone owned more than 5,000 acres, planted mostly in wheat and corn. The plantation had all the mills, shops, and work areas necessary to be self-sufficient.

The two homes on the plantation, one dating from 1763, the other from about 1803, are examples of architecture that combines medieval English, Georgian, and neoclassical traits, reflecting the changing needs and knowledge of North Carolina colonists. Touring them, you see examples of how they might have been furnished, based on research about the plantation. The project continues to develop, so that eventually you'll be able to study a reconstruction of the kitchen on its original foundation, inspect relocated and restored outbuildings, and examine historically authentic vegetable and flower gardens. Moderate admission charged. Open Monday through Saturday from 10:00 A.M. to 5:00 P.M. and Sunday from 2:00 to 5:00 P.M. Closed Thanksgiving and Christmas Day. For full information write to the plantation at 32 Hope House Road, Windsor 27983, or call (252) 794–3140. Web site: www.albemarle-nc.com/hope.

The second plantation also deserves much wider attention. ***Somerset Place,*** a nineteenth-century coastal plantation near Creswell, belonged to Josiah Collins, a successful merchant who came to Edenton from England in 1774. He and other investors formed the Lake Company, which acquired more than 100,000 acres of land next to Lake Phelps. They dug (or, more accurately, had slaves dig) a 6-mile-long canal through an area known as the Great Alligator Dismal, to join the lake to the Scuppernong River and drain the swamps. When things were going well, gristmills and sawmills produced rice and lumber to ship down the canal in flatboats. But the flooding it takes to grow rice bred mosquitoes that made the slaves sick, so eventually the plantation grew corn and wheat instead.

Collins bought out his partners in 1816 and at his death passed the property on to his son. Later, Josiah Collins III took over. It seems Josiah Three, who went to Yale and graduated from law school in Connecticut, had a head for business. He turned Somerset Place into one of the state's largest plantations, working more than 300 slaves by 1860. Most North Carolinians didn't own slaves; Collins was one of only four planters in the state with more than 300.

The great fascination in visiting Somerset Place lies in the uncommonly detailed records the Collins family kept, especially about the black people on the plantation. The records detailed not only births, deaths, and marriages but also jobs and skills. Thus today we know that the cook was Grace and that one slave, Luke Davis, had only one job, cleaning carpets. We know that two sons of Collins III were playing with two slave boys one winter when all four boys drowned in the canal.

Additional information comes from the accounts of Dr. John Kooner, a physician who used to stay at the plantation for several weeks at a time, treating the slaves and the Collins family. He described an elaborate African dance that slaves Collins had imported directly from Africa apparently taught to the rest of the slave community. They performed it every year at Christmas, beginning at the great house, snaking to the overseer's house, and ending up at the slave quarters. Everyone on the plantation participated, either as a slave dancer or a spectator.

Archaeological exploration has turned up the remains of slave houses, a hospital and chapel, and the plantation's formal garden, as well as the original brick boundary walls.

This kind of priceless information continues to come to light at Somerset Place, where personable and knowledgeable guides work hard to pass it on. You won't experience a routinized, canned tour here.

Ultimately, the Civil War did in the plantation. The Collins family died elsewhere, and today the site is run by the state.

Somerset (252–797–4560) is open April 1 through October 31, Monday through Saturday from 9:00 A.M. to 5:00 P.M., Sunday from 1:00 to 5:00 P.M.; November 1 through March 31, Tuesday through Saturday from 10:00 A.M. to 4:00 P.M., Sunday from 1:00 to 4:00 P.M. Closed Monday during winter when hours are shorter. All hours may vary; for details contact the site manager (P.O. Box 215, Creswell 27928). Admission is free. At Creswell, the turn for the plantation is marked with a sign. The address is 2572 Lake Shore Road, Creswell. Web site: www.ah.dcr.state.nc.us.

It's a quick drive from here to the office and main parking lot of ***Pettigrew State Park*** (252–797–4475), 2252 Lake Shore Drive, Creswell, bordering on Lake Phelps. Actually, Somerset Place State Historic Site lies within the park, too. And a hiking trail from the parking lot takes you to the Somerset Place buildings in about five minutes. The trail continues to the Pettigrew cemetery. Another part of the trail, known as "Carriage Trail" because the Collins family used to like taking carriage rides along the route, leads to an overlook from which you can tread a boardwalk through the cypress woods. Some families like to settle in a picnic area in the park, then walk over to the historic site, rather than starting out at Somerset Place.

A park entrance and parking lot are 9 miles south of Creswell, off US 64 on State Route 1166. One of the park's main draws is fishing—largemouth bass, yellow perch, and pan fish are plentiful. The lake is also good for shallow-draft sailboats, canoeing, and windsurfing. The park forest has a variety of deciduous trees, along with wildflowers and lower shrubs, all in enough variety to keep nature travelers with botanical interests happy. As for wildlife, a variety of waterfowl, owls and other birds of prey, and lots of woodland animals, including deer, frequent the area. Pettigrew has a few campsites but no hookups.

Finally, you can inspect some displays of prehistoric Indian culture, including dugout canoes, that will help give you a sense of the area's history over a long period of time. The park is open from about dawn to nightfall, varying with the season. Call ahead to check hours for your visit. Admission is free.

Places to Stay in the Northern Coast and Islands

BEAUFORT

Beaufort Inn
101 Ann Street
Beaufort 28516
(252) 728–2600

Elizabeth Inn
307 Front Street
Beaufort 28516
(252) 728–3861

Inlet Inn
Corner Queen and Front Streets
Beaufort 28516
(252) 728–3600
(800) 554–5466

Langdon House
135 Craven Street
Beaufort 28516
(252) 728–5499

Pecan Tree Inn
116 Queen Street
Beaufort 28516
(252) 728–6733

KILL DEVIL HILLS

Best Western Ocean Reef Suites
107 Virginia Dare Trail
Kill Devil Hills 27948
(252) 441–1482
(800) 937–8376

Days Inn–Oceanfront
101 North Virginia Dare Trail
Kill Devil Hills 27948
(252) 441–7211
(800) 325–2525

KITTY HAWK

Beach Haven
4104 Virginia Dare Trail
Kitty Hawk 27949
(252) 261–4785
(888) 559–0506

MANTEO

Duke of Dare Motor Lodge
100 South Virginia Dare Road
Manteo 27954
(252) 473–2175

Tranquil House Inn
405 Queen Elizabeth Street
Manteo 27954
(252) 473–1404

MOREHEAD CITY

Best Western Buccaneer Inn
2806 Arendell Street
Morehead City 28557
(252) 726–3115
(800) 682–4982

Comfort Inn
3100 Arendell Street
Morehead City 28557
(252) 247–3434
(800) 422–5404

Hampton Inn
4035 Arendell Street
Morehead City 28557
(252) 240–2300
(800) 467–9375

NEW BERN

Comfort Suites
218 East Front Street
New Bern 28560
(252) 636–0022

Days Inn
925 Broad Street
New Bern 28560
(252) 636–0150

Holiday Inn Express
3455 Martin Luther King Jr. Boulevard
New Bern 28562
(252) 638–8266

THE NORTHERN COAST AND ISLANDS WEB SITES

New Bern
www.newbern.com

Outer Banks
www.outerbanks.org

Kitty Hawk Kites, hang gliding
www.kittyhawk.com

OUTER BANKS

Holiday Inn Express
58822 Highway 12
Hatteras 27943
(252) 986–1110
(800) 361–1590

Places to Eat in the Northern Coast and Islands

BEAUFORT

Net House
Turner Street
Beaufort 28516
(252) 728–2002

The Spouter
218 Front Street
Beaufort 28516
(252) 728–5190

KILL DEVIL HILLS

Flying Fish Cafe
2003 Croatan Highway
Kill Devil Hills 27948
(252) 441–6894

Port-O-Call Restaurant
504 South Virginia
Dare Trail
Kill Devil Hills 27948
(252) 441–7484

MANTEO

Clara's Seafood Grill
400 Queen Elizabeth Street
Manteo 27954
(252) 473–1727

1587 Restaurant
405 Queen Elizabeth Street
Manteo 27954
(252) 473–1587

MOREHEAD CITY

Mrs. Willis' Restaurant
3002 Bridges Street
Morehead City 28557
(252) 726–3741

Sanitary Fish Market and Restaurant
501 Evans Street
Morehead City 28557
(252) 247–3111

NEW BERN

Henderson House
221 Tryon Palace Drive
New Bern 28560
(252) 638–3205

Pollock Street Delicatessen
208 Pollock Street
New Bern 28560
(252) 637–2480

OUTER BANKS

Austin Creek Grill
12 Marina Way
Southend Ferry Landing
Highway 12
Hatteras 27943
(252) 986–1511

The Upper Piedmont and Sandhills

Sir Walter's Country

You should probably get here soon if you want to enjoy the Raleigh area. Although the population hovers around a few thousand less than 210,000, depending on your source, the entire area is developing or at least spreading out rapidly, especially in the direction of Durham. Driving along rural roads, you often come upon heavy equipment and newly cleared land. Tomorrow that land will be home to a new development. But the area is so rich in history, culture, and amenities that it would be a shame to skip it.

Raleigh, the state capital, named for Sir Walter Raleigh, offers a variety of historical sites, museums, and fine old architecture in addition to the government buildings downtown.

Plan on stopping at ***Historic Oakwood,*** at North Person Street between Jones and Boundary, if you're interested in Victorian homes. This historic district of more than 400 homes, many restored, is considered one of the best examples of an unspoiled Victorian neighborhood in the country. Pick up a free walking-tour map that includes some history and descriptions of some of the buildings at the Capital Area Visitors Center, 301 North Blount Street. The center (919–733–3456) is open Monday

THE UPPER PIEDMONT AND SANDHILLS

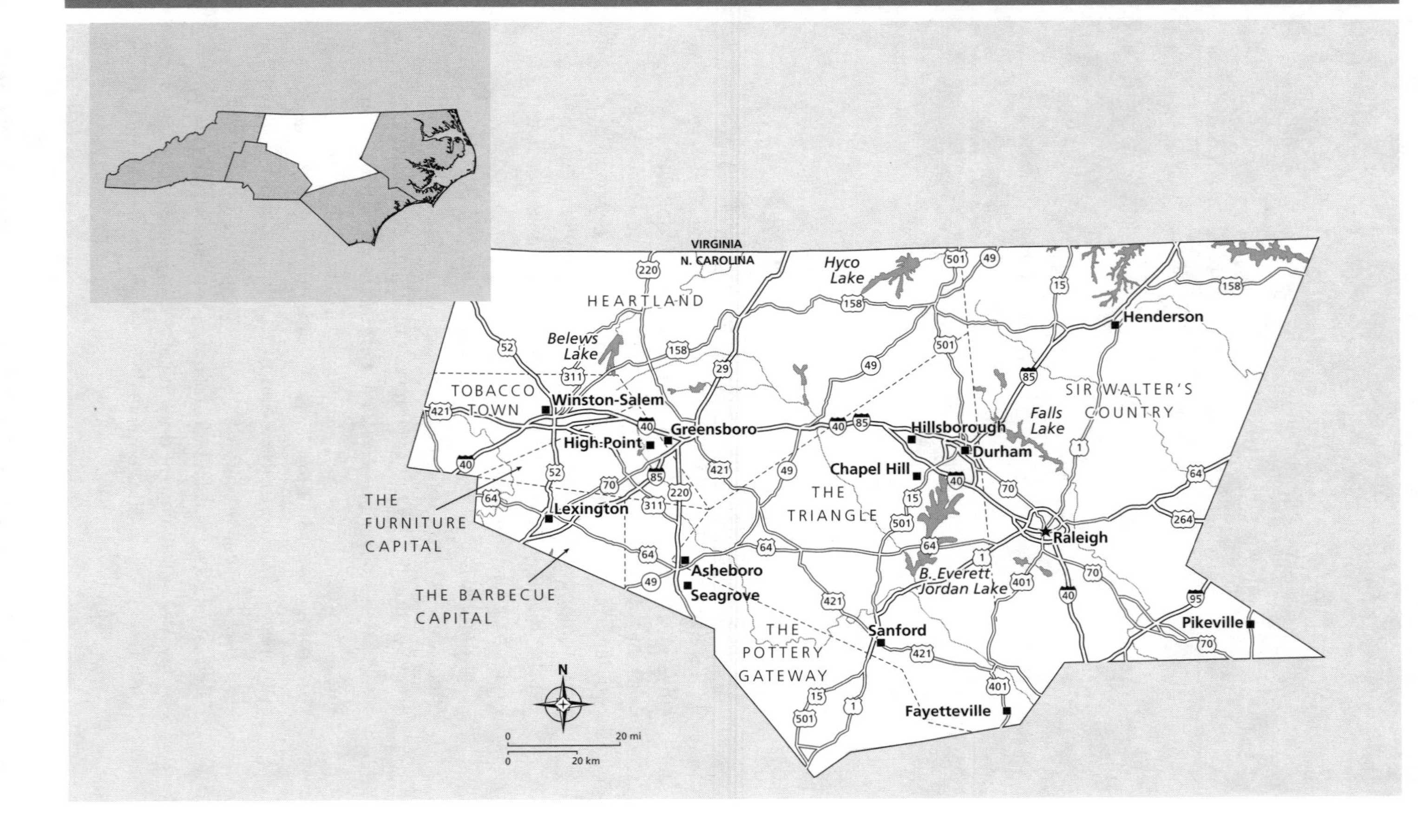

through Friday from 8:00 A.M. to 5:00 P.M., Saturday from 10:00 A.M. to 5:00 P.M., and Sunday from 1:00 to 4:00 P.M. Closed Thanksgiving, December 24 and 25, and New Year's Day.

The ***Oakwood Inn,*** 411 North Bloodworth Street, offers you an opportunity to spend the night in an 1871 Victorian home in the heart of the historic district. The proprietors, Doris and Gary Jurkiewicz, know a lot about the area and keep maps with lots of information about the old houses on hand to guide you through the historic neighborhood. The inn, which has six guest rooms, is attracting increasing numbers of business travelers during the week and because of that has put telephones and cable television in every room and offers high speed wireless Web connection. Gas log fireplaces add coziness to every room. Oakwood breakfasts fall in the gourmet category: croissant French toast, pumpkin pancakes, orange waffles, and so on. Breakfast is included in the rates. Phone (919) 832–9712 or (800) 267–9712; Web site: www.OakwoodInn.BB.com.

As for the museums, several deserve your attention. ***The North Carolina Museum of History,*** 5 East Edenton Street, 4650 Mail Service Center, concentrates on exhibits, artifacts, and dioramas related to state history, transportation, and, of course, the Revolutionary and Civil Wars. It also has good exhibits about women in North Carolina. A recent addition is a huge exhibition about health and healing as it has been practiced in different cultures and times in the state. It covers everything from polio hospitals to herbal medicine. Guided tours are available Monday through Friday, but you need a reservation. The museum (919–715–0200) is open Tuesday through Saturday from 9:00 A.M. to 5:00 P.M. and Sunday from noon to 5:00 P.M. Closed major holidays. Admission is free. Web site: www.ncmuseumofhistory.org.

The ***North Carolina Museum of Natural Sciences*** is between Jones Street and Edenton on North Salisbury Street (919–733–7450 or 877–462–8724). Here you divide your attention between stuffed and skeletal remains of what once was and living specimens of what still is from across the state. In the

ANNUAL EVENTS IN THE UPPER PIEDMONT

Old Salem
Reenactment of original Fourth of July held in 1783
July 4
(336) 721–7300

Winston-Salem
Annual Piedmont Crafts Fair
(mid-November)
(336) 725–1516
www.piedmontcraftsmen.org

whale hall a 50-foot whale skeleton hung from the ceiling dominates the exhibits. Another highlight is "Willo," the first dinosaur discovered with a fossilized heart. The living conservatory here is filled with live monarch butterflies and ruby-throated hummingbirds, in a re-creation of a dry tropical forest that also has cacti, heliconias, and orchids. Museum hours are the same as those at the museum of history. Admission is free. Web site: www.naturalsciences.org.

Black history is beginning to receive organized, formal recognition in this area. The ***African-American Cultural Complex,*** 119 Sunnybrook Road, displays a large collection of items created by African Americans in three houses along a nature trail. They include innovations in science, art, business, medicine, politics, and sports. Hours by appointment. Call (919) 250–9336 for details. Web site: www.aaccmuseum.org.

The ***Martin Luther King Memorial Gardens*** (919–834–6264), 1500 Martin Luther King Jr. Boulevard, features a life-size statue of Dr. King and a two-tone granite water monument honoring twenty-five pioneers in civil rights and education in a setting of more than 8,000 flowers. The King Memorial Wall surrounds the statue and includes 2,400 bricks inscribed with the names of people who have helped support the facility. The park is open twenty-four hours a day. Admission is free. Web site: www.king-raleigh.org.

For insight into life in Raleigh's early days for both plantation owners and their slaves, visit ***Mordecai Historic Park,*** at the juncture of Wake Forest Road and Mimosa Street, on Person Street, just a mile from the state Capitol and downtown Raleigh. With several thousand acres, this was one of the largest plantations in Wake County before the Civil War, growing corn, wheat, cotton, and food for the people on the plantation. To give you an idea of its size, the area now known as Historic Oakwood stands on what used to be Mordecai property. Five generations of the same family lived in ***Mordecai***

A True Story

Each year in July, the African-American Cultural Complex presents the outdoor drama, *Amistad,* the story about a mutiny on a slave ship that resulted in what is now considered the first civil rights case in America. It is the only outdoor drama in the United States written, produced, and directed by African Americans. In song, dance, and speeches, performers dramatize how the Africans were taken from their native land, were imprisoned on the ship, revolted at sea, and went to trial in America. The drama's producers say the episode stands as an early example of people of different cultures, races, genders, and faiths uniting in a democratic action. Call (919) 250–9336.

House, and their eighteenth- and nineteenth-century furnishings, art, and books still fill the place.

Slaves did all the labor on the plantation. Records show that some of them grew their own rice and practiced traditional African farming, crafts, cooking, and music there.

The park includes a re-created kitchen garden of vegetables, herbs, fruits and flowers typical of the mid-nineteenth century. Only two of the plantation's outbuildings, known as "dependency" buildings, remain; an 1842 kitchen from Anson County has been set up next to the garden where the original kitchen probably stood.

On one street in the park, you'll find the little house where Andrew Johnson, seventeenth president of the United States was born, December 29, 1808. His mother was a weaver; his father cared for horses.

Other historic buildings from Raleigh and the nearby area have been brought to the park as well—an 1812 law office, an 1847 post office, and a chapel built by slaves in 1840 on a plantation in Chatham County. Open Tuesday through Saturday, 10:00 A.M. to 4:00 P.M. Tours begin on the hour. Admission $6.00 for adults, $4.00 for children ages seven to seventeen, free for children six and under. Phone (919) 834–4844.

Also allow time for the ***North Carolina Museum of Art*** at 2110 Blue Ridge Avenue (take the Wade Avenue exit off Interstate 40), 4630 Mail Service Center. The building, designed by the architect Edward Durrell Stone, who designed the John F. Kennedy Center in Washington, D.C., and the original Museum of Modern Art in New York, is important; so are the eight major collections. Arranged in chronological order, they cover 5,000 years of art, displaying work by artists from Botticelli to Monet to Andrew Wyeth. You'll also find exhibits of Jewish ceremonial art along with Greek and Roman sculpture. Tours are available at 1:30 P.M. A cafe and gift shop operate during museum hours. The museum also offers varied, changing programs of festivals, films, and performing arts events for the family. The museum (919–839–6262, extension 2154) is open Tuesday through Saturday from 9:00 A.M. to 5:00 P.M. (until 9:00 P.M. Friday) and Sunday from 10:00 A.M. to 5:00 P.M. Closed Monday and major holidays. Admission is free. Web site: www.ncartmuseum.org.

Another approach to art is ***Artspace,*** 201 East Davie Street (919–821–2787), a nonprofit visual arts center in downtown Raleigh with more than twenty-five working studios where you can watch artists at work and also visit shows in two galleries. Artists sell work out of their studios as well as from the galleries and in the gift shop. Artspace is open from 10:00 A.M. to 6:00 P.M. Tuesday through Saturday. The first Friday of every month, Artspace is open until 10:00 P.M. Admission is free. Web site: www.artspacenc.org.

The ***Raleigh City Museum,*** 220 Fayetteville Street Mall, gives you an intensely local, idiosyncratic look at the people and history of the town. This is one of those places that came into being because of the determination of people who live here. Beth Crabtree, a local historian, determined that the city needed some special home to honor its history and collect its artifacts before they became scattered, and in the early 1990s she began working to make it happen. After her death, another local woman, Mary Cates, picked up the torch and marshaled even more support. The resulting museum, with both changing exhibits and displays of artifacts, is housed in the ground and first floors of the old Briggs Hardware Store, a building dating from about 1890–1900. (Other tenants are the A.J. Fletcher Preservation Foundation and Special Olympics.) The private, nonprofit museum collects artifacts through the effective device of asking for them: "Share your artifact and its historical story." The results range from eighteenth-century tools and portraits to photographs and household items, and the collection continues to grow. Typical exhibits also include such topics as the history of business in Raleigh, Raleigh's beginnings on 1,000 acres, and the development of the Civil Rights Movement in Raleigh. The museum is open Tuesday through Friday, 10:00 A.M. to 4:00 P.M., Saturday 1:00 to 4:00 P.M. Admission free. Fayetteville Street Mall is between Salisbury and Wilmington Streets, a block from the Capitol. Phone (919) 832–3775. Web site: www.raleigh citymuseum.org.

Attending to your dinner, a restaurant in the area really appeals to the kinds of people who read a book like this. ***Jean-Claude's Cafe*** serves French country food in a small, unassuming dining room, mostly to local folks who believe they're keeping the place a secret. The restaurant is in North Ridge Shopping Center, unlikely as that sounds for such a find. (Take the Old Wake Forest Road exit from the beltline, and go north 3 miles on what becomes Falls of Neuse Avenue.) The menu includes a country pâté that could be a meal in itself; soup du jour specialties, such as cream of pumpkin; and entrees such as French sauerkraut with pork and mixed sausages to make your mouth water and bust your belt, at surprisingly moderate prices. You can order nice wines and imported beers here, too. Open Monday nights for dinner and Tuesday through Saturday for lunch and dinner. Call (919–872–6224).

People who enjoy Jean-Claude's also like the ***Irregardless Cafe,*** at 901 West Morgan Street. When they describe it, people tend to call it the "vegetarian restaurant," but it does serve chicken, steaks, and duck as well as the vegetarian entrees. Don't be fooled by the sprouts in the salads. These aren't old hippies or young health-food nuts; they're folks who've figured out how to get the best flavor out of fresh ingredients with the least amount of doctoring. The menu changes daily to take advantage of fresh vegetables and meats. To dispel the notion that you're doing something that's good for you, you can order anything you like from the full bar. The homemade desserts will keep you on the sinful side, too. Open for lunch Tuesday through Friday from 11:30 A.M. to 2:30 P.M.; dinner Tuesday through Thursday from 5:30 to 9:30 P.M., Friday and Saturday to 10:00 P.M. Dancing until midnight Saturday. Sunday brunch 10:00 A.M. to 2:00 P.M. Call (919) 833–9920 for a mouthwatering description of the day's dinner menu and to make reservations. Web site: www.irregardless.com.

Greenshield's Brewery and Pub acknowledges the Brit influence in Raleigh's culture by serving a variety of traditional English foods as well as an American menu and an assortment of beers made on the premises. The establishment is in downtown Raleigh's historical City Market, at 214 East Martin Street, around the corner from Artspace. Some of the British offerings include bangers and mash (sausage and mashed potatoes), fish and chips, and shepherd's pie, although it is made with beef rather than the more traditional lamb. A dish called "Scotch egg" seems designed to keep a country man warm whilst he's out walking the cobbles. It consists of a hardboiled egg wrapped in sausage, rolled in bread crumbs, and fried! Some of the American fare is pretty sturdy, too. The beer batter onion rings, for example, come in absolutely huge servings. The shrimp and grits, of course, is entirely Southern, but don't forget that the early colonists survived by being flexible, so go ahead and enjoy the grits, even in an English-themed pub. Greenshield's beers are popular enough to be sold all around the city, but the brewery and bottling facilities are here. You can take in a tour on Saturday afternoons. In addition to two pubs, the establishment has a beer garden, from which you can watch the brewing activity, and a patio that is nice enough to use almost year-round. Greenshields is

AUTHOR'S FAVORITE PLACES IN THE UPPER PIEDMONT

- North Carolina State University Arboretum
- Cedar Creek Gallery
- Hillsborough
- Mt. Airy
- Harley Museum
- Seagrove
- Old Salem
- Selma
- Museum of Early Southern Decorative Arts
- Furniture Discovery Center
- Nahunta Pork Center
- Ava Gardner Museum

open seven days a week, beginning at 11:30 A.M., and usually closes about midnight, an hour later on weekends when they have live music. Phone (919) 829–0214. Web site: www.greenshields.com.

Squids, at the junction of the U.S. Highway 15/501 Bypass and Elliott Road, specializes in fresh seafood—steamed jumbo shrimp, wood-grilled fish, blackened fish, and fried fish—all served up with a fluffy, sweet version of hush puppies. In season you can order oysters on the half shell. The oyster bar is open for a seafood happy hour daily from 4:00 to 6:00 P.M. Dinner begins at 5:00 P.M. Phone (919) 929–0025.

If you like gardens and plants and farmers, you'll want to add several more stops to your itinerary—the ***Raleigh Farmers Market*** and the ***J. C. Raulston Arboretum*** at North Carolina State University. The Farmers Market, 1301 Hodges Street in the warehouse section of town, draws crowds of locals with fresh produce sold by local truck farmers. Even if you're traveling and don't want to haul a lot of carrots across the state, it's fun to wander around watching the people and sampling the wares. Depending on your taste in fresh fruits and vegetables, it might be a little more fun to visit here during spring strawberry season or summer peach time than, say, for fall turnips or winter squash, but the market is open year-round from 5:00 A.M. to 6:00 P.M., Sunday 8:00 A.M. to 6:00 P.M. Phone (919) 733–7417. Web site: www.ncdamarketing.org. The arboretum at North Carolina State University, 4301 Beryl Road (919–515–3132, take the Hillsborough Street exit off the beltline), grows thousands of plants from around the world. In addition to special interest areas, such as the silver-and-white garden and a Japanese garden, a long perennial garden shows what it's possible to grow outside in North Carolina every month. Open daily from 8:00 A.M. to dusk. Admission is free.

Two more gardens appeal to horticulture enthusiasts: ***Joel Lane House Gardens,*** at the corner of St. Mary's and West Hargett Streets, and the ***Raleigh Municipal Rose Garden,*** at 301 Pogue Street, in a residential neighborhood near North Carolina State University. The Joel Lane House Gardens are authentic colonial Revival style, with espaliered fruit trees, pomegranate tress, a grape arbor, and, in the herb garden, medicinal and culinary herbs. The gardens are open daily from sunrise to sunset, with tours available March to the first of December, Tuesday through Friday from 10:00 A.M. to 2:00 P.M. and 1:00 to 4:00 P.M. Saturday. Admission free. Phone (919) 833–3431 for details. The rose garden, which has an amphitheatre for concerts and stage productions, contains sixty different varieties of roses, about 1,200 plants, with something in bloom from late May until fall. Seasonal flowers, trees, and shrubs are included in the garden. Open daily, sunrise to sunset. Admission free. Phone (919) 821–4579. Web site: www.raleigh-nc.org/parks&rec/.

For a nice break from the city, head north, either on U.S. Highway 1 or on U.S. Highway 401 and State Highway 39, to Henderson, not far from the Virginia border. The ***Kerr Lake State Recreational Area,*** 269 Glasshouse Road (252–438–7791), is a 50,000-acre lake that stretches from North Carolina into Virginia, with 800 miles of shoreline. You'll find everything from picnic areas to camping facilities and hiking trails. The area has 700 campsites, fourteen boat ramps, fourteen picnic shelters, and three community buildings. Admission to the park is free, but there is a fee for camping: $20 for electrical and water or $15 for nonelectrical, just water, for both tents and recreational vehicles. The Vance County Tourism organization sponsors July 4 fireworks and a Labor Day Parade of Lights flotilla. Web site: www.kerrlake-nc.com.

While you're in the area, treat yourself to the ***Cedar Creek Gallery,*** 1150 Fleming Road, a workplace and sales outlet for top-quality craftspeople. Their brochure says, "Expect to be overwhelmed," and that's not hype. The gallery displays are spread through many rooms. Much of the work is pottery, but you'll also find fine glass, handmade stereopticons, stringed instruments, jewelry, and toys that are too splendid to put into the hands of kids. The quality is so outstanding that people tend to walk along talking in hushed tones, though that's not at all the demeanor of the artisans themselves. In the rear of the gallery, the ***Museum of American Pottery*** displays the entire range of local pottery, from the old folk pottery of places such as Cole and Jugtown to the works of contemporary studio potters. The exhibits include information about basic potting procedures and such things as salt glazes, too. From Henderson go south on Interstate 85, take the second Butner exit (186), turn left on US 15 North, turn right at the first crossroads, and left on Fleming Road

Courtesy in the Capital

As a newspaper reporter, I sometimes have to spend time in the courthouses in Raleigh. Full of lawyers, clerks, defendants, and mounds of paperwork, this is nobody's favorite place. And I've been around a lot of overworked, unpleasant people in a lot of courthouses, so I went into the state and county courthouses here with a chip on my shoulder.

I got lost. I got into the buildings but couldn't figure out what exit to use to find my car. Here are the people who helped me and smiled while they were doing it: two clerks, three guards, and a lawyer. The lawyer went with me on the elevator and through some back halls to a shortcut that got me out to the parking lot where I'd left my car. As the door was closing on the building, he actually waved bye.

to the gallery. Open daily from 10:00 A.M. to 6:00 P.M. (919–528–1041). Web site: www.cedarcreekgallery.com.

As a final indulgence in this area, stop at ***Bob's Bar-B-Que,*** on State Highway 56 between Creedmor and I–85. Not only can you get good eastern-style North Carolina barbecue here, but you can also dig into a serving of bunter stew, made with beef, pork, limas, and potatoes. The traditional beverage is iced tea, sweet or unsweetened, served in plastic cups with the name of the restaurant on the side. Open Monday through Saturday from 10:00 A.M. to 8:00 P.M. Phone (919) 528–2081.

From Raleigh you can go off in a number of directions, all with their own peculiarities and pleasures. Interstates 40 East and then 95 South take you to Fayetteville. US 70, toward Goldsboro, takes you to ***Selma, Pikeville,*** and ***Smithfield,*** which you can easily visit on the same day. If you are an antiques lover, you may decide to devote a day to the town of Selma. As you head in this direction, the landscape gradually flattens out.

Signs from US 70 (as well as from I–95 and I–40) will direct you to Selma, a small town that has pulled itself from the doldrums of empty old buildings to become an antiques mecca. The story begins in 1997, when Bruce Radford, town manager, was trying to figure out a way to restore the town to its earlier vibrancy. The town needed a theme, he thought. And it came to him during a golf game. He swung at the ball and got an inspiration, more or less at the same time. The golf ball went into the woods and Bruce has since moved on, but his idea flourishes.

Using some financial incentives, promise of advertising support, and a lot of local enthusiasm, the town of Selma has seen its downtown buildings re-

Who Cares about Royalties Anyway?

I was sitting in Bob's Bar-B-Que enjoying a barbecue sandwich and fried onion rings, my usual treat here, when I noticed an unusual amount of activity going on as some customers paid their bill at the cash register. The woman went out to the car and came in carrying a book I recognized right away as *North Carolina Off the Beaten Path*. She showed it to the proprietors, who were surprised.

They didn't know they were in the book.

I walked over to the counter and asked, "Do you like that book?"

Fortunately they said they did, so I told them, "I wrote it."

They acted suitably impressed, then the woman said to me, "I'd ask you to autograph it, but I didn't buy it. I checked it out of the library."

Oink

Larry Pierce, manager of Nahunta Pork Center, wearing the white smock and hat that is standard dress for anyone going into any of the buildings where pork is handled, is headed into the ham house. As he opens the door he turns slightly and says, "You know about the chicken and the pig planning what each will contribute to an important breakfast?

"The pig says, 'I'm contributing bacon.'

"The chicken says, 'I'm contributing eggs.'

"The pig says, 'You're making a commitment. I'm making a sacrifice.'"

And grinning at his own pork humor enough to wiggle his thick brown mustache, Pierce goes on into the chilly building.

The same offbeat humor shows up in the bumper stickers stacked beside the cash register: PROMOTE PORK. RUN OVER A CHICKEN.

stored as antiques malls and shops, many with living quarters upstairs, artisans' studios, and shops for such antiques-related activities as upholstering.

The town is into the swing of it and will probably grow fast enough to cease being off the beaten path before long. While you are searching for antiques, take the time to stop in ***Short's Grill,*** a lunch place in the center of town where you can get a burger all-the-way made of fresh ground beef, served with a fountain Coke that tastes like Coke tasted in the old days. For further information about Selma, call the town hall (919) 965–9841.

In this same area, the ***Nahunta Pork Center,*** 200 Bertie Pierce Road, Pikeville, is a family operation that has grown from early slaughterhouse days, when they supplied hogs to barbecue houses, into a plant that includes a retail store where you can buy pork products so fresh that you can almost still hear the squeal. The difference in flavor between this and grocery store meat that has spent several days in storage, transit, and case-life is obvious after a single bite. The sausage is made from an old family recipe, as is the barbecue coating sauce the store sells.

When Nahunta Pork Center went retail, a lot of people predicted the center wouldn't make it because there weren't enough customers in the area. They were wrong. In 1984 it claimed to be America's largest retail pork store. It had forty employees and processed about one hundred hogs a day.

Today the center claims to be the largest all-pork retail displayer in the eastern United States.

The same old family home, with the same carpet and a bit of the furniture still there, now serves as offices. The center employs about eighty people and processes up to 150 hogs a day. Part of the beauty of the place is that it's oriented to small farmers, not agri-industry producers. The Nahunta Pork Center is especially known for its hand-rubbed country hams. The center is open from 8:00 A.M. to 5:30 P.M. Monday through Friday, 8:00 A.M. to 3:00 P.M. Saturday. Phone (919) 242–4735.

When you're through here, hop back on US 70 and follow the signs a few miles to Smithfield and the ***Ava Gardner Museum.*** Ava Gardner was born in this area, lived here when she was young, and is buried here. The museum was started by Tom Banks, who met Ava while she waited for rides near the campus of Atlantic Christian College, which he was attending, in the little town of Wilson.

Later he became a publicist on one of her movies, *My Forbidden Past.* No matter what else he did in a career that took him from New York to Florida, he kept up with what was happening to Ava, making scrapbooks of newspaper clippings about her. He also collected photographs, posters, audio- and videocassettes from her movies, and anything else he could find. In the 1970s he visited her in London and told her he was going to donate everything to start a museum in her honor.

In 1981 he bought the teacherage in Smithfield where she had lived when her mother taught school. He moved his collection there and opened the museum in 1982.

Since then the museum's had a few different locations, and the collection has continued to grow with donations of costumes, Ava's good china from her years in London, even her collection of Frank Sinatra records, until there are now more than 100,000 items.

And the museum has finally moved into a permanent location at 325 East Market Street. The museum's recent move to its new site, in what used to be a Belk's Department Store, also marks a change in its status. For the first time the

A Mellow Fellow

When I talked to Bruce Radford about how things continue to prosper in Selma, the mellowness of his voice reminded me of the first time I talked to him on the telephone, before I'd been to Selma to meet him. I said that he had "a radio voice."

"Actually," he said, "I have a radio face."

He doesn't. He's a nice-looking man, but what a great line!

It Started with a Kiss

According to local lore, Tom Banks would speed past Ava on his bicycle and yell, "Hey Girlfriend." One day, she ran after him, pulled him off the bike, and kissed his cheek. Banks was smitten permanently.

museum has a full-time professional director and is being promoted by a thirty-second television commercial narrated by Gregory Peck.

Museum space has nearly doubled, from 3,500 to 6,500 square feet, and includes a 2,200-square-foot gallery with large panels as a self-guided tour covering her life from early childhood to her final days, with scenes from such movies as *Night of the Iguana* and *Show Boat*. Her career spanned forty-four years and included seventy-two films.

A video theater with a 61-inch projection TV can hold up to fifty people, and a fifteen-minute video about Ava Gardner can be seen here.

The museum is open Monday through Saturday, 9:00 A.M. to 5:00 P.M., Sunday 2:00 to 5:00 P.M. Admission is $4.00 for adults, $3.00 for senior citizens sixty-five and older, $3.00 for teens thirteen to sixteen, $2.00 for children three to twelve. Children under three admitted free. Phone (919) 934–5830. Web site: www.avagardner.org.

From Raleigh, if you decide to head south to ***Fayetteville*** instead of east, in a little less than an hour you'll find yourself in the sandhills, countryside that is more flat than the area in the center of the state. Fayetteville is probably best known as the home of ***Fort Bragg Air Force Base*** and Pope Air Force Base. Pope is closed except to people with military or Department of Defense identification, but Fort Bragg is open to visitors. Interest in the base has increased since the September 11, 2001, terrorist attacks on the World Trade Towers and the Pentagon.

Fort Bragg began as "Camp Bragg" in 1918 as an army field artillery site. Today it's the world's largest airborne troop facility and, since 1952, has been headquarters for the Green Berets. The base covers 220 square miles and holds 42,000 soldiers, as well as 8,500 civilian employees.

You can visit a number of museums and interesting sites on the Fort Bragg base. The ***82nd Airborne Division War Memorial Museum,*** at Ardennes and Gela Streets, gives you a look at weapons, uniforms, aircraft, parachutes, and other items from World War I through Operation Desert Storm. Some aircraft are displayed outside, too. The museum is open Tuesday through Saturday, 10:00 A.M. to 4:30 P.M. Admission free. Phone (910) 432–3443.

Fore

The Fayetteville area has ten public golf courses, three driving ranges, and three military golf courses open to active duty and retired military personnel, Department of Defense civilians, NAF employees, and the family members and guests of all these.

Fayetteville is the birthplace and corporate headquarters of Putt-Putt golf. Two of Fayetteville's native sons—Ray Floyd and Chip Beck—are well-known golfers.

Methodist College is one of only five colleges in the country to offer a degree in professional golf management.

At the ***JFK Special Warfare Museum,*** in Building D, at Ardennes and Marion Streets, you'll see exhibits emphasizing Special Forces operations and the Green Berets' role in "unconventional warfare." The museum is open Tuesday through Sunday, 11:00 A.M. to 4:00 P.M. Admission free. Phone (910) 432–4272.

The military influence remains strong in Fayetteville, even away from the military bases. The ***Airborne and Special Operations Museum,*** at 100 Bragg Boulevard, bills itself as "the only place on earth where you can see, hear and experience the story of the U.S. Airborne and Special Operations units." Life-sized and walk-through dioramas, a motion simulator, and a large-screen theater give you the chance to develop a sense of what it would've been like to be a paratrooper on D-Day, fly low over treetops, or participate in a combat mission. The museum was built to be a showplace. Its 59,000 square feet include a main exhibit hall of 23,000 square feet and a center lobby of 5,000 square feet that is five stories of glass walls and windows. For perspective, consider that the average four-bedroom house is often less than 3,000 square feet. The museum is open 10:00 A.M. to 5:00 P.M. Tuesday through Saturday, noon to 5:00 P.M. Sunday. Closed Monday, except open on federal holiday Mondays. Museum admission free; $3.00 each for the large-screen theater and motion simulator or $5.00 for both. Phone (910) 483–3003. Web site: www.asomf.org.

No Escaping the Civil War

The federal government commissioned an arsenal in Fayetteville in 1838. The Confederacy took it over when the Civil War started, and General Sherman targeted it when his troops marched through the South. He seized the city in March 1865.

Perhaps the most notable thing about Fayetteville these days is its energy and the vigor with which citizens have been revitalizing the downtown historic district. Some of the old buildings are open for tours, others not. The ***Museum of the Cape Fear Historical Complex,*** at the corner of Bradford and Arsenal Avenues, combines three historic elements about the development of southeastern North Carolina—museum galleries, the 1897 Poe House, and part of an old federal arsenal. The museum exhibits focus on Native American culture, the area's early settlers, the antebellum years, the Civil War, the role of the textile industry, and traditional pottery. The 1897 Poe House, a late Victorian home, is open for tours. The complex is open Tuesday through Saturday, 10:00 A.M. to 5:00 P.M., Sunday 1:00 to 5:00 P.M. Admission is free. Phone (910) 486–1330.

Heritage Square, 225 Dick Street, is owned by the Fayetteville Woman's Club and includes three buildings listed on the National Register of Historic Places: the 1800 Sanford House, a freestanding 1818 oval ballroom, and the 1804 Baker-Haigh-Nimocks House. You need an appointment to get inside. Phone (910) 483–6009.

The ***Historic Haymount*** area, near Fort Bragg on Bragg Road near downtown Fayetteville, features some interesting specialty shops and pleasant eating places. The newest inhabitants of a house built in the 1840s market themselves as the ***Belmont Village.*** The house, which has an impressive Palladian window and a grand staircase, contains a photo studio, which is probably not of much interest if you're traveling, but the gift and home furnishings boutique and the tea room will be. The Belmont Village is open 10:00 A.M. to 5:00 P.M. Monday through Saturday. A few shops open later. Closed Sunday. The tea room serves lunch from 11:00 A.M. to 3:00 P.M. Monday through Friday. Phone (910) 485–8433. Also in Historic Haymount, at 1213 Hay Street, the shop ***Angels and Antiques*** claims to have the largest selection of angels in the United States. Open Monday through Friday 10:00 A.M. to 5:30 P.M., Saturday to 5:00 P.M. Phone (910) 433–4454. ***Hilltop House Restaurant,*** 1240 Fort Bragg Road, has an upscale restaurant in a restored home in the heart of Historic Haymount, which serves steaks, seafoods, pasta, chicken, and pork as well as daily specials, prepared with a touch of creativity. Don't expect an intimate little place, though; it can accommodate up to 150 people. The restaurant is open for lunch and dinner Monday through Friday, 11:00 A.M. to 9:30 P.M., Saturday, 5:00 to 10:00 P.M., and Sunday 10:00 A.M. to 9:00 P.M. Phone (910) 484–6699.

In the ***Market and Carolina Dream Makers,*** at 302 Russell Street, more than fifty local artists and crafters sell their work, including baskets, pottery, jewelry, and Americana folk art. The market is open Tuesday through Saturday, 10:00 A.M. to 4:00 P.M. Phone (910) 483–3111.

Food and Flowers

Fayetteville hosts two especially popular annual festivals. The Dogwood Festival, started in 1982, is traditionally held in mid- to late April for three or four days to celebrate spring and the blooming of an 18-mile dogwood trail. Most of the events, including major entertainment, take place in the downtown area. The festival culminates in the multi-arts event known as Sunday-on-the-Square. Phone (910) 323–1934.

The ***International Folk Festival,*** started in 1978, happens in historic downtown Fayetteville on Hay Street, in the Market House vicinity, late in September on a Sunday afternoon from noon to 5:00 P.M. The festival features entertainment and dancing typical of the countries represented, but the big draw is food. Visitors can sample fare ranging from Thai egg rolls and Liberian rice bread to cassava cake from the Philippines. This festival typically attracts as many as 60,000 people. Phone (910) 323–1776.

A collective of more local artists and crafters display and sell their work at ***Cape Fear Studios,*** 148-1 Maxwell Street. An annex, the ***Mill House,*** is open on Cool Spring Street. The studios are open Tuesday through Friday, 11:00 A.M. to 5:00 P.M., Saturday 10:00 A.M. to 4:00 P.M., Sunday 1:00 to 5:00 P.M. Admission free. Phone (910) 433–2986. Web site: www.capefearstudios.com.

In downtown Fayetteville, ***Rude Awakenings Coffee Shop,*** at 227 Hay Street, operates in a renovated building that is a hallmark of the downtown revitalization of which the community is justifiably proud. The coffeehouse, right next to the Cameo Art House Theater, offers the standard varieties of coffees, teas, and baked goods. Their Web site provides insight into how the building and downtown were renovated: www.rudeawakening.net.

For something a tad stronger than coffee, try ***Huske Hardware Brewing Company,*** at 405 Hay Street. This building used to be a hardware store. It has been converted into a brew pub where you can see the brewing in process and sample a variety of ales. The dining menu includes seafood and beef. Open for lunch and dinner Monday through Wednesday, 11:00 A.M. to midnight, and Thursday through Saturday, 11:00 A.M. to 2:00 A.M. Phone (910) 437–9961.

Another brewery and restaurant, the ***Mash House,*** at 4150 Sycamore Dairy Road, has won a silver medal for its English-style India pale ale, called Hoppy Hour IPA, and prepares American-style food to go with it. Some of the most popular menu items are a seafood newburg with lobster sauce, grilled salmon with Caesar salad, and chicken breast grilled with seven herbs. You can order pizza with homemade crust, calzone, burgers, and sandwiches, too. Thursday through Saturday, from 11:00 P.M., live bands perform everything from oldies and blues to covers of newer pop songs. The bands come mostly out of Raleigh, a pert server said, because that's where the booking agent lives. The Mash House is open for lunch, dinner, and snacks from 11:30 A.M. daily. Phone (910) 867–9223.

The Triangle

In a sense, ***Durham*** is closer to Raleigh than it used to be. With both communities expanding laterally, it's not hard as you drive between the two places to imagine that they'll soon run together. And when people speak of "The Triangle," they're typically including Raleigh. But the increasing development has brought more traffic, which slows driving between Raleigh and Durham, and Chapel Hill and Durham more often package themselves as a tourist unit not necessarily including Raleigh. Durham is a tobacco town; Duke University was endowed by and named for the Duke family, which made Durham a tobacco center.

Although tobacco is not as important in the area as it once was, criticizing smokers is not a good way to make friends here. The Duke family pioneered in marketing cigarettes in America. You can understand something of the mystique and importance of tobacco by visiting the ***Duke Homestead State Historic Site and Tobacco Museum,*** established on the Duke family farm. Take the Guess Road exit off I–85 to 2828 Duke Homestead Road. Depending on when you're here, you'll see tobacco being planted, cultivated, harvested, or prepared for market and have the opportunity to participate in part of the processing.

On the property, the old family house, two tobacco factories, a curing barn, and a packhouse show you how it used to be. In the visitor center, tobacco-related exhibits include advertising, signs, machinery, and an old cigar store Indian. A seventeen-minute documentary film, *Legacy of the Golden Leaf,* describes the history and importance of tobacco in the state in a more positive light than most of what you see and hear today. Open Tuesday through Saturday 10:00 A.M. to 4:00 P.M. Hours change, so it's a good idea to call ahead (919–477–5498).

The Duke Homestead holds four major festivals a year: the Herb, Garden, and Craft Festival in June; the Tobacco Harvest Festival in September; an Evening at the Homestead, for children, in October; and Christmas by Candlelight in December.

Duke money also made possible a dominant institution in this area, ***Duke University.*** In 1924 a $6 million gift from the family made it possible to expand what was then Trinity College. A large endowment and subsequent grants followed. The result is Duke University's two large campuses spread west and east

Calling it "Vale-Vale" Wouldn't Work

When Don Clayton designed and built his "improved" miniature golf course as a way to take a break from working too hard, he had to open a bank account for the business. He gave up calling the place Shady Vale when he realized he didn't know how to spell Vale. Since the game is about putting, he decided to call it Putt-Putt instead. He knew how to spell that.

of Durham, with great stone buildings and acres of grass and woods seeming to be enough for a huge student population. In fact, everything is large except the student body. Enrollment is in the neighborhood of 10,000 students, most of whom have to walk a lot to cover the large distances. The campuses are called, appropriately enough, East Campus and West Campus. You get to East Campus by following the signs from US 15/501 Bypass to State Road 751 onto Duke University Road. The Georgian buildings of the original college are here.

To get to West Campus take the Hillsborough Road exit from I–85 and go east on Main Street. On the West Campus the massive Gothic ***Duke University Chapel*** dominates (919–684–2572). James Duke, founder of the university, planned it that way. In March 1925, when he was walking the woods that have become West Campus, he designated the highest ground as the chapel site, saying that he wanted the central building of the campus to be "a great towering church" so dominating that it would have a spiritual influence on the young students who studied there. This edifice is worth a visit.

Horace Trumbauer of Philadelphia, who designed Duke's mansion on Fifth Avenue in New York, was the architect. The chief designer was Julian Able, the first black architect graduated from the department of architecture at the University of Pennsylvania.

Duke chose to have the church built of gray stone from a quarry in nearby Hillsborough. The result is a Gothic church patterned after the original Canterbury Cathedral. A 210-foot tower soars skyward, housing a fifty-bell carillon. A 5,000-pipe organ was built into the rear of the nave several decades after the chapel's construction.

The organ, designed by Dirk Andries Flentrop of Holland, is based on an eighteenth-century organ of classical design, constructed of solid wood and using no electricity except to power the blower. It was built in Holland, where it was played to assure its quality. It was then totally dismantled, with each pipe wrapped separately, and shipped to Duke University. After the organ's first official use at Christmas 1976, one critic wrote that the organ "breathes

Duke University Chapel

music." In daylight the red, green, and gold trim on its mahogany seems to combine with the glow of its 5,000 long slender pipes.

Sunlight streams through seventy-seven stained-glass windows. These and the ornamental lead and gold symbols in the doors of the building were designed and created by G. Owen and Bonawit, Inc., of New York.

Instead of kings and saints at the portals, the chapel memorializes Protestant heroes such as Luther, John Wesley, Thomas Jefferson, and Robert E. Lee.

James Duke, his brother Benjamin, and their father Washington are entombed in a small memorial chapel. Statues, showing all three men lying comfortably pillowed and gracefully draped, are carved in marble atop their tombs beneath the windows. Charles Keck of New York was the sculptor.

The elaborate ironwork of the gates to the memorial chapel was done by William H. Hackson Company of New York.

Fine woodwork throughout the building was done by Irving and Casson, A. H. Davenport Inc., Boston; the stone carving was by John Donnelly, Inc., of New York.

BETTER-KNOWN ATTRACTIONS IN THE UPPER PIEDMONT

Raleigh
North Carolina State Capitol
(919) 733–4994 or 733–3456

Winston-Salem
Old Salem
(336) 721–7300
(336) 725–1516

It may seem strange that so much work in this Southern chapel was done by New York and Boston craftsmen until you realize that James Duke was living in New York when the project was in process.

The chapel is open daily from 8:00 A.M. to 8:00 P.M. Interdenominational worship services are at 11:00 A.M. on Sunday. Web site: www.chapel.duke.edu.

Also on the West Campus, the ***Sarah P. Duke Memorial Gardens*** (418 Anderson Street; 800–367–3853) have lots of open grass for kids to romp on and paths through wooded areas, as well as all kinds of seasonal flowers, a gazebo, and a lily pond. The fifty-five acres feature more than 2,000 kinds of plants, including the Blomquist Garden of Native Plants and the Asiatic Arboretum. Admission is free. Web site: www.hr.duke.edu/dukegardens/duke gardens.html.

Another stop to feed your fascination with natural science is the ***Museum of Life and Science & Magic Wings Butterfly House,*** 433 Murray Avenue. Spread over seventy-eight acres, the museum has a variety of science and nature displays, including a mock-up of the Apollo 15 and a nature center with native animals. A train ride through the outdoor park gives you a chance to see everything from bears and wolves to farm animals. And the tropical butterfly house, the largest museum butterfly house east of the Mississippi, features species from Asia, Africa, and Central and South America. Open from 10:00 A.M. to 5:00 P.M. Monday through Saturday, noon to 5:00 P.M. Sunday. Closed New Year's Day, Thanksgiving, and Christmas. Admission is $8.50 for adults, $7.50 for seniors, and $6.00 for children. Miniature train ride is $1.50 extra. Phone (919) 220–5429. Web site: www.ncmls.org.

Two attractions in Durham pay homage to the role of African Americans in the region. ***Hayti Heritage Center,*** 804 Old Fayetteville Street, features works and artifacts of African Americans, visual arts galleries, and dance and community meeting spaces. Both contemporary and traditional art, by local, regional, and national African-American artists, is on display. Hayti was once a focal African-American marketplace with thriving neighborhoods. The center is downtown, easy to find by taking Expressway 147 to exit 12. It is open from 9:00 A.M. to 7:30 P.M. Monday through Friday, 9:00 A.M. to 3:00 P.M. Saturday. Weekend hours may vary depending on special events and activities. For details call (919) 683–1709. Web site: www.hayti.org.

St. Joseph's AME Church, at 804 Old Fayetteville Street, was one of the first autonomous African-American churches in America. The church was originally the sanctuary for St. Joseph's AME Church, which was begun in 1869. Phone and Web site are the same as Hayti Heritage Center.

Historic Stagville, 5825 Old Oxford Highway, is a center for African-American studies and a place to learn about African-American plantation life, culture, and society before the Civil War. Historic Stagville has an eighteenth-century plantation house, part of which contains offices, with the rest open to the public. Four slave houses and an 1860 barn are on the property as well. Displays and research here emphasize the various cultures from which the slaves came, forming a new African-American culture in which self-reliance flourished. The barn, for instance, was built by master-craftsmen carpenters: slaves. Research here also demonstrates that there was more to the lives of the slaves than working all day for the master, although they certainly did that. But in their own community and homes, they also cultivated vegetable gardens, participated in athletic events, and took part in community affairs. Artifacts found on the property suggest that slaves brought from various parts of Africa kept some of their traditions and secret religious practices, which they used to create a new African-American culture. Historic Stagville is open from 9:00 A.M. to 4:00 P.M. Monday through Friday. Admission is free. Phone (919) 620–0120. Web site: www.ah.dcr.state.nc.us/.

While you're in the Triangle, take a picnic to the ***B. Everett Jordan Lake,*** a 47,000-acre lake created by the U.S. Army Corps of Engineers for flood control. All water recreation is available at some part of the lake—boating, swimming, and fishing—as well as hiking and camping. As you drive around in the area, you'll probably notice several different roads, all marked with signs, leading into access areas. One is US 64 at State Highway 51, which leads to several recreation areas. Another is off US 64 going north on US 15/501, a point southwest of Durham, which takes you from Pittsboro, through Bynum and into Chapel Hill, home of the ***University of North Carolina at Chapel Hill.*** Chapel Hill and Durham are so close together that residents frequently live in one community and work in the other. The area south of Chapel Hill is still fairly rural and is a popular living area for university people with an itch to rusticate.

About 8 miles south of Chapel Hill, on US 15/501, just outside the community of ***Pittsboro,*** you'll find one of the most unusual examples of gentrified rural living imaginable. ***Fearrington Village,*** built around what used to be a barn, silo, farmhouse, and a few outbuildings, now comprises an inn with thirty-three rooms, a restaurant, a market and cafe, a series of shops, a residential area with town houses and freestanding homes, and such services as a pharmacy, bank, and beauty shop. It really is a village—an upscale one—in the middle of perennial gardens and fields dotted with cows. Not just any cows, of course: Scottish Belted Galloway cows, black at both ends and white in the middle, like walking Oreo cookies. Nobody milks these cows or eats them. They're pets. Or stage setting.

More than twenty-five years ago, R. B. and Jenny Fitch bought the Fearrington family dairy farm and started work on a planned community here. They didn't tear down existing buildings, and they built new ones to fit in unobtrusively. For instance, the granary became the market, deli, and cafe. The old milking barn houses a home-and-garden shop. The Potting Shed, in the old corncrib, sells plants propagated from the Fearrington gardens.

Living here isn't for anybody with shaky finances, and neither is staying at ***Fearrington House Inn,*** with rates running to more than $325 a night. The prices at the ***Fearrington House Restaurant*** or the ***Fearrington Market Cafe,*** however, are comparable to those in restaurants anywhere. The inn does offer every creature comfort you can think of, in rooms decorated in English style.

Pretty Kitty

Every year the Chatham Animal Rescue and Education (CARE) holds the "My Friend My Cat Show."

One participant said, "It's not a fancy cat show, it's just a cat show." But it does have awards in thirteen classes, including longest tail and whiskers; best long hair; best black, best white; best calico; best senior; best rescue/handicapped; best tabby red, best tabby gray; and best particolor. Local folks can tell you what cats they're entering and what cats their friends and families have entered in previous years. It's a party. Food and vendors are part of the day.

The rules specify an entry fee of $5.00 per class, limit two classes per cat. Cats must be in carriers, have current rabies certificate, and be feline leukemia negative. And no unaltered male cats over a year old may participate.

Profits go to the humane society.

The show is held at the Senior Center on State Highway 87 North, Pittsboro. Judging begins at noon on a Saturday late in February. Visitors are welcome. Phone (919) 542–5757. Web site: www.chathamanimalrescue.org.

Activities such as touring the gardens, which are wonderful, are free. And you can browse in McIntire's, a good independent bookstore, shop for wine and gourmet treats, pick up handmade pottery and jewelry, and perhaps attend a reading by a well-known author in the renovated barn.

For more information about food, lodging, and activities in Fearrington Village, call (800) 316–3829. Web site: www.fearringtonvillage.com.

The town of Pittsboro is worth wandering through, too. It has lots of antiques shops and the kinds of stores that cater to people fixing up old houses, as well as a natural foods store and several restaurants. This is the kind of place where "real" farmers still mix on the sidewalks with men in Bermuda shorts and Birkenstocks.

The earliest settlers of this area were families who moved from the plantations on the coast to get away from the humid summer heat and the illnesses that came with it. The town of Pittsboro was formed in 1787. The early buildings were modest frame structures, but the new courthouse in 1843 was the first brick building. For a small town, Pittsboro had a lot of activity. Crowds gathered to see a Confederate statue unveiled, a murderer hanged, and President Theodore Roosevelt coming through. When electricity came in 1922, people danced in the street. This and a good bit more about the town's history is detailed in an outstanding little brochure, "Pittsboro Historic District," which includes a map of local structures and short paragraphs about their history. Most of the stores and restaurants in town have copies.

Another brochure, "Chatham County," also free in the stores, suggests a self-guided walking tour that begins at the present courthouse. The courthouse is at the center of a highway circle typical of many small Southern towns, with shops and restaurants lining the circle as well as streets radiating out from the curve.

A brochure called, "Historic Pittsboro Antiques Walk," maps antiques, collectibles, and memorabilia shops within easy walking distance.

A potter, Lyn Morrow, has a shop and studio just 5 miles north of Pittsboro on US 15/501 that is a "must stop" if you enjoy places that are offbeat but still deal in quality. ***Lyn Morrow Pottery*** is located inside a house she's painted in cobalt blues and turquoise. Assorted metal sculptures stand around the front yard. Lyn says people sometimes wonder why she painted her house in such psychedelic colors, but when you see her pottery, you understand. It's not remotely psychedelic, but blue and turquoise are her predominant colors, and in that way her pottery stands out from that of the thirty or so other potters whose work she sells. She's been a potter for more than thirty years and not only knows her craft but knows all the potters in a wide region as well. Lyn Morrow Pottery is open Tuesday through Saturday 10:00 A.M. to 5:00 P.M.; Sunday noon to 5:00 P.M. Phone (919) 545–9078.

Just a mile or so north of Lyn, still on US 15/501, Joyce Bynum's ***Stone Crow Pottery*** has become an established studio and shop over more than twenty-five years, in an old log cabin. The stairs to the second floor of the display area bear a sign warning visitors to limit the number of people on the second floor at one time to ten. The showroom atmosphere is rustic. Joyce's work includes some unusual platters, mugs, and bowls decorated with three-dimensional figures such as fish and animal faces. She also works a lot with slip trail decorating. Her pieces tend toward whimsy and humor, and she likes the concept of functional art. Stone Crow Pottery is open Tuesday through Saturday 10:00 A.M. to 5:00 P.M., Sunday 1:00 to 5:00 P.M. Phone (919) 542–4708.

Also on US 15/501, shortly after you pass the access roads to the lake between Bynum and Pittsboro, two more women practice their craft in a ramshackle building beside the road. Neolia and Celia Cole make pottery in the North Carolina production tradition, specializing in spongeware, a soft brownish glaze called "butterware," and a shocking red glaze. The pots at ***Cole's Pottery,*** 3410 Hawkins Avenue, Sanford, are not the sleek stylish pieces of studio potters but the made-for-use mugs, bowls, pitchers, and teapots of the kind that served local people for daily use in earlier days. The sisters also make a variety of miniature tea sets and vases. They sign each piece with a comment like, "Love, Neolia Cole," and "Let me go home with you." Their stock, like that of most North Carolina potters, fluctuates with demand. Sometimes they can hardly keep up, and the shelves will be sparsely filled; other times pots crowd every available inch. Nobody gets upset if you stop in, look around, and leave without having bought anything. Open Monday through Friday from 8:00 A.M. to 5:30 P.M. and Saturday from 8:00 A.M. to 3:30 P.M. (919–776–9558). New potteries spring up regularly in this area and their numbers grow steadily, so when you drive through, you will certainly see signs for some places not mentioned here that will be worth a look. Generally, the newer places produce studio-art pottery rather than traditional folk pottery.

The attractions and people of this Pittsboro area reflect its proximity to Chapel Hill and the influence it has on the area.

Chapel Hill, almost the geographical center of North Carolina, is recognizably a college town, the kind in which the campus and the town meet at a wall running along the campus green, where students sit on the wall to see and be seen, and where the businesses across the street are mostly campus oriented. Visitors actually tour the campus, less because of its history than because it is so Norman Rockwellish, sort of an artist's conceptualization of a campus, with trees and grass and historic buildings—even some ivy here and there.

Franklin Street, running along the edge of the university campus and bordering the town, is where town and gown meet. Local people pride themselves on having prevented the street from turning into nothing more than a row of souvenir shops, as has happened in many college towns. Lindsay Chappell, writing for *Images Magazine,* said, "If you could stand at one end of Franklin Street and see all the way to the other, you'd pretty much be glimpsing the soul of Chapel Hill." Along this street you find art galleries, coffeehouses, restaurants, beer spots, and shops. ***Top of the Hill Restaurant and Brewery,*** at the corner of Columbia and Franklin Streets, isn't exactly a hangout because it's too upscale, but it is a landmark of sorts. The establishment overlooks downtown Chapel Hill from a third-floor patio, which is served from a shining curved bar inside. It has won awards for best restaurant in Chapel Hill, best microbrew in the Triangle, and best outdoor dining. Top of the Hill is open daily 11:00 A.M. to 2:00 A.M. Phone (919) 929–8676. Web site: www.topofthehillrestaurant.com.

At ground level, ***Crook's Corner,*** 610 West Franklin Street, seems to serve townspeople, students, and visitors in about equal numbers. The restaurant's signature dish is shrimp and grits. The restaurant offers a huge variety of beers. Phone (919) 929–7643.

A couple of blocks away, ***Carolina Brewery*** claims the title of Chapel Hill's first microbrewery and serves contemporary American fare, including many dishes made with beer. Carolina Brewery was named "best brew pub in the southeast" one year. It features live blues on Thursday nights. The pub is open Sunday through Tuesday 11:30 A.M. to midnight; Wednesday and Thursday 11:30 A.M. to 1:00 A.M., and Friday and Saturday 11:30 A.M. to 2:00 A.M. Phone (919) 942–1800.

A college standard at 452½ West Franklin Street is the ***Cave.*** Every college town has one. Bills itself as the oldest bar in town—established 1970. The Cave serves beer only, in cans or bottles. Live music seven nights a week is the big draw, especially rock and roll, blue grass, country, and folk. The place has games such as pool and pinball, too. Open daily 2:30 P.M. to 2:30 A.M. Phone (919) 968–9308.

ghosts in the tower

A castle stands on the campus of the University of North Carolina that has all the elements of a legend, even though it's only been there since the 1920s. The Order of the Gimghouls, a secret fraternity, apparently met here. And a young man died fighting a duel over a girl named Fanny and was buried under a rock in the castle, where you are supposed to see his bloody hand print.

In the college atmosphere, ***Womancraft,*** a retail gallery of area artisans, seems to be just what you'd expect. For years they were part of the Franklin Street scene, but they have moved. About seventy-five crafters, mostly women, sell their work in the cooperative. The offerings range from Appalachian mountain crafts such as basketry to sophisticated stained glass and stitchery. You'll find handmade quilts, weavings, jewelry, pottery, artwork, and sculpture. The children's toys and clothes are especially popular with shoppers. The shop doesn't have the hit-or-miss feeling that tends to pervade some cooperatives, probably because it is so well established. Womancraft is in its third decade in business.

The crafters take turns working in the shop; they hire no outside help. This means that whenever you shop, you have the opportunity to talk with some of the people who have made the things you're inspecting. Items are arranged in appealing displays throughout the space rather than each member's work being confined to a particular booth. The shop is a pleasure to visit anytime, but it is especially rewarding around holidays. They take pains to offer seasonally appropriate items for Christmas and other special times.

The folks at Womancraft say they now feel truly off the beaten path, because they've moved from downtown to a store in Meadowmont Village, a multi-use shopping area with retail space downstairs and condos and offices on the upper floor, at 406 Meadowmont Village Circle. This is a concept that is catching on in Chapel Hill. The new store is just across the Orange County line, traveling State Highway 54 from Durham County. Turn off Highway 54 onto Meadowmont Lane and then onto Meadowmont Village Circle. This is straight across the highway from Friday Center, a large conference center for the University of North Carolina. You'll see a well-marked entrance to Meadowmont Village. Womancraft is open Monday through Wednesday 10:00 A.M. to 7:00 P.M., Thursday and Friday 10:00 A.M. to 9:00 P.M., Saturday 10:00 A.M. to 7:00 P.M., Sunday 1:00 to 5:00 P.M. Phone (919) 929–8362. Web site: www.womancraft.com.

Chapel Hill is known for the quantity and quality of its arts and crafts, not just in the retail arena but also in its programs at the University of North Carolina and in the university's ***Ackland Art Museum,*** at the corner of Columbia and Franklin Streets. The museum claims its collection of Asian art is the most significant in North Carolina. Other exhibits in the museum show collections of Indian and Western art, as well as pottery and wood carvings, two areas especially intrinsic to the state. The entire collection totals some 15,000 pieces, including a broad representation of the history of European painting and sculpture, with works by Rubens, Delacroix, Degas, and Pissarro. African and Asian art are also well represented. The museum is open Wednesday through Saturday 10:00 A.M. to 5:00 P.M., Sunday 1:00 to 5:00 P.M. Admission free. Phone (919) 966–5736. Web site: www.ackland.org.

Right next door to the Ackland, students, faculty, and visiting artists in the university's art program exhibit their work in ***Hanes Art Center.*** Admission free. Call (919) 962–2015 for hours.

Carrot Stuff

Well over a decade ago, my husband and I ate at the Fearrington Market Cafe for the first time. We both took a fancy to the cold carrot concoction served with our sandwiches. When I asked about the recipe, the waitress said the carrots were so popular they sold them in the deli. She also told me the recipe was in Jenny Fitch's cookbook, *The Fearrington House Cookbook,* which had been published not long before and was for sale in the market. She suggested I go take a look at the recipe, but I decided the only decent thing to do was buy the book.

The recipe is titled "Carrots in Smooth Tomato Sauce," and the main ingredient in the sauce is canned tomato soup. My crest was fallen. This was during one of my "purist" food periods, and I tried everything to make the recipe with something other than canned soup, but nothing else worked.

Ultimately, I capitulated and made very good carrots in smooth tomato sauce. I took the dish as my contribution to a communication studies department party at UNC/Charlotte while I was teaching there.

The head of the department was ecstatic. It was his favorite, he said. His roommate used to make it all the time. Did he know what the recipe was called? I asked.

"No," he said. "We just called it 'carrot stuff.'"

To make "carrot stuff," steam sliced carrots until just crispy-tender. Mix them with chopped onion and green pepper and pour over them a sauce made by combining a can of tomato soup with ½ cup salad oil, ¾ cup vinegar, 1 cup (or less) sugar, and a dash each of Worcestershire sauce and prepared mustard. The carrots taste better if you refrigerate them overnight before serving. (Note: Use as much carrots, onion, and green pepper as you'd like.)

Also on the university campus, in the Wilson Library, the ***North Carolina Collection Gallery*** contains re-created rooms of important people and places in the state's history. These include room settings with sixteenth- and seventeenth-century furnishings, the inside of a Quaker-style house, and an antebellum gentleman's library. The gallery also displays some of the personal items of Sir Walter Raleigh and North Carolina novelist Thomas Wolfe. The gallery is open Monday through Friday 9:00 A.M. to 5:00 P.M., Saturday 9:00 A.M. to 1:00 P.M., Sunday 1:00 to 5:00 P.M. Closed during university holidays. Admission free. Phone (919) 962–1172.

More art in the ***Morehead Galleries*** of the university's Morehead Planetarium deserves attention. The walnut walls below the rotunda are hung with a variety of American and Old Master paintings, including portraits of the Morehead family, which was prominent in the state's history. In the North Gallery you can view the huge Bruxelles Tapestry, reaching to the ceiling. The galleries are open Sunday through Friday 12:30 to 5:00 P.M. and 7:00 to 9:45 P.M., Saturday 10:00 A.M. to 5:00 P.M. and 7:00 to 9:45 P.M. Closed Monday evenings. Gallery admission free. Phone (919) 962–1236. Call for planetarium show details or check the Web site: www.moreheadplanetarium.org.

The ***North Carolina Botanical Garden,*** on Old Mason Farm Road, off US 15/501 Bypass, is one of the largest natural botanical gardens in the Southeast, with 600 acres of land that includes nature trails, aquatic plants, herbs, and a surreal-looking collection of carnivorous plants, some of which make the Venus Flytrap look mundane. Collections of regional plants are arranged in settings to simulate their natural habitat. The gardens are open weekdays from 8:00 A.M. to 5:00 P.M., 9:00 A.M. to 5:00 P.M. Saturday, 1:00 to 5:00 P.M. Sunday. During daylight savings time months the gardens are open an hour later. Admission is free. Phone (919) 962–0522 for more information. Web site: www.ncbg.unc.edu.

Make a quick 12-mile side trip north on State Highway 86 to ***Hillsborough,*** where a lot of history is condensed in a small area. Hillsborough was a capital of colonial and revolutionary North Carolina and a center of politics. During the Revolution Cornwallis's troops grouped for deployment here. The state convention to ratify the federal Constitution met here in 1788; in 1865 the Confederate general who signed the surrender in the Civil War headquartered here. Colonial, antebellum, and Victorian architecture mingle comfortably along the streets. The Hillsborough Historical Society likes to say that the town is a living, not a reconstructed, community.

As you drive toward the town, no matter which way you take, your first reaction is going to be that this guidebook has made some kind of mistake, because you'll be driving past all the standard convenience stores, fast-food restaurants, and grocery chains that ring most communities these days. But keep going, because moving on into town is kind of like discovering Brigadoon.

They Won't Eat People

Several of North Carolina's botanical gardens grow a variety of carnivorous plants. The more you see of them, the more fascinating they become in their shapes and colors and growth patterns. The common Venus Fly Trap you find mixed in with houseplants in retail stores doesn't begin to suggest the differences of these exotic plants. If you get interested in them as you tour gardens, North Carolina horticulturists sometimes suggest the book, *The Savage Garden* (Ten Speed Press, 1998), by Peter D'Amato. It is packed with pictures and information about the different species, where to get them, how to grow them, and (if you really get hooked) how to propagate them.

Everybody Celebrates

The first Sunday in December, the community celebrates the ***Christmas Candlelight Tour,*** which begins at the Dickson House. People of all ages help get ready for it. A volunteer inside the Dickson House jokes about being almost as old as the building. Outside, volunteers have lined the walkway with luminaria and a little boy who can't be more than a year or two old, is carefully inserting a candle into each holder, while his parents and their friends watch and help.

The town has become more aggressive about advertising to attract tourists in the past few years. One of the town's ads says it is "an easy day trip from just about anywhere." This is true, but Hillsborough is also rather removed from other attractions in the area, sitting, as it does, almost at the Virginia border.

To pick up a map for a walking tour, stop at the ***Orange County Visitor Center,*** 150 East King Street. You can also get information about shops, museums, and restaurants in the area.

The visitor center is in the ***Alexander Dickson House,*** an eighteenth-century farmhouse with marvelous woodwork. The small rooms remind you that people lived in this area without grandiose mansions. One room has a fireplace of brick and slate, the floors are pine, and the walls are painted in subdued blue and cream shades. Because you're in the South, you're inevitably going to get a bit of Confederate lore here. The Dickson House was the last headquarters of the commander of the largest Confederate armies to surrender to the Union. The house does not stand in its original location, which was at the southwest intersection of what are now I–85 and Highway 86. The Hillsborough Preservation Fund bought the house and the outbuilding General Wade Hampton had used as an office and moved them a mile and a quarter to the center of town.

Part of the charm of the house and the town is that the preservation and activities seem to be family affairs, with people of all ages involved in taking care of the area, planning tours and special events, and greeting tourists. In Hillsborough, historic preservation doesn't feel like a stuffy look back so much as an ongoing community activity.

A good example of this is the garden and courtyard outside the Dickson House, maintained by volunteers. ***Helen's Garden*** was dedicated in 1990 in the name of Helen Blake Watkins and her late husband, who moved to Hillsborough in 1956 and contributed to local landscaping and preservation projects. After her husband died, Helen donated land she owned as the new site for the Dickson House. A Chapel Hill landscaper designed the garden to show plants that were typically used for food and medicine, with something growing almost all year long. Even in December a few blue flowers bloom, Carolina Jessamine climbs across the roof of the outbuilding, and rosemary grows as high as a tall man. Crows circle lazily overhead as though they are watching over the garden. The garden is free and open to the public every day. Visitor center hours are Monday through Saturday 10:00 A.M. to 4:00 P.M., Sunday 1:00 to 4:00 P.M. Admission free. Phone (919) 732–7741. Web site: www.historichillsborough.org.

Montrose Gardens (320 St. Mary's Road; (919) 732–7787) is a nationally known complex of gardens that Gov. William Alexander Graham and his wife, Susan Washington Graham, began in the mid-nineteenth century. In addition to gardens for sun-loving plants, you'll find a rock garden and a woodland garden.

Another interesting site in Hillsborough is the ***Burwell School Historic Site,*** 319 North Churton Street. The house and outbuildings were built about 1821 and served as a school for women—they called it a "female school" back then. The house includes furnishings from the days when the Reverend and Mrs. Burwell lived in and ran the school there. The property has a nice formal garden as well. Call (919) 732–7741 for details. Admission free. Web site: www.historichillsborough.org.

The Hillsborough Garden Club founded the ***Orange County Historical Museum,*** at the corner of Churchton and Tryon Streets, in the Confederate Memorial Building, to show how people lived in Orange County from the days of the Indians to the end of 1865. Mostly the museum contains local pieces, including a display of old dental instruments, a 160-year-old working loom, and an old hand-pumped organ from the local Presbyterian Church. The museum is open every day but Monday, 1:00 to 4:00 P.M. Admission free. Phone (919) 732–2201. Web site: www.historichillsborough.org.

Find more history at ***Occaneechi Indian Village,*** downtown on South Cameron Avenue by the Eno River, a reconstructed village with huts, a cooking area, and a sweat lodge that appear as they would have from the late 1600s up to about 1710.

The reconstruction is a cooperative effort by the Occaneechi Band of the Saponi Nation, the town of Hillsborough, Orange County, and the University of North Carolina. Although the village attracts tourists, it is also a tool the tribe uses to teach the history and customs of the Occaneechi people. They lived in North Carolina in the early 1700s but moved with other small tribes to Virginia by 1710. By the 1780s, the Indian people began moving back to the piedmont, settling near Hillsborough to farm, hunt, and fish. The tribe reorganized in 1984 and has been working to educate its own people and their neighbors about their practices. This includes holding pow-wows and festivals and making presentations in schools. For more information about their activities, call (919) 304–3723. Web site: www.occaneechi-saponi.org.

After your Hillsborough side trip you can follow US 64 west from Pittsboro to Asheboro. This little community of something more than 16,000 is home to the ***American Classic Motorcycle Company and Museum*** (336–629–9564), a meeting spot for Harley-Davidson enthusiasts at 1170 U.S. Highway 64. Ed Rich, proprietor, distinguishes between enthusiasts and bikers. "The bikers, they're more the party types. The enthusiasts are into history and restoration."

Rich started collecting old Harley-Davidsons in 1971 and has been building the collection ever since. He bought most of the bikes in the 1980s then cut down on the number of purchases when their cost went up in 1988.

He opened the museum in 1980. The collection of thirty-one bikes fills the second floor of his store. A long row of old bikes gleams behind a glass-enclosed display area. One of his treasures is a red 1936 model El61 knucklehead, one of only two known to exist in original condition. It has the original paint and 17,000 miles on the odometer.

Knuckleheads, shovelheads, blockheads, and flatheads have engines fitting those descriptions. If you get confused you can buy a magnet replicating each kind of engine head in miniature.

The museum also has a collection of toys, old advertisements, and other memorabilia, including a picture of a smiling young Elvis on *his* Harley.

What We Do for Love

Larry Kessler is proof that a good mechanic is made, not born. For eleven years he drove a truck coast-to-coast, averaging 4,500 miles a week. He lived in Columbus, Ohio. One Friday night when he and a friend were having a cold beer in the garage, they hatched a plan to go to the Harley-Davidson school in Orlando, Florida. They agreed that first one, then the other, would do it.

Kessler went first. He, his wife, and child moved to Orlando, struggling to earn enough money for Orlando's high rents and food. Kessler's wife worked, and he worked too—whenever he wasn't in class. "I didn't sleep much," he says.

They bought their food a day at a time, sometimes not sure they'd be able to eat the next day. At one point Kessler was ready to give up and go back to Columbus, but his friend insisted on helping him financially.

"The thing is, I'm here and he's still in Ohio, so only half the plan worked out," Kessler says. Was it worth it? Kessler looks up from the shiny machine he's working on and grins, "When I'm done with this, I gotta go ride it." Larry has moved on, but his pleasure in riding a Harley flourishes here.

You don't have to know anything about Harleys to enjoy this place. It's enough to enjoy the enthusiasm of others. Rich and his mechanic, Larry Kessler, are almost missionaries when it comes to teaching people about the world of Harleys. "A lot of heritage and history go with it," Rich says.

Going in every direction from Asheboro, you have wonderful possibilities.

The Pottery Gateway

Although the area bustles with activity, don't look for anything special in the way of food or lodging. Steakhouses and a few motels are about all you'll find, but these are pleasant and entirely acceptable when you just need a meal and a night's sleep, not an experience.

For an experience, go to the south side of Asheboro on U.S. Highway 220, where signs and arrows direct you to the ***North Carolina Zoological Park.*** The zoo (800–488–0444) is big, on more than 1,000 acres, though not all are being used yet. It's famous, and it's certainly not far off the beaten path. Go anyway. It got to be big and famous because they're doing such a good job with the concept of keeping the animals in natural environments without bars. Sometimes a natural gulf separates the people from the animals, sometimes a clear barrier. For instance, the aviary, under a glass dome, houses hundreds of exotic birds along with thousands of tropical plants. In other sections you can watch elephants, herds of antelope, and even crocodiles, all apparently blissfully unaware of an audience or confinement.

If you are traveling with an eye to understanding the state of North Carolina, the North Carolina Streamside exhibit is special. It depicts the wildlife and habitat from the mountains to the coast in a series of displays with everything from fish and snakes to otters splashing in a pool. The impression you get in many of these displays is that someone has simply glassed in a slice of nature and set it there, but in fact you're looking at artfully created ponds, streams, and woodlands, all suited to creatures displayed there. It isn't really natural. For instance, the "rocks" in the habitats of some indigenous snakes are really made of lightweight molded composition with heaters inside that keep the temperature exactly right for the snakes. A few live plants grow, but many of the "trees" and "bushes" have been fabricated with stunning accuracy. And on the back side, doors open to allow attendants access to the habitats for feeding and caring for the animals.

Seeing everything involves walking a couple of miles or more, but for a modest fee you can ride in a tram that follows the same route as the footpaths. There is also a modest admission fee to the park itself. Open daily from 9:00 A.M. to 5:00 P.M. Closed an hour earlier in winter. Web site: www.nczoo.org.

Pisgah Covered Bridge, one of only two left in North Carolina, on US 220, in the little community of Pisgah, spanning a branch of Little River, has hiking trails, picnic tables, and parking, but the bridge itself was damaged in 2003 and renovation has been on-going and expensive. It should be complete by publication time, but call for updates (800–626–2672) and check the Web site: www.visitrandolph.org.

From the natural to something near the ultimate in machinery, the ***Richard Petty Museum*** displays race cars, trophies, and films of famous races on the grounds of Petty's garages. Most of the awards belong to Richard, but some belong to Lee Petty, his father. Sometimes the garages are open for tours. Showcases commemorate Petty's 200th win and his 1,000th start. If you know about NASCAR racing fans, are aware of the intense partying that goes along with any race day for some of them, and have seen the huge banners advertising Goody's Headache Powders that go up at convenience stores on big race weekends, you may find humor in the Goody's Mini-Theater and Photos. Among the displays are a Chrysler Hemi engine and several race cars, all number 43. (Every car Richard Petty drives is number 43.)

Racing is so important in North Carolina that the results of all races in which local drivers participate are broadcast on local television sports news. Petty is a much-loved North Carolina hero. He has received honorary degrees from North Carolina colleges. It would be a mistake, however, to suppose this is a uniquely North Carolina phenomenon. Among Petty's artifacts are letters of congratulations from Presidents Ford, Reagan, and Bush.

Petty's racing days have ended, but his reputation as the king of racing remains intact. Even if you neither know that Petty is the king of racing nor care a fig for the sport, you might find spending some time among people who do a fascinating cultural experience. Signs off US 220 near the zoo south of Asheboro at the Level Cross exit direct you to the museum. Modest admission fee; children under twelve free. Open Monday through Saturday from 9:00 A.M. to 5:00 P.M. Phone (336) 495–1143.

You could spend all day at the zoo; the Richard Petty Museum needs only an hour or so; the next attraction, ***Seagrove,*** and the potteries could take a week.

The Asheboro area has at least half a dozen motels from which you could make an easy jog to Seagrove. Or you could stay right in the Seagrove community.

The ***Duck Smith House Bed and Breakfast,*** 465 North Broad Street, is a fully restored turn-of-the-twentieth-century hostelry with a fireplace, furnished with antiques and original artwork. It has four guest rooms and serves breakfast as part of the rate. Phone (336) 873–7099 or (800) 869–9108.

Restaurants are in such short supply in pottery country that several potteries have picnic tables for shoppers who bring lunch. A good restaurant in Seagrove, on US 220, is the ***Jugtown Cafe*** (336–873–8292). The food ranges from subs, croissant sandwiches, and burgers to country-cooking plate specials with several vegetables. The food is good and prices are moderate. The cafe is open Monday through Wednesday from 6:00 A.M. to 2:00 P.M., Thursday through Saturday 6:00 A.M. to 8:00 P.M., Sunday from 7:00 A.M. to 2:00 P.M.

Also on US 220 in Seagrove, ***Seagrove Family Restaurant*** serves breakfast, sandwiches, salads, and such dinner items as hamburger steak with cheese and grilled onions, baked ham, and fried chicken. Call (336) 873–7789 for hours of operation.

Before you start, accept the fact that it's physically impossible to stop at every pottery in one day. It was impossible a few years ago when they numbered in the thirties; now that there are more than one hundred, your only alternatives are to choose your stops selectively or to plan several trips. New places open regularly, so don't limit your stops to those mentioned here.

The people whose job is to promote tourism in the area have all but thrown up their hands in despair over keeping up with the growing number of potteries or with trying to tell you when they are open. As a representative for Randolph County Tourism puts it, "If somebody decides to go to the beach for a week, they just close down and go."

This is not true of all the potteries; many run thoroughly professional businesses with enough staff to keep things going even during vacations. But as Dan Triece of DirtWorks Pottery explains, potters in the area these days fall into roughly three groups: those open seven days a week, those open five days a week (usually Tuesday through Saturday), and those that operate on weekends. The weekend potters generally have other jobs and throw pots as a hobby.

Another recent development is the opening of consignment shops in Seagrove, where work by various potters is for sale. This is a good way to see the work of several potters at one stop, but you'll miss the action of the actual potting.

Two stops at the beginning of your excursion into pottery country can help you decide which potteries you want to visit. The ***Museum of North Carolina Traditional Pottery,*** 112 Main Street, provides information, maps, and brochures about potteries in the area. A collection of work by various potters in the window will give you an idea what kind of work each does, so you can seek out those that appeal to you the most. The museum is open from 10:00 A.M. to 2:00 P.M. Monday through Friday, from 9:00 A.M. to 3:00 P.M. Saturday. Admission free. Phone (336) 873–7887. Web site: www.tourseagrove.com.

Barely a fast walk away, the ***North Carolina Pottery Center,*** at the junction of US 220 and State Highway 705, has exhibits that trace the history and development of North Carolina pottery from the prehistoric Native Americans to the present, with more than 200 items on display. One large display behind glass shows the current work of more than ninety potters in the area. Brochures and maps are also available here. The center is open 10:00 A.M. to 4:00 P.M. Tuesday through Saturday. Admission $3.00, children $1.00. Phone (336) 873–8430. Web site: www.ncpotterycenter.com.

Seagrove's best-known annual event is the ***Seagrove Pottery Festival,*** sponsored as a fund-raiser by the Museum of North Carolina Traditional Pottery. Each year on a Saturday and Sunday in mid-November, the festival includes an auction of signed and dated limited edition pottery by local potteries, as well as booths by local potters and other traditional crafters, who demonstrate, display, and sell their wares. In true Tarheel tradition, the festival provides lots of pork barbecue and chicken, too. For exact dates phone (336) 873–7887.

A second big event is the annual ***Seagrove Winterfest,*** in mid-February. This is when most pottery shops have taken a rest after the Christmas rush and have their shelves restocked. This is when potteries often introduce their new shapes, glazes, and colors. For more information call (336) 873–7887, (336) 873–7300, or (336) 873–7280.

Originally this part of the country attracted production potters who made the storage jugs, pitchers, crocks, and bean pots farmers used every day because both the heavy red clay for potting and the timber stands for fueling the kilns were right here. No doubt local moonshine was one of the products that got stored in the jugs. A rich culture developed around potting, complete with family traditions in design and glazing. Some potters, such as Ben Owen, earned reputations for being excellent turners.

upclose

The North Carolina mystery writer Margaret Maron wrote *Uncommon Clay,* a mystery novel set in Seagrove that gives you a good idea of how the people of the community relate to each other and their work. She spent a lot of time here to learn about the potting world, and although her story is fiction, the kinds of rivalries and friendships she describes really do exist.

As other materials came along for making utensils to cook and store food, the potters turned more to producing items for tourists. But the actual potting stayed basically the same. Over three and four generations, feuds and disagreements came up, and sometimes a member of a famous potting family, such as the Owens, would splinter off to start an independent pottery.

The old families continue making the same kinds of pottery today. Tourists and gift shop owners buy it up faster than the wheels can turn.

Newcomers fill out the scene with more artistic studio pottery, which is usually more elaborately shaped, decorated, and glazed. These pieces take longer to make.

Some of the new potters are local young people who have studied in the well-respected program at Troy Technical College nearby. Others, transplants from elsewhere, have been attracted by the concentration of potters that draws customers and ensures support. It would be wrong to say that all new potters make studio pottery and all old-timers practice production pottery, however. You'll find a good bit of crossover. The best thing to do is simply look at the work, talk to the potters, and make your choices.

Many of the materials these days are shipped in from elsewhere rather than dug from local ground, and some kilns are fired by oil, gas, or electricity rather than wood. But the atmosphere is still that of a unique culture engrossed in a hands-on kind of work.

Some people say the old-timers don't think much of the new crowd because they're too fancy. Some people say the newcomers look down on the "production mentality" of the old families. Those attitudes may exist, but what you'll usually hear is encouragement from the long-established potters for the

Potting in North Carolina

new ones, and deep respect and admiration from the newer people for the speed and accuracy with which a good production potter can turn. As one young man said, "I've been futzing with this lid for two hours now. Those guys would've finished a dozen pots in that time."

Wherever you stop, talk to the people. They're used to it, they like it, and it's an integral part of the experience. As you do, you can't help noticing the arthritic hands of some of the old potters. As a younger artisan explained it, "My pots will never be quite as good as theirs, because you need to keep wetting the clay with *cold* water for the very best results, and I use warm water. I've seen what twenty and thirty years of cold water and clay does to your hands. I'm afraid I'm not quite that dedicated."

The largest concentration of potteries begins on Highway 705, off US 220. The state road numbers are clearly marked, so it is easy to follow the map through the countryside, traveling from one pottery to another. No two are alike, nor are their wares. Part of the fun is in the discovery and surprise; you don't need full information ahead of time about each place, but the following are a few guaranteed to be special. They are all marked on the free maps available at every pottery. The following listing is far from complete but gives you an idea of the various kinds of work done by some of the established potters.

Phil Morgan Pottery (336–873–7304) features Phil's elegant crystalline glazes on porcelain and his wife's more traditional earthenware, much of it in pleasing muted rose and blue tones and decorated with flowers. These people love to talk and can give you what seems like a complete course in the intricacies of crystalline glazing. Although more people are producing crystalline these days, Morgan is still considered a master. Web site: www.seagrovepotteries.com.

Potts Town Pottery (336–879–4295) is a newer endeavor by Jeff and Linda Potts. Linda's grandmother was a Cole—the Potts say they represent the ninth generation of Coles, famous traditional folk potters. They use local clay and produce traditional earthenware tableware and serving pieces. Some of the glazes, especially the blue, resemble those of the old Cole pottery, but you will see differences in sheen.

Ben Owen Pottery (336–879–2262 or 910–464–2261) displays the work of Ben Owen III, who was recognized as a boy for having superior talent, on a par with that of his grandfather. Young Ben works as an artist, producing shapes and designs inspired by Egyptian and Japanese work. His pots are on display in museums around the country. The display rooms usually aren't heavily stocked, but you do find an interesting variety. The Owen family has been famous for its bright red glazes. Web site: www.benowenpottery.com.

At ***Westmoore Pottery*** (910–464–3700), open since 1977, Mary and David Farrell make reproductions of the earthenware and salt-glazed stoneware typical of the eighteenth and early nineteenth centuries. They also make stunning reproductions of Moravian pottery as well as create new designs in the old traditions. Web site: www.westmoorepottery.com.

Mary can throw a pot or apply a Moravian-design slip trail without a flaw and chat with customers at the same time. The couple and the pottery have received national attention in more than one country-oriented magazine for their work and the unique new home they built behind their new pottery. Their work is especially popular with people involved in authentic historic restoration and representation.

The people at ***Cady Clay Works*** (910–464–5661), John Mellage and his wife, Beth Gore, produce wood-fired pieces with vibrant colors and contemporary designs. They usually have some spectacular, extra-large bowls that are surprisingly lightweight for their size.

At ***Walton's Pottery*** (336–879–6650), Don and Susan Walton make lead-free stoneware pottery that you can safely subject to the oven, microwave, and dishwasher. The Waltons have some gorgeous glazes and unique contemporary designs. They make some small, oval dishes with straight sides that are just right for individual servings of gratinéed casserole-type foods. Also, you can buy some unusual jewelry, such as earrings—hand cut, glazed, and fired—here.

DirtWorks Pottery (336–873–8979), is the permanent showroom of Dan Triece. Triece has won awards in the Southeast, especially for his copper lus-

I'm Sorry, Ben, and I'll Never, Never Do it Again

Ben Owen is considered by many to be the best potter in North Carolina. He has been on tour, his work is displayed in museums, and he put in a stint as resident potter at a college less than 5 miles from where I live. Sharing the general enthusiasm for his work, I've visited his studio, visited with his father who has since passed away, and purchased three pieces of Ben's work over the years. I've written about him in this guidebook since its earliest editions. An annoyed reader has pointed out that I've spelled Ben's name wrong—Owens instead of Owen—everywhere except in his Web site address.

"Couldn't be," I thought. "Surely not, not all these years." I went right to the source, the signed bottom of his pots in my house. Ben Owen. No "S." I really have had it wrong all these years.

To complicate matters further, there is an Owens in the lineup—The Original Owens Pottery at 3728 Busbee Road.

As the old song says, "Little things mean a lot." I'll get it right from now on, Ben.

ter raku. He also works in stoneware, ranging from pastels to midnight blue. The shop also carries woodcrafts, basketry, jewelry, and other North Carolina crafts as well as work by other regional potters.

Turn and Burn (336–873–7381) produces unusual hand-carved face jugs and snake jugs inspired by jugs made locally in the 1600s satirizing political problems. David Garner, who says he grew up so surrounded by the craft he can't remember the first time he saw a pot made, has been potting for more than twenty years. One favorite jug shows Ross Perot's face upside down. This pottery produces traditional salt glaze and wood-fired stoneware.

Milly McCanless of ***Dover Pottery*** (336–879–4340) started as a first-generation potter but now has children handling much of the design and production. Initially, she got into it because she had a dollhouse and wanted to learn to throw miniature pots for her miniature dining table. In the process she discovered that she was also good with big pots. She saw that while there wasn't much market for miniatures, she could sell as much full-sized pottery as she could produce. She's especially known for pieces beautifully decorated in painted floral and bird designs. "It's functional art. I love the idea," she says. Dover potters also have been working with crystalline and raku glazes. The business has grown so much, Milly says, that she does much less potting herself these days. Web site: www.doverpottery.com.

The Poole Family owns and operates ***Rockhouse Pottery*** (336–873–7887), specializing in handcarved pottery, Tarheel (North Carolina) themes, stoneware, saltware, and large and small planters.

Charles Tostoe, at ***Fat Beagle*** (336–873–9673), relies on production pieces that he can sell in craft shows to pay the bills, but his personal passion is sagger firing, a Korean process in which unglazed, raw clay pots are put inside a larger clay container with sawdust and other ingredients such as copper and salt, then fired. Later he burnishes the pot by rubbing it with the back of a spoon. The result is a softly glowing finish that looks almost like tinted ivory.

Holly Hill (336–873–7300) produces traditional, hand-turned functional stoneware in the tradition of J. B. Cole, from one of the earliest potting families around.

At ***Whynot Pottery*** (336–873–9276) you'll find stoneware in a variety of contemporary shapes and glazes, pieces that are especially well balanced. Web site: www.whynotpottery.com.

In addition to traditional hand-turned stoneware, ***Southern Visions*** (336–879–6990) makes folk art figures, face jugs, and Noah's arks. Web site: www.kingspottery.com.

Johnston & Gentithes (336–873–9176) bills itself as a source of museum quality wood-fired pottery and visionary sculpture.

Jugtown (910–464–3266) operates somewhat more commercially than the other potteries, including handwoven rugs and placemats, handmade toys, and other North Carolina folk crafts in its retail stock. Jugtown has been operating since 1920. The Jugtown stoneware is uniform enough in appearance to look nice beside the more regular, mass-produced commercial dinnerware and seems practically indestructible. Most of the pieces reflect traditional local styles and glazes. There is a bathroom here, too. That may seem like a small thing, in the abstract, but after you've spent some time driving these country roads where you don't find pit stops every few miles, it's something to appreciate. You may also enjoy eating your picnic lunch at the tables under the trees provided for visitors.

The hours of the various potters may vary by a half-hour or so in opening and closing, but most are open from 8:30 A.M. to 4:30 P.M. Tuesday through Saturday. Many are closed all day Sunday, though some open Sunday afternoon. The best time to go is Friday afternoon, when most of the kilns are opened to bring out the new pots. Saturday morning is a good time, too, but by afternoon the wares will already be thinning out. It's almost a waste of time to go around Christmas or in late summer. The shoppers then simply buy faster than the potters can pot.

Although some early glazes contained lead, today's are lead-free and safe for table use. If you have any concerns about lead, ask in the pottery.

Heartland

Another possible trip from Asheboro is the short hop up US 220 to ***Greensboro,*** a pleasant city with a historic downtown and lots of surprises. There's some Revolutionary War history here, in a strange sort of way. Cornwallis won a battle against General Nathanael Greene's American troops, but in the process he lost so many men that he ultimately had to surrender at Yorktown. The Guilford Courthouse National Military Park, 6 miles north of Greensboro on US 220, commemorates the loss and the win with exhibits on the battlefield and displays and films in the visitor center (336–288–1776). The center is open daily from 8:30 A.M. to 5:00 P.M. The gate to the tour road closes at 4:30 P.M. Admission is free.

Drawing on more recent events, Greensboro holds special significance for blacks. In 1960 black students from ***North Carolina A & T State University*** (originally the Agricultural and Mechanical College for the Colored Race) began the first sit-ins at Woolworth's segregated lunch counter. A & T is Jesse Jackson's alma mater, and he still comes to town from time to time.

On the campus of North Carolina A & T State University, the ***Mattye Reed African Heritage Center*** displays African masks, paintings, black history books, and art objects. Open Monday through Friday. Call for current hours (336–334–3209). Admission is free.

Less than 10 miles east of Greensboro, the ***Charlotte Hawkins Brown Memorial State Historic Site*** (336–449–4846), honors Dr. Brown's fifty years as head of another school for blacks, Palmer Memorial Institute. The buildings are gradually being restored, and plans are to make the memorial a center for contributions of North Carolina blacks, including a research center with collection and computer facilities devoted to North Carolina black history. The complex includes cottages and dormitories, outdoor exhibits and trails, a visitor center in the old teacher's cottage, and a picnic area. Dr. Brown's house has been restored, and some of her original furniture reupholstered. Open Monday through Friday from 9:00 A.M. to 5:00 P.M. Winter hours are 10:00 A.M. to 4:00 P.M. Admission is free. Web site: www.ah.dcr.state.nc.us.

Local history from the time of the early Indians to date shapes the displays at the ***Greensboro Historical Museum,*** 130 Summit Avenue, Greensboro, in what used to be the First Presbyterian Church. In a re-creation of nineteenth-century Greensboro, the museum displays a general store, the drugstore where William Sydney Porter (O. Henry) once worked, a post office, a law office, a firehouse, a cobbler's, and a blacksmith's.

Other exhibits include room settings from historical homes, an exhibit of household items and clothing of Dolley Madison (a Greensboro native before she became First Lady), and a collection of antique automobiles. Open Tuesday through Saturday 10:00 A.M. to 5:00 P.M. and Sunday from 2:00 to 5:00 P.M. Closed holidays. Admission is free. Phone (336) 373–2043. Web site: www.greensborohistory.org.

If you're traveling with kids (or even if you're not, come to think of it), don't miss the ***Natural Science Center,*** 4301 Lawndale Drive (336–288–3769), where you can easily spend a day immersing yourself in the sights and sounds of everything from dinosaurs to star systems. This is a "participation museum," where you don't have to tell the kids "look, don't touch." For instance, you can put your hand into a real dinosaur footprint, pet and feed animals in the zoo, observe sunspots in the live solar observatory, and turn your imagination loose in the planetarium. The transparent anatomical mannequin, which you might want to save until after lunch, lets you study what goes on inside the skin of the human body. The museum is open Monday through Saturday from 9:00 A.M. to 5:00 P.M. and Sunday from 12:30 to 5:00 P.M. The zoo is open Monday through Saturday from 10:00 A.M. to 4:30 P.M. and Sunday from 12:30

to 4:00 P.M. A moderate admission fee covers the museum and zoo. Planetarium shows daily at 2:00, 3:00, and 4:00 P.M. are $1.00 extra.

When you've had enough of indoor attractions, Greensboro has three gardens worth some attention, collectively known as the ***Greensboro Gardens.*** The Greensboro Arboretum, Bog Garden, and Bicentennial Garden feature most of the plants native to the Piedmont region. The arboretum is on West Market Street at Lindley Park. It has nine labeled collections of indigenous species. The bog garden is at the corner of Hobbs Road and Starmount Farms Drive and features a variety of plants that thrive in wet areas. The Bicentennial Garden is at the corner of Cornwallis Drive and Hobbs Road. It emphasizes mass plantings of bulbs, annuals, and perennials, along with flowering trees and shrubs. Admission to the gardens is free. Call (336) 373–2199 or (800) 344–2282 for more information. Web site: www.greensborobeautiful.org.

If you are interested in regional folk art and pottery, you should know about two Greensboro collectors with galleries in their homes. Mike Smith and his family run the ***At Home Gallery,*** and Mike's cousin, ***Lynn Melton,*** has a gallery to display and sell the pottery she has been collecting for more than thirty years. Smith's emphasis is on the type of art that has come to be called "self-taught" and sometimes "visionary" and "outsider." The artists he represents include James Harold Jennings, Sarah Rakes, G. C. DuPree, M. C. Jones, Mose and Annie Tolliver, Mary T. Smith, and Jimmy Lee Sudduth. To the beginning collector, some of this art looks like something your kids could do, but on closer inspection, there's a lot more to it. Smith has added photographs he's taken to the Web site, showing some of the artists at work in their home environments. Lynn Melton specializes in regional pottery dating back to the earliest days of potters here. She has everything from swirl pottery (striped with mixed clays in colored swirls around the pot in the throwing process) to face jugs of every description. You have to make an appointment to visit Lynn and Mike because the galleries are in their private homes. To see a sample of At Home Gallery's art, check the Web site: www.athomegallery.com. To make an appointment, e-mail him at athome05@earthlink.net or call (336) 286–0131. To contact Lynn, e-mail her at LMELTON222@aol.com.

aw, nothing to it!

Nothing annoys people who are serious about self-taught art more than people who look at it and dismiss it as something the kids did. Mike Smith likes the line he heard that goes something like this, "Yes, my kids did all the pictures. I wrote all the Shakespeare plays, and this is my wife, she wrote all the sonnets."

See art in a more formal setting at the ***Weatherspoon Art Museum,*** Spring Garden and Tate Streets, on the campus of the University of North

Carolina/Greensboro (336–334–5770). The museum, which has six galleries and a sculpture courtyard, is nationally known for its collections of modern and contemporary art, 6,000 objects mostly created after World War II. The permanent collection includes Matisse prints and bronzes, the Dillard Collection of Art on Paper, with 500 items, and 600 Japanese woodblock prints from the eighteenth through the twentieth centuries. The museum is open Tuesday, Wednesday, and Friday from 10:00 A.M. to 5:00 P.M., Thursday 10:00 A.M. to 9:00 P.M., Saturday and Sunday 1:00 to 5:00 P.M. Admission is free. The museum's Web site (weatherspoon.uncg.edu) offers an excellent overview of museum holdings and samplings of work from various collections. It also details changing exhibits.

Drop your weary head on a pillow at a small, older, European-style hotel downtown—or at the Greenwood Bed and Breakfast, in one of Greensboro's first suburban areas, about 10 blocks from the business district. The ***Biltmore-Greensboro Hotel,*** 111 West Washington Street (336–272–3474 or 800–332–0303), has had what the cliché makers would call "a checkered past." It was built to be corporate headquarters for a textile company in the 1800s, then was used as a post office, and later was turned into a hospital during World War II. In the twenty years before it was rescued and renovated, it had been either a house of ill repute or a flophouse, depending on whose story you believe. A little of both may have been true. Now the lobby is a pretty little area of brass and crystal chandeliers and eighteenth-century reproductions and art. The rooms are tasteful and comfortable, with small refrigerators to cool your traveling comestibles. Web site: www.biltmorehotelgreensboro.com.

The ***Greenwood Bed and Breakfast,*** 205 North Park Drive (336–274–6350 or 800–535–9363), built in the early 1900s, has also been renovated. Old oaks and the neighborhood park surround the home with greenery and shield the backyard swimming pool from the curious. Inside, wood carvings and art collections from around the world attract your attention. The proprietors, Bob and Dolly Gerton, serve a continental breakfast with fruit and homemade breads, which is included in the rates. The inn has five guest rooms, all with private baths. Web site: www.greenwoodbb.com.

Tobacco Town

From Greensboro you're looking at a drive of only about 20 miles west on I–40 to ***Winston-Salem,*** the tobacco town. It would be hard to overstate the influence of the R. J. Reynolds Tobacco Company. While Richard Joshua Reynolds was directing a rapidly growing business and hiring increasing thousands of people in the tobacco factories, his wife, Katharine, set about a long series of community improvement activities for the benefit of those same families. With

Reynolds money and Moravian artistic influence, the area developed into a cultural center that still ranks high in the country today.

Perhaps the most audacious Reynolds act in later years was the lock-stock-and-barrel move of Wake Forest University from Wake County to Winston-Salem in 1950. President Truman came to wield the shovel in the groundbreaking ceremony. The ***Museum of Anthropology,*** on the campus, is billed as the only museum devoted to the study of world cultures, covering Africa, Asia, Oceania, and the Americas. Call (336) 758–5282 for details. Web site: www.wfu.edu.

To learn more about the tobacco industry and the Reynolds influence in it, visit ***R. J. Reynolds Tobacco U.S.A.,*** 3 miles north of Greensboro on U.S. Highway 52. Call (336) 983–1290 to arrange a guided tour of the plant that produces 450 *million* cigarettes a day and a stop in the museum that depicts the development of the industry. Notice the heavy sweet smell of tobacco that permeates the air. Line workers who are close to the actual tobacco products will tell you that the smell gets into their clothes and remains so strong that when they get home after work, they may shuck their work clothes at the doorway to keep the smell out of the house.

As background on the R. J. R. dynasty, you should read the book by Patrick Reynolds (who has come out strongly against using tobacco) and Tom Shachtman, *The Gilded Leaf: Triumph, Tragedy, and Tobacco—Three Generations of the R. J. Reynolds Family and Fortune.* Larry Hagman (who played ruthless J. R. Ewing in the Dallas television series) wrote of the book that it made *Dallas* look "like a bowl of warm milk toast." Be careful about trying to discuss the book while you're here, though. Criticizing tobacco in a community built upon it rouses the ire of some residents. So does speaking ill of the First Tobacco Family.

About half a century ago, the town was shocked when Zachary Smith Reynolds, usually called Smith, son of R. J. and Katharine, was shot through the head during a boozy party at the family home, less than a year after his marriage to the torch singer Libby Holman. Apparently Smith Reynolds caught Libby flirting (or more) with a friend, fighting erupted, and Smith either shot himself or was killed by Libby. Newspapers suppressed much of the story at the time, and even today, polite society doesn't talk about it, though that hasn't stopped brazen authors from writing about it. An interesting source, should you decide to pursue the subject further, is the biography, *Libby Holman: Body and Soul,* by H. D. Perry.

After studying the impact of Reynolds and tobacco, turn your attention to the Moravians. Moravians came from Pennsylvania to settle the area in 1753. They built Salem as a totally planned, church-governed community in 1766.

Winston wasn't founded until 1849. In Salem, arts and crafts flourished; in Winston, it was tobacco and textiles. By the early 1900s the two towns had grown together and consolidated. It would be hard to say whether tobacco or the Moravians left the greater mark on the area, nor is it really pertinent; in the early days tobacco wasn't a dirty word, and nobody saw anything wrong with a strong relationship between church and chew.

If you see only one attraction here, it certainly should be ***Old Salem,*** a Moravian town restored so carefully that when you walk the streets and go into the buildings, you feel as though you've entered a time warp. To give you an idea of the pains staff people take with getting it right, people responsible for demonstrations of cooking and household activities take turns preparing research papers and consulting old diaries, journals, and letters to discover exactly how the households might have run. Unlike traditional historians who mainly study battles, politics, and industrial development, these re-creators also try, as well, to piece together the elements of day-to-day life. This isn't the only historic site where such activities are going on, but it's hard to imagine one where they're being treated any more earnestly or where the subject matter is any more fascinating. This attention to detail extends even to the food cooked from old Moravian recipes. The original gingerbread recipe used fresh ginger root, but recipes in later years have shifted to powdered ginger because it's easier to find and keep. The Old Salem recipe still specifies fresh, grated ginger. At the ***Winkler Bakery,*** costumed bakers make cookies and bread in a wood-fired brick oven. The baked goods are for sale.

Old Salem

Costumed guides in the old kitchen cook in the huge fireplace and iron with flatirons heated there, all the while sweating genuine sweat—a fascinating reminder in this age of air-conditioning that just getting from one day to the next once took a lot of energy. Among the demonstrations offered in Old Salem are music from an organ built in 1797, potting, baking, and spinning.

Not all the buildings in the historic district are restored as tour buildings. Some are private homes. The presence of automobiles and real people living real lives doesn't seem to detract from the atmosphere; indeed it simply makes it feel more alive. Whatever tours you take, start at the visitor center (336–721–7300 or 888–653–7253). Moderate to high admission fees, depending on how many features you wish to tour. Get tickets for all Old Salem tour attractions at the visitor center, open from 8:30 A.M. to 5:00 P.M. Monday through Saturday and from 12:30 to 5:00 P.M. on Sunday. Web site: www.oldsalem.org. All hours for attractions at Old Salem may vary. Call the visitor center or check the Web site for specifics.

Old Salem Gardens are reputed to be the best-documented, restored community gardens in America. Their authenticity is possible because the Moravians kept meticulous records. Many of the gardens have been re-created on their original sites and produce the same varieties of vegetables, flowers, and herbs described in old records. The attention to horticultural detail goes beyond the garden squares to include old cultivars of fruit trees in orchards, flowering vines on fences, and native trees in the landscape.

Having toured Old Salem, you'll need to eat at the ***Old Salem Tavern Dining Rooms*** at 736 South Main Street in the district (336–748–8585). Continuing the sense of reenactment, costumed staff serve Moravian-style cooking by candlelight. Specialties include game and gingerbread from the old recipes. For the faint of palate, standard beef and chops entrees are also available. All spirits served. The restaurant is open for lunch every day, and for dinner every day but Sunday.

Also in Old Salem, the ***Museum of Early Southern Decorative Arts*** (336–721–7300 or 888–258–1205; Web site: www.mesda.org/mesda.html) gives you a close look at the results of extensive research into the regional decorative arts of the early South. The exhibits include furniture, paintings, textiles, ceramics, silver, and other metalware. You can't just wander in here. Guides take you through the building in small groups. You may buy tickets at the Old Salem Visitors Center. Museum hours are Monday through Saturday from 9:30 A.M. to 5:00 P.M. last tour at 3:30 P.M., and Sunday from 12:30 to 5:00 P.M. You can spend the night in Old Salem at the 1840 ***Augustus T. Zevely Inn,*** a privately owned bed-and-breakfast at 803 South Main Street, Old Salem. This fine old brick building is furnished with pieces of the Old Salem Collection so that it feels much as it would have in the 1840s. Some of the twelve guest rooms have fireplaces. Some also have microwaves, refrigerators, and whirlpools, which, of course, feel nothing at all like the 1840s but are kind of nice after a day of walking. Phone (336) 748–9299 or (800) 928–9299.

An alternative end to a day in this historic manufacturing and artistic town is a night's lodging at ***Brookstown Inn,*** a restored 1837 textile mill at 200 Brookstown Avenue (336–725–1120 or 800–845–4262). The history of the inn matches that of the city for interest. Moravians opened the Salem Cotton Manufacturing Company and later sold it, and the buildings were subsequently used as a flour mill and then as a moving-company storage house. The conversion to an inn created large guest rooms with odd nooks and crannies and high ceilings. An upstairs wall is covered with the graffiti (protected by an acrylic plastic sheet) of the young factory girls who boarded there. A boiler room with catwalk now serves as a restaurant in which one of the old boiler faces is a focal point. The decor is early American, with many handmade quilts and country accents. Rates include wine and cheese in the parlor, homemade cookies and milk, and continental breakfast in the dining room.

While you are in the Winston-Salem area, take a few minutes to drive to the old ***Shell gas station*** at the corner of Sprague and Peachtree Streets. You'll know you're there when you come to a huge orange and red structure shaped like a seashell, with two old gas pumps standing in front. This old gas station sold Quality Oil products in the 1930s and then fell into disuse and disrepair. It had a big crack sealed with a strip of black tar, and vandals had broken windows and fixtures and littered the ground.

Sarah Woodard, who wasn't even born when the station was in its glory days, oversaw the renovation, which was completed in 1997. Almost any time you stop in, some old-timers who remember when the station was operating are

Sweet Stuff

Southerners have a notorious sweet tooth. The tea-drinking habits of North Carolinians are a good example. We drink tea iced—year-round, not just in summer. We put sugar in it and call it "sweet tea"; if you want it any other way, you have to say so by ordering "unsweet tea." Even then, if you don't want a mouthful of sugar, taste just a little sip when the tea comes, because the request for unsweet tea is so rare servers may well bring you the sweet kind out of habit.

apt to be standing around reminiscing about earlier times. One of them says he always thought the Shell was the prettiest thing in town—and he still does.

As you leave the area, to move swiftly back into the twenty-first century you might stop at the ***Sciworks,*** 400 West Hanes Mill Road, 7½ miles north of the intersection of I–40 on US 52 on Museum Drive off the Hanes Mill Road exit. The participatory exhibits cover natural science and physical science and technology. A three-dimensional solar system display puts you in the middle of the planets, and a model of the moon shows the landing sites of Apollo. Children especially enjoy the saltwater touch tank and the petting zoo. Admission is $8.00 for adults, $6.00 for children ages six to nineteen, $6.00 for senior citizens fifty-five and older, $4.00 for children ages three to five; children younger than three are free. The museum (336–767–6730) is open Monday through Friday 10:00 A.M. to 4:00 P.M. and Saturday 11:00 A.M. to 5:00 P.M. Admission is free the second Friday of every month from 4:00 to 8:00 P.M. in June, July, and August. Web site: www.sciworks.org.

The Barbecue Capital

On US 52, about 20 miles south of Winston-Salem, the town of ***Lexington*** is a must-stop for barbecue freaks. More than a dozen restaurants in this little town serve pork barbecue (if it's made with anything but pork it isn't really barbecue!) "Lexington style." The town has at least twenty barbecue restaurants, mostly, maybe even entirely, run by people whose families have been involved with barbecue for several generations. The first barbecue restaurant was in a tent in the middle of town, opened by Sid Weaver in 1919. Lexington barbecue is generally called "western style," though you need to be careful about what you say, because a slip of the tongue regarding barbecue in North Carolina is grounds for deportation to another country—preferably vegetarian. Authentic Lexington barbecue is made by cooking pork shoulders slowly over hickory wood fires until the meat is falling-apart tender, basting it with a "dip" of vinegar, ketchup, water, salt, and pepper. Some barbecuers may add a few other ingredients such as red pepper. As the dripping from the meat falls into the hot coals, the smoke rises to flavor the meat. Then the pork is chopped by hand to be served in sandwiches or on plates accompanied by red slaw and hush puppies. Bits of tomato make the slaw red.

Each year in the fall, the Lexington Barbecue Festival attracts in the neighborhood of 100,000 visitors. It's held in eight roped-off blocks of uptown Lexington and goes on with a variety of events besides eating. Check www.barbecuefestival.com for all kinds of details about Lexington barbecue, including current dates.

Eastern barbecue, typical on the coast and for some distance inland, uses the whole hog. After roasting over a wood fire, the meat is pulled from the bones by hand and chopped. The baste contains no tomato. And the barbecue comes with white or yellow slaw.

Complications arise in the disagreement about which is where and which is better because, inevitably, some places begin blending techniques and it's possible to come across eastern barbecue in the western part of the state and vice versa. "Real" North Carolinians can get testy on the subject. You can plunge into huge discussions on the subject, as well as participants' recommendations for their favorite barbecue spots, simply by typing "eastern nc barbecue" and "western nc barbecue" into a Web browser.

Lexington's most popular celebrity is Bob Timberlake, the painter and designer, whose ideas have mushroomed into a multimillion-dollar business. Timberlake grew up in the area, made contact when he was young with Andrew Wyeth and, with Wyeth's encouragement, decided to try to paint for a living. His style is something of a cross between Norman Rockwell's nostalgia and Wyeth's detailed realism. Mostly Timberlake paints scenes from the farm and lake where he lives. His prints sell these days for more than he once got for his originals. The early prints bring as much as $3,500. And an original Timberlake painting may bring up to $50,000.

How the Experts Rate North Carolina Barbecue

Blind Taste Judging

Judge No.________
Code No. ________

	Poor	Fair	Good	Very Good	Excellent
Appearance	2 4 6 8	10 12 14 16	18 20 22 24	26 28 30 32	34 36 38 40
Tenderness	2 4 6 8	10 12 14 16	18 20 22 24	26 28 30 32	34 36 38 40
Taste	4 8 12 16	20 24 28 32	36 40 44 48	52 56 60 64	68 72 76 80

Total Score:________

Key:
Appearance: Texture, color, fat to lean ratio, burnt meat.
Tenderness: Moist and tender vs. dry and tough.
Taste: Sauce too hot, too mild, or excessive vs. a pleasing blend of sauce and meat.

Timberlake has thrown his energy into designing everything from upholstery fabric and men's shirts to log cabins. His furniture company provides employment for thousands of people in the area, as do his other ever-growing enterprises. He has created a series of dolls made to look like his grandchildren. "It just keeps pouring out," he says. The best way to get a glimpse of the scope of Timberlake's activities is at the ***Bob Timberlake Gallery*** (800–244–0095), which opened in 1997. It is a combination gallery, museum, and salesroom. You can see everything from his new furniture to his earliest paintings. The gallery is at 1714 East Center Street. From I–85 take exit 94, then drive west on US 64. Signs direct you. The gallery is open Monday through Friday 10:00 A.M. to 6:00 P.M., Saturday 9:00 A.M. to 5:00 P.M., closed Sunday. Admission is free. Web site: www.bobtimberlake.com.

The Furniture Capital

High Point is mostly about manufacturing and selling furniture. The town, already active in the lumber business, first got into furniture building in the early 1880s, when a local lumber salesman noticed the big difference between the price of wood as it left the sawmill and the price it brought once it had been shipped away and turned into furniture. Sensibly, he and two local merchants risked all they had to start a furniture company close to the source of the wood. It was the right idea in the right place at the right time. Sales took off and the future was set. Today High Point has 125 furniture manufacturing companies.

Unless you are professionally involved in the furniture business, avoid High Point in April and October, when for the better part of two weeks in both months the town hosts the Southern Furniture Market, usually referred to simply as "market." Said to be the largest furniture show in the world (it fills 150 buildings totaling between five and six million square feet), this trade show attracts interior decorators and furniture retailers—in other words *buyers*—from all over the world. More than 1,500 furniture company exhibitors show up for each market show. Multiply that by the staff each company brings to work the booths and add all the buyers who come looking for the latest goodies, and you get an image of a town, normal population on the shy side of 70,000, so overloaded that if it were a ship it would sink. Finding a place to stay or to eat is a challenge.

A valuable museum in the area is the ***Springfield Museum of Old Domestic Life,*** established in 1935 in the third meetinghouse of the Springfield Meeting, 555 East Springfield Road (336–882–3054). Museums, like history books, tend to focus on extraordinary events, wars, and politics and not on the commonplaces of day-to-day life. This museum is an exception. Here you can inspect the artifacts of daily life that have been used in the neighborhood for 200 years or more—spinning equipment, utensils, farm items, clothing, pictures from homes, toys, and a slew of fascinating odds and ends. The curator says, "Most of what we have has been donated by local Quakers."

She likes to emphasize the items that were commonplace in their day, objects crudely made to fill an immediate need. If you didn't know the way in which many of them had been used, you probably could never figure out what they were for. Such artifacts simply cannot be replaced.

One example is the log lifter. It looks like a crutch for a giant. Log lifters were devices created to get logs from the ground to high points in the walls when building log cabins. One man stood at each end of the log with a lifter and heaved.

Another example is a homemade Noah's Ark, with all the animals two-by-two. This was a Sunday toy, made during the time when children in the community weren't allowed to play on Sundays with their regular toys or do much else. It was carved about one hundred years ago by Yardley Warner for his twins, probably because he sympathized with the children's restlessness and wanted to make them a religious toy to keep them occupied on Sundays.

Another uncommon exhibit is the 4-foot-long tin horn the coachman blew at each stop of the stagecoach along the Old Plank Road. The number of blasts blown told people at upcoming stops, such as Nathan Hunt Tavern, what passengers would be wanting when they got there. Old Plank Road was built between Fayetteville and Winston-Salem by laying down boards next to one another to form a firm-surfaced highway. Part of the old road is now Main Street. A plank from the road and a notched mile marker are also in the display. A traveler in the dark could stop at the marker and feel the number of notches on it to know how far it was to Nathan Hunt Tavern. A model shows a stagecoach on a plank road with markers to give you an idea how it all worked.

Visiting here is more like going into an attic than a museum. "There's so much stuff, and you can handle it. You don't get the feeling of things resting on velvet that you can't touch," the curator says. The museum is open by appointment. Admission is free.

The ***High Point Historical Museum,*** 1895 East Lexington Avenue (336–885–1859), exhibits more traditional kinds of material related to the town's history, including military displays. The numbers "1859" in the phone number and the address stand for the year the town of High Point was founded. You have to admire a museum that can pull off something like that. There is also a display of old telephones that takes you back to before Ma Bell, a collection of furniture made in High Point, and, appropriately, woodworking tools that take you back to the first manufacturing in town. Also on the property are the restored 1786 John Haley House, a weaving house, and a blacksmith shop. Demonstrations are offered in these buildings on weekends. The museum is open Tuesday through Sunday. Admission is free. Web site: www.highpointmuseum.org.

The next two attractions are in the same building at 101 West Green Drive, but they really don't have much to do with each other. The ***Angela Peterson Doll and Miniature Museum*** (336–885–3655) contains more than 1,700 dolls collected by Angela Peterson from around the world. She picked up everything—crêche dolls, a Shirley Temple collection of 120 dolls, and Bob Timberlake dolls, as well as enough dollhouses and furnishings to create a miniature village. Before the collection was housed here, it was in several rooms of the retirement home where Peterson lived. In fact, she said she chose that particular place to live after "auditioning" a number of possibilities because this place expressed an active interest in her doll collection. The home may have ended up being more interested than she was. Somewhere along the way, when she was in her late eighties or early nineties, she began referring to the collection as "the damned dolls," because it took so much work to keep their costumes clean and properly pressed. The dolls were moved into the building on West Green Drive after her death. The museum is open 10:00 A.M. to 5:00 P.M., Monday through Friday, Saturday 9:00 A.M. to 5:00 P.M., and 1:00 to 4:30 P.M. Sunday. Admission is $4.00 for adults, $3.50 for people age sixty-five and over, $2.50 for children six to fifteen. Combination ticket with the Furniture Discovery Center is $8.50.

At the ***Furniture Discovery Center*** (336–887–3876), in the same building as the doll museum, you can learn more than you realized there was to know about how furniture is designed and made. The center, which has been around less than a decade, is a place for entertainment and education. It was started partly as a substitute for tours of specific furniture manufacturing plants, a practice that has been abandoned because of safety hazards and liability problems.

Actually, you can learn more about how furniture is made and about its history in the center than you could touring a factory, because the displays are set up to explain industry issues concerned with everything from eight-way-hand-tied cone coils to ergonomics.

Here are some of the topics the exhibits cover: furniture market history, miniature bedroom displays, Drexel salesmen's miniatures, wood and trees, furniture designed to fit people rather than spaces, upholstery fabric, and furniture reproductions.

The exhibits are numbered to guide you through the offerings in a logical manner, giving you a sense of the flow of production. Signs explaining the exhibits are conspicuously posted.

The museum offers a variety of hands-on experiences. You can try the air-powered tools, sit in the chairs of the ergonomics exhibit, study a half-built love seat, and play with the computer design program to see what various fabric colors and patterns look like on different-shaped furniture pieces.

For kids one of the most popular exhibits is Harvy Hardwood, the talking tree, who gives recorded lessons about hardwoods and their uses. Another popular exhibit is the wood exhibit, a series of eleven different wood panels with appropriate leaves etched on the outside. You guess the kind of tree, lift the panel, and read the description to see if you are right. The center is open Monday through Friday 10:00 A.M. to 5:00 P.M., Saturday from 9:00 A.M. to 5:00 P.M., Sunday from 1:00 to 5:00 P.M. Admission is $5.00 for adults, $4.00 for senior citizens and students over fifteen years, $2.00 for children six to fifteen; children under six are free with accompanying adult. Web site: www.furniturediscovery.org.

A pleasant place to stay while you're in High Point is ***Toad Alley Bed and Bagel,*** a six-room bed-and-breakfast inn at 1001 Johnson Street (336–889–8349). It's a completely renovated 1907 neocolonial home in the center of High Point's historic district. The house used to be known as Mrs. Jones's house and accommodated female schoolteachers in what were considered modest quarters then. The ladies would scarcely recognize the place today.

The decor is luxurious and eclectic, reflecting the taste of a good designer with a flash of humor. Old botanical prints and Dali prints hang side by side in rooms with classic quilts, Oriental rugs, antique wicker, and comfortable contemporary chairs. The colors lean toward pastels, grays, and white, with surprising splashes of brighter colors. In one downstairs bedroom, four huge white posts that were originally part of the side porch mark the four corners of a luxuriously festooned bed. The posts are painted so that blooming vines seem to grow toward the ceiling and match the comforter covering the bed.

Partly because of the efforts of a previous innkeeper, the house is surrounded with good perennial borders, so that you enjoy peonies, foxgloves, daisies, and the like, brightening the area along the privet hedge. The back doorstep of the house looks toward the historic district, which features in its old buildings a growing number of specialty shops, including a children's shop, a nature shop, a bookstore, and a gourmet shop. Whatever stores are in business when you visit here, the "boutique row" is always fun to browse through.

The inn has attracted celebrities but has done it so quietly that folks didn't know they were in town. Cher is reported to have stayed here. While it's easy to see that she would enjoy the inn, one wonders what in the world she was doing in High Point in the first place.

Within walking distance of the inn, you can dine at ***J Basul Noble Restaurant,*** at 114 South Main Street (336–889–3354), a restaurant described by one local resident as "nouvelle American but kind of French and almost four-star." You'll find such offerings as fresh lamb, foul, and seafood, always interestingly prepared. The restaurant has a full liquor license and an excellent wine list. The proprietor, J. Basul Noble II, emphasizes fresh ingredients of top quality. Open Monday through Thursday from 6:00 to 10:00 P.M. and Friday and Saturday from 6:00 to 11:00 P.M.

In a busy part of town, near the intersection of East Chester and Main Streets, ***Act 1 Restaurant,*** 130 East Paris Avenue, draws customers for entrees such as grouper, duck, and veal prepared in interesting, contemporary ways. In addition to dining rooms, the restaurant has an atrium and a lounge. It is open for lunch and dinner. Call (336) 869–5614 for reservations.

Places to Stay in the Upper Piedmont

ASHEBORO

Comfort Inn
242 Lakecrest Road
Asheboro 27203
(800) 526–3766

Hampton Inn
1137 East Dixie Drive
Asheboro 27203
(336) 625–9000
(800) 426–7866

DURHAM

Comfort Inn University
3508 Mt. Moriah Road
Durham 27707
(919) 490–4949
(800) 228–5150

Hampton Inn
1816 Hillandale Road
Durham 27705
(919) 471–6100
(800) 426–7866

Red Roof Inn—I-40
5623 Chapel Hill Boulevard
Durham 27707
(919) 489–9421
(800) 843–7663

GREENSBORO

Battleground Inn Motel
1517 Westover Terrace
Greensboro 27408
(336) 272–4737

Comfort Inn
2001 Veasley Street
Greensboro 27407
(336) 294–6220
(800) 424–6423

Courtyard by Marriott
4400 West Wendover
Greensboro 27407
(336) 294–3800
(800) 321–2211

Holiday Inn Express
3114 Cedar Park Road
Greensboro 27405
(336) 697–4000
(800) 284–1493

HIGH POINT

Biltmore Suites Hotel
4400 Regency
High Point 27265
(336) 812–8188
(888) 412–8188

Toad Alley Bed and Bagel
101 Johnson Street
High Point 27262
(800) 409–7946

RALEIGH

Best Western Hospitality Inn
2800 Brentwood Road
Raleigh 27604
(919) 872–8600

Holiday Inn Brownstone Hotel
1707 Hillsborough Street
Raleigh 27605
(919) 828–0811
(800) 465–4329

THE UPPER PIEDMONT WEB SITES

Durham
www.visitdurham.info

Greensboro
www.visitgreensboro.com

High Point
www.highpoint.org

Lexington
www.visitlexingtonnc.com

Raleigh
www.VisitRaleigh.com

Winston-Salem
www.visitwinstonsalem.com

Red Roof Inn Raleigh
3520 Maitland Drive
Raleigh 27603
(919) 231–0200
(800) 843–7663

Sleep Inn
2617 Appliance Court
(near I–440 and Capital Boulevard)
Raleigh 27604
(919) 755–6005

WINSTON-SALEM

Brookstown Inn Bed and Breakfast
200 Brookstown Avenue
Winston-Salem 27101
(800) 845–4262

Courtyard by Marriott
3111 University Parkway
Winston-Salem 27105
(336) 727–1277
(800) 321–2211

Hampton Inn
1990 Hampton Inn Court
Winston-Salem 27103
(336) 760–1660
(800) 426–7866

Innkeeper
2115 Peters Creek Parkway
Winston-Salem 27127
(336) 721–0062
(800) 466–5337

Places to Eat in the Upper Piedmont

ASHEBORO

Bamboo Garden Oriental Restaurant
405 East Dixie
Asheboro 27203
(336) 629–0203

CHAPEL HILL

Crook's Corner
610 West Franklin Street
Chapel Hill 27516
(919) 929–7643

HIGH POINT

J Basul Noble Restaurant
101 South Main Street
High Point 27262
(336) 889–3354

LEXINGTON

Jimmy's Barbecue
1703 Cotton Grove Road
Lexington 27292
(336) 357–2311

Lexington Barbecue
10 Highway 29/70
Lexington 27295
(336) 249–9814

SEAGROVE

Seagrove Family Restaurant
Highway 220
Seagrove 27341
(336) 873–7789

SMITHFIELD

Café Monet
146 South Third Street
Smithfield 27577
(919) 989–3039

The Lower Piedmont

Statesville

In less than an hour, you can drive west on I–40 from Winston-Salem to ***Statesville,*** where you'll find several delightful stops known mostly to local folks. ***Farm House Gardens*** is on the east side of town on US 70 (704–873–2057). If you like gardening and houseplants, you'll find that you simply must buy some plants here, even if it means driving 500 miles home with them in the back seat. Kay Kincaid started the business more than ten years ago with the encouragement of her husband, Randy, as the obvious expression of her lifelong passion for plants. "I always loved plants. So did my mother and before her, my grandmother. When I was little, I spent all my time around the farm at my grandmother's knees in the garden," she says. The force of that passion produced a nursery-greenhouse-gift shop combination that stuns you with the variety and quality of the offerings. This isn't the kind of place where anybody counts the number of plants for sale or measures in terms of how many greenhouses are open (that number changes with the seasons anyway).

Farm House Gardens surely isn't the largest retail plant operation in North Carolina, but it is the place you go for the

THE LOWER PIEDMONT

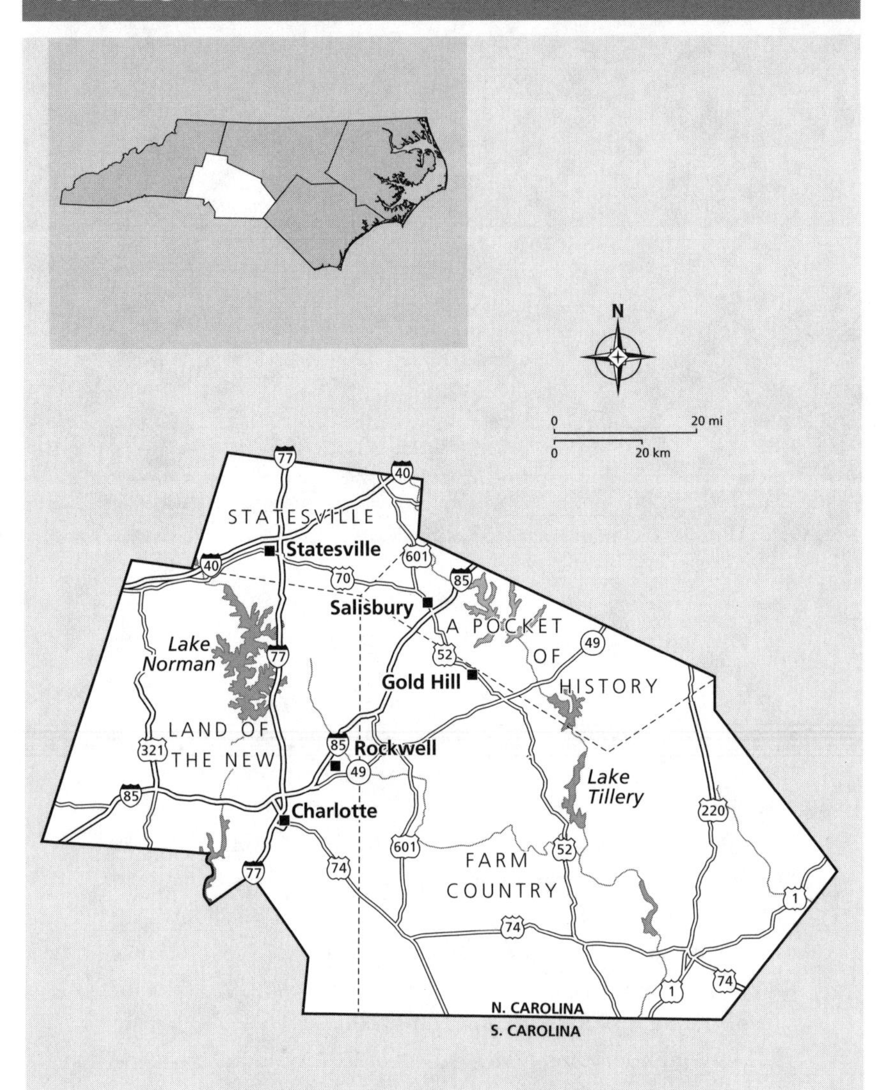

N
0
20 mi
0
20 km
STATESVILLE
Statesville
Salisbury
A POCKET OF HISTORY
Lake Norman
Gold Hill
LAND OF THE NEW
Rockwell
Lake Tillery
Charlotte
FARM COUNTRY
N. CAROLINA
S. CAROLINA
77
40
601
70
85
52
49
321
220
74
1

special plants you haven't been able to find anywhere else. In spring you can buy tomato plants and pepper plants, but that's rather like choosing peanut butter in a gourmet shop. The perennials fill benches and the spaces under them and are lined up along the paths of the back gardens. In the greenhouses houseplants, including little myrtle topiaries and several different maidenhair ferns, tempt you to exceed your budget with every step you take. All the common herbs and many more that are hard to find are here, too, along with Japanese maples in great variety, enough different hostas to fill a small catalog, and rare dwarf shrubs. One gardener, nursing sore feet the day after a visit to Farm House Gardens, complained that she'd been there for four hours and hadn't seen everything.

As if the variety weren't enough, you deal with people who so obviously love and know the plants that it's more like swapping cuttings with Aunt Elizabeth than a commercial transaction. If you mistakenly zero in on a not-for-sale stock plant and are crushed that you can't have it, someone will cut off a little start for you and tuck it into the soil of another plant you've purchased, along with instructions, if you need them, on how to root the slip. If you're one who boasts that you have a black thumb and can kill anything, don't go here. They mean for your plants to thrive, and any other attitude would be an insult. At

a symbol is not a goddess

One of the most controversial frescoes ever created by North Carolina artist Ben Long is on display in the civic center on Center Street. The larger-than-life fresco depicts the goddess Hectate and a number of Christian figures. Some local citizens said a pagan goddess had no place in Statesville.

Ben Long said Hectate was the goddess of crossroads and stands as a symbol because Statesville is at a major crossroads of Interstates 77 and 40. So far Hectate remains.

ANNUAL EVENTS IN THE LOWER PIEDMONT

Charlotte
Southern Ideal Home Show
(mid-October)
(800) 849–0248

Gold Hill
Gold Hill Founder's Day
(late September)
(704) 279–5674

Autumn Jubilee
(early October)
(704) 636–2089

Statesville
National Balloon Rally
(mid-September)
(704) 873–2892

the outdoor sales station they keep a hand-lettered sign listing the people who are mad at them. The way to get on the list is to sign it. A great joke. New owners who have taken over continue with the same passion. Open from 9:00 A.M. to 5:00 P.M. Monday through Saturday. Closed Sunday. Write Route 7, Box 27, Statesville 28677.

Don't leave Statesville without seeing the ***Iredell Museum of Arts and Heritage,*** 1335 Museum Road (704–873–4734). This is a truly local museum, and the story of its beginning and growth makes you feel good. The center is housed in a turn-of-the-twentieth-century building that was the Statesville waterworks until 1940. In 1956 a group of local citizens decided that the area needed a museum and put their energy and money into making it happen. Today it operates with a $100,000-a-year budget that allows for three full-time professionals on the staff. Enthusiasm for it practically shoots out the ears of people working there. The museum features ten temporary exhibits a year, runs thirty-five educational programs in association with the local school system each year, and displays 3,000 objects in the permanent collection. The glassware pieces number more than 1,000. The staff say the quality of the items varies, but it's important to have it all. "Somebody has to save all those Avon pieces." Plans for the future include identifying all the glassware. A geologist has already put in a marathon rock-identification day to tag and group the 500 rocks in the collection.

In the small toy-and-doll collection, you'll see a Victorian doll with brown eyes—a rarity, because Queen Victoria had blue eyes, and most dolls were modeled on her.

One of the museum's founders insisted that it deal with science as well as art to attract people not interested in the arts. To help fill that need, two partly restored pioneer cabin sites have been included. Nature trails have been developed outside for short walks.

But what captures the imagination of the public here is the homeless mummy. Well, it has a home now, but nobody has been able to say for sure how it got there. They know she died when she was thirty-five years old, that her remains are 2,000 years old, and that she was mummified at a time when practitioners were getting a little sloppy about the process, but all people know about her recent history is that the museum and the mummy have both been there since 1956. Nobody knows where the mummy came from before that. One staff member said, "A lot of the people involved are still alive, but not all of them remember where the trucking company went to get things. One woman who might know has long since moved, and we can't find her."

The best rumor about the mummy is that another museum rejected it because it was cursed. Maybe it was a good curse. Good things certainly have

BETTER-KNOWN ATTRACTIONS IN THE LOWER PIEDMONT

Charlotte
Charlotte Knights Baseball Stadium
(704) 357–8071

Discovery Place
(704) 372–6261

North Carolina/South Carolina Border
Paramount's Carowinds Theme Park
(704) 588–2600
(803) 548–5300
(800) 888–4386

been happening while Ms. Mummy has lived at this museum. Some of the permanent collection is not at the farmstead but is housed in the Fairintosh Building at 541 Gaither Road. Call for directions and to check hours, which may vary seasonally. Admission by donation. Web site: www.iredellmuseum.com.

Take time to wander around Statesville's historic downtown. Many of the commercial buildings and homes are on the National Register of Historic Places, including the 1892 City Hall, considered by preservationists to be a fine example of the Richardsonian Romanesque style. Web site: www.downtown statesvillenc.org.

Stop next at the ***Fort Dobbs State Historic Site*** (704–873–5866), 438 Fort Dobbs Road, the site of a French and Indian War fort with archaeological sites, artifacts, nature trails, and recreational facilities. Open 9:00 A.M. to 5:00 P.M. Monday through Friday. Admission free. Web site: www.ah.dcr.state.nc./us/hs/dobbs/dobbs.htm.

This next stop isn't near anything else. Although it is located a ways north, almost at the Virginia border, the most direct way to get to ***Mt. Airy*** is to drive a couple of hours from Statesville straight up I–77. (This avoids the slow, sometimes treacherous, drive over the Blue Ridge Mountains.) Mt. Airy is ***Andy Griffith's home town.*** As a visitor you can approach it in one of two ways—visiting a shrine to Andy Griffith in his incarnation as Sheriff Andy Taylor, the Hero of Mayberry, or experiencing the spirit behind the Mayberry fiction.

How long Mt. Airy will remain off the beaten path is anybody's guess. The thing is, local people are starting to live the fiction. Griffith has always insisted that Mayberry was not really based on Mt. Airy, and while he did go back there from time to time when his parents were alive, he doesn't often any more. He retired to Manteo. But ever since Tanya Rees, of the Surry County Arts Council, got together with Jim Clark, publisher of *The Bullet: Official Newsletter of the Andy Griffith Show Rerun Watchers Club,* to create

Mayberry Days with tours and contests and parades, Mt. Airy keeps moving toward becoming Mayberry.

There is an old jail. It really is the old Mt. Airy jail. You can tour it. It bears no resemblance to the Mayberry jail, but the old squad car outside looks an awful lot like Sheriff Taylor's.

The most authentic place in Mt. Airy is probably ***Snappy Lunch,*** 125 North Main Street, which, according to its menu, is "Mt. Airy's Oldest Continuous Eating Establishment at the Same Location Since 1923!! Home of the Famous Pork Chop Sandwich." Mentioned by Andy on the show, they tell you. Snappy Lunch seems to have translated straight from fact to fiction. It looks the same as it did at the time of the show: wooden booths, grill in the window, pictures on the wall. The famous pork chop sandwich still sells for much less than the tourist trade would pay, because as Mary and Charles Dowell, who own the restaurant and work here see it, they are "making it OK." Call (336) 786–4931. Web site: www.snappylunch.com.

whoneedsandy?

Mt. Airy has at least some claims to fame quite apart from Andy Griffith.

Mt. Airy has been nicknamed "The Granite City" because the world's largest open-faced granite quarry is just east of town.

The original Siamese twins, Eng and Chang Bunker, who married sisters and lived here, are buried in the cemetery of White Plains Baptist Church, right next to Mt. Airy.

Country singer Donna Fargo is a Mt. Airy native.

Right next door is ***Floyd's Barber Shop.*** It used to be called City Barber Shop, but the proprietor, Russell Hiatt, got on the bandwagon. Lots of people come in not just to get a haircut but also to take Hiatt's picture. He doesn't mind at all. But in turn, he whips out his Polaroid and takes two pictures of the customers, one for them to take home as a souvenir and one to add to the collection on the wall. Open Monday, Tuesday, Wednesday, and Friday, 7:00 A.M. to 5:00 P.M. Phone (336) 786–2346.

The ***Andy Griffith Museum,*** in the visitor center, 615 North Main Street (800–576–0231), contains several rooms of memorabilia, including the white suit Griffith wore as Matlock. Both a walking tour of some of the town's older neighborhoods and a guided step-on tour are available.

As for ***Mayberry Days,*** it's hard to give exact dates because the thing keeps growing, but they're always in late September. For specifics, call the Surry County Arts Council (800–286–6193). Mt. Airy Web site: www.visitmayberry.com.

Mt. Airy is in Surry County, and although "Mayberry" gets the most attention, the county has a number of other interesting, lesser known places to visit,

Pork Chop Sandwich Snappy Lunch Style

Although the pork chop sandwich for which Snappy Lunch is famous starts with a piece of pork tenderized by a special machine and includes a chili and slaw made from Charles Dowell's secret recipes, you can make a pork chop sandwich using Charles' basic recipe.

Start with six boneless pork chops, each about ¾ inch thick, flattened to measure about 4 to 6 inches in diameter, patted dry and seasoned with salt and pepper.

Prepare a batter by beating together the following ingredients:

2 large eggs
2 cups all-purpose flour
2 tablespoons sugar
¼ teaspoon salt
1 to 1¼ cups milk

Heat enough vegetable oil in a heavy skillet to come about ¼ inch up the side of the pan. The oil should be hot but not smoking.

Dip the chops in batter, let the excess drip off and fry until golden brown, 8 to 10 minutes on each side.

Serve on soft hamburger buns topped with tomato and onion slices, coleslaw, ketchup, mustard, and relish.

Recipe makes enough batter for six sandwiches.

including the largest open-face granite quarry in the world, according to Surry County publicists. It is in Mt. Airy. It Runs 1 mile long, a third of a mile wide, and is so deep geologists estimate it can continue yielding stone at full operation for the next 500 years.

Now, to get a taste of a more authentic version of rural North Carolina, get out your N.C. Transportation map and look at the blue highways just off U.S. Highway 601, south of Mt. Airy. Go south on the blue highway that crosses State Highway 268 at Level Cross. This takes you into rural Surry County. Comparatively speaking, you might consider Mt. Airy the "urban" part. Head for the little town of Rockford and ***Old Rockford Village.*** This is what country folk used to call a "poke and plum" spot: Poke your head out the window as you drive, and you're plum out of town.

The focal point here is Annie Barnett's ***Rockford General Store.*** It's a hard place to define—partly touristy, partly a local source for everything from lye soap to pickled eggs and homemade fried apple pies, as well as more than

Braggin' Rights

A clerk in the Rockford General Store was trading one-liners with a customer about how small the town of Old Rockford Village is. The customer won with, "This town is so small that the person who left the porch light on last December won a prize for best Christmas decorations.

one hundred kinds of old-fashioned candy. The store, located on Rockford Road, meanders in several directions, with wooden-floored rooms filled with reminders of earlier times. Outside the store on the porch, a red wooden bench invites you to sit, and a checkerboard is set up with rocks as playing pieces, ready for anybody who wants a game. Annie Barnett died in 2003 and it is not clear how long the "temporary closing" of her store will last, but it is still an important part of the community. The best way to find out, and to make sure the store will be open if you want to stop in, is to call ahead (336–374–5317).

Whether you actually go into the store or not, driving these back roads gives you a glimpse of rural North Carolina as it really is, not as parts of it have been gussied up for tourists. Driving along these two-lane macadam roads with the car windows down, you can hear a "bobwhite, bobwhite, bobwhite" bird call. The warm air in summer smells of recently cut hay, although the fields are planted mostly in corn and tobacco. New orange Allis Chalmers tractors, sometimes standing right beside old ones, dot the landscape.

This stretch has as many trailers as conventionally built homes, and cable TV probably doesn't come out this far, because TV satellite dishes stand in many yards. Here and there an old log building has been restored. Others are crumbling to the ground. Driving these miles slows you down and reminds you that not everyone lives strapped with cell phones and pagers. From these roads you can drive easily over to US 601 South and head down to Salisbury.

A Pocket of History

From Statesville, head east on US 70 for twenty or thirty minutes to ***Historic Salisbury***. Two kinds of people live here—those whose families have been in place for generations and those who have moved in recently, mostly from up north. Both share an almost smug conviction that theirs is one of the most congenial, historically interesting communities in North Carolina. I say *almost* smug because they're right. Although this is one of the oldest towns in the area, and the entire 23-block downtown community of commercial and residential buildings dating from 1820 to 1920 is on the National Register of Historic Places, it receives relatively little attention from outside. The Historic Salisbury Foundation and an active group of supporters are trying to change that. Web site: www.visitsalisburync.com.

They point to the 1898 Grimes Mill, a roller mill with all its original machinery in five floors; the Civil War Salisbury Confederate Prison Site and National Cemetery, where the largest number of unknown Civil War soldiers are buried; and the restored Railroad Depot. All of them are open to the public.

Then there's the Historic Salisbury walking tour, which includes the homes in the National Register Historic District. Some of these homes are open to the public. The ***Dr. Josephus Hall House,*** 226 South Jackson Street, for instance, is a large, 1820 antebellum house that sits among old oaks and boxwoods that have been in place nearly as long as the house. Dr. Hall was chief surgeon at the Salisbury Confederate Prison during the Civil War. After the war the Union commander used the house as headquarters. Somehow the grounds and the interior escaped the destruction typically associated with Yankee occupation in the South, and the Hall House contains nearly all its original furnishings. Open Saturday and Sunday from 1:00 to 4:00 P.M. Modest admission fee. (704) 636–0103.

Just about a block away, the ***Utzman-Chambers House*** museum, 116 South Jackson Street, is a notable example of architecture from the Federal period. It shows the life of a prominent local family during the early 1800s. An early nineteenth-century garden features four formal beds of flowers and herbs native to the Piedmont in 1815. Open Thursday through Sunday from 1:00 to 4:00 P.M. Modest admission fee. Phone (704) 633–5946.

The ***Rowan Museum*** has exhibits related to Rowan County history in the old courthouse, 202 North Main Street. The old courthouse building was built in 1857, for the princely sum of $15,000, and was used as a court building until 1914, when it became the community building. Since then, at one time or another, it has served as almost everything for which the town needed a build-

AUTHOR'S FAVORITE PLACES IN THE LOWER PIEDMONT

Farm House Gardens

Waterworks Visual Arts Center

Kluttz Piano Factory

Cline's Country Antiques

Reed Gold Mine

Mint Museum of Art

ing: public library, American Red Cross headquarters, chamber of commerce, and adult night school. When the flu epidemic hit the town in 1918, the community building became an emergency hospital and kitchen. Open Thursday through Sunday 1:00 to 4:00 P.M. Modest admission fee. Phone (704) 633–5946.

The Rowan Museum includes another house a few miles outside of town that gives you a glimpse of early country life in the county. The ***Old Stone House,*** built by Michael Braun between 1758 and 1766, reflects the traditions of the German Rhinelanders who settled in the county in the early 1700s. Braun came to the area from Philadelphia, Pennsylvania, and the stone house will look familiar to anyone who has traveled the county roads in Pennsylvania and seen houses built on the Quaker plan. The house has been beautifully restored, and the museum is working to continue developing the property. The house is furnished with a collection of North Carolina and Pennsylvania pieces and looks much as it probably would have when Braun lived in it. One piece, a weaving loom in an upstairs room, has been in the house as long as anyone can remember.

To get to the Old Stone House from Rowan Museum, turn right on Innes Street, and go 4.2 miles (Innes Street becomes U.S. Highway 52 South) into Granite Quarry, and turn left on East Lyerly Street, which is also called Old Stone House Road. The house sits on the right, beside the road, about 0.6 miles farther on. Modest admission fee. The house is open from 1:00 to 4:00 P.M. Saturday and Sunday, April through November. The hours may change, and sometimes you can arrange to see the house at another time. Call the museum at (704) 633–5946 for more information.

Moving from the historic to the contemporary, the ***Waterworks Visual Arts Center,*** 123 East Liberty Street, features changing exhibits of contemporary art. The outdoor sculpture garden is especially pleasant on clear, sunny days. The gallery used to be in a building that was first used as the Salisbury Waterworks and then as the city police station. Now it is in a renovated and expanded building that used to be a car dealership. Its large open spaces are especially suited to displaying art. Open Tuesday through Saturday 10:00 A.M. to 5:00 P.M. Donations are suggested. Call (704) 638–1882.

In downtown Salisbury, which you really must see for its remarkable old factory, old train station (where Amtrak now stops), and business buildings, you can break the fast-food habit by having a bite of lunch at ***Spanky's,*** an old-fashioned ice-cream parlor that serves not only homemade ice-cream concoctions but also good soups, salads, deli sandwiches, and cheesecake (corner of Main and Innes Streets; 704–638–0780). Spanky's actually makes seventy-five different flavors of ice cream, but the owner explained, almost apologetically, that they keep only twenty-five flavors on hand at a time! The restaurant is in an old building that in 1859 was the tallest in North Carolina. Open Monday through Saturday from 9:00 A.M. to 8:00 P.M., and Sunday from noon to 8:00 P.M.

Of the many barbecue restaurants in the area, ***College Bar-B-Que,*** 117 Statesville Boulevard (704–633–9953), is a long-established place where the waitresses have known some of the regulars for years. It's almost always busy, and don't be confused by the word "College" in its name. Old timers, families with little kids, and "just folks" all come here, though it is close to Catawba College and attracts students too. As you approach the restaurant sometimes you can smell the wood smoke from the barbecue fire, and inside you will hear the steady thumping sound of knives against cutting boards as the pork is chopped. The restaurant serves all the breakfast standards—eggs, biscuits, sausage—as well as sandwiches and menu specials, and you can expect your glass of iced tea to be kept full until you leave, but barbecue is the defining offering. The restaurant opens every day at 7:00 A.M. and closes at 8:00 P.M. except on Monday, when it closes at 2:00 P.M., and Saturday, when it closes at 3:00 P.M.

Almost any day you are in Salisbury, you'll see people wearing earphones and consulting booklets as they walk the streets, following one of the self-guided tours. You may borrow the brochures, tapes, and tape players for two of the tours, free, from the Visitor Information Center at 204 East Innes Street. Brochures and guide maps for the African-American Heritage Trail are available at the Visitor Information Center and also at W. J. Walls Heritage Hall on the campus of Livingstone College.

The ***Salisbury Heritage Tour*** (audio, walking) is a 1.3-mile walking tour that provides details about the history and architecture of Historic Downtown Salisbury and the large homes of the West Square Historic District. The ***Civil War Heritage Tour*** (audio, driving) provides insights into Salisbury's role during an infamous time, including a Union prisoner-of-war camp where 11,700 died. Nothing remains of the Salisbury Confederate Prison. The Union soldiers are memorialized at the Salisbury National Cemetery. The ***African-American Heritage Trail*** (brochure, driving) self-guided tour notes important moments, leaders, and lives of generations of African Americans who lived and worked in Salisbury.

When you are on Innes Street, orient yourself so the winged ***Confederate Monument*** in the center of town is to your back, turn left on Main Street (or turn right if you are facing the statue), and drive a few minutes into the neighboring town of ***Spencer*** to visit the ***North Carolina Transportation Museum*** (877–628–6386) on 411 South Salisbury Avenue. This is the site of what was once the largest service facility or shops for Southern Railway Company. The museum's collection includes all kinds of transportation-related

Humiliation

I had just begun exploring the area around Salisbury and Spencer. People kept asking me if I'd been to the Spencer Shops yet. I wasn't in a big hurry to find them, because shopping isn't my idea of a good time, but eventually I figured that anything so many people mentioned would be worth a visit. The idea of gift shops in an old transportation museum seemed OK.

I went into the museum office and after checking all the signs, asked the receptionist where the gift shops were. Was it like a row of specialty shops in converted train buildings or what? I asked.

Her face changed from polite-receptionist to local-citizen-horrified-at-such-ignorance. The Shops at Spencer, she said, are machine shops where mechanics once repaired Southern Railway's steam locomotives. Those trains hauled passengers and such freight as furniture, textiles, and tobacco, and the shops at one time employed nearly 3,000 people.

Gift shops, indeed! Sniff.

artifacts—antique automobiles, railroad cars, and an airplane. The roundhouse, with thirty-seven bays, is an inevitable hit with train enthusiasts. You can watch a video about the railroad in the visitor center. Train rides in restored cars are available when there are enough people. Admission to the museum is free. Train rides are $5.00 for adults, $4.00 for children and senior citizens. Train rides and museum hours vary seasonally. It is a good idea to call ahead.

Right across the street the ***Little Choo Choo Shop*** (704–637– 8717), 500 South Salisbury Avenue, is a serious, well-stocked model-railroad shop handling supplies for scales from "G" to the tiny "Z." They buy, sell, trade, and repair. One room is devoted to books and videos about model railroading, and you can get top-notch advice from the people who work here, too. Another small room is filled with wooden toy trains to occupy kids while you browse among the grown-up toys. The store is open Tuesday through Saturday 10:00 A.M. to 5:30 P.M.

One interesting side trip from Salisbury is a quick jog south on I–85 to ***Cannon Village at Kannapolis.*** Cannon Village is a shopping outlet now, but it and the town are a fascinating, almost unspoiled glimpse of a once-prosperous mill town.

Another interesting dimension is that Fieldcrest-Cannon was taken over by Pillowtex, which has since gone bankrupt and, finally, in 2003, closed entirely, putting several thousand local residents out of work. Few of them have found new jobs.

The first thing you notice about Cannon Village and its outskirts is that everything matches—not sheets and towels or skirts and blouses, but the white-trimmed brick shops and brick sidewalks, bounded by the great brick walls of the Fieldcrest-Cannon mill buildings; the brick schoolhouse, the church, and even the supermarket that are part of the larger community. About the only things that aren't brick are the mill houses—tidy, modest, mostly white homes that reflect pride of ownership in their neatly clipped hedges and mowed lawns. You pass these homes that run along the railroad tracks and the streets of Kannapolis on your way into Cannon Village.

Confederate Monument

Cannon Village is at the center of the town of Kannapolis. The village is a center for off-price, outlet, and specialty shopping, especially home furnishings. Back in 1887 this was a mill town founded by Charles Cannon as a community for the employees of Cannon Mills.

In the early 1980s Fieldcrest Corporation and Cannon Mills combined, and Fieldcrest's founder, Benjamin Franklin Mebane, restored the buildings along Oak Avenue, West Avenue, and Main Street to create a shopping complex that is a mixture of colonial and early twentieth-century structures trimmed by full-grown trees and green strips of lawn.

In the ***Cannon Village Visitors Center and Museum,*** 200 West Avenue, a museum display traces the development of textiles from some early Inca cotton to present day fabric woven on high-speed, air-jet looms. Call (704) 938–3200 for days and hours of operation in the Village and Visitors Center.

Here's another side trip you can easily make from Salisbury that gives you a glimpse of earlier mill life in the area without the shopping hype. ***Cooleemee*** is a well-preserved but not gentrified mill town. To get there, go to Jake Alexander Boulevard, which becomes US 601/70. Follow 601 North into Davie County. At Greasy Corner turn left onto State Highway 801, and

Early Kannapolis

They say George Washington never slept here—but he could have. The area attracted many important travelers, and Washington passed through at least once. Francis Asbury, the English preacher who brought the Methodist faith to the United States, also stopped here several times. The "Great Road" between Charlotte and Salisbury in colonial days ran through the center of Kannapolis, just about where Cannon Village is now. One favorite stopping place was Murph's Inn, which stood near what is York Avenue today.

Earlier, Catawba and Waxhaw Indians traveled about the same route as they made trading trips between South Carolina and Virginia. They probably stopped at springs near what are now the South Main underpass, the east side of the North underpass, and the west side of Woodrow Wilson School.

drive about 1 mile to Cooleemee. Go right onto Marginal Street, then left onto Church Street. This will bring you to the ***Mill Village Museum,*** in the Zachary-Holt House at Old 14 Church Street. It is well marked with signs. The Mill Village Museum offers an honest, down-to-earth look at life in a Piedmont cotton mill village a century ago, and the old homes in the town show how the town grew up around the Cooleemee Cotton Mill. The museum bills itself as "telling the story of Carolina cotton mill folks," and although the emphasis is on how the town developed around the Cooleemee Cotton Mill, later called Erwin Mills #3, the information about the people and the town gives you a good idea of what many mill towns in the Carolina Piedmont were like. The mill closed in 1969.

The Cooleemee Historical Society has actively collected artifacts, photographs, and stories from people who remember when the mill, which opened in 1898, was the center of life. Exhibits in the museum are organized under the categories Country Roots, Cooleemee is Born, From Cotton to Cloth, Like One Big Family, Establishing a Society, the Old Square, a New South, Honoring Their Memory, and This Old House. A detailed and engagingly written museum guide explains each exhibit.

After looking around the museum, a walk or slow drive around the town, where most of the mill houses are still occupied, gives you a further sense of what a mill village was like. For instance, the addresses of the houses used to be numbered so that the lowest numbers were for the houses closest to the mill.

The historical society wants to clear up what they consider misrepresentation of Southern mill towns by some historians. Michael Myerson, in his book, *Nothing Could Be Finer,* wrote about mill hands: "Tied to their machines day and night and housed in mill-owned shanty villages, the developing North Carolina lived an existence out of a Dickens nightmare." But that's not the picture drawn by the exhibits in the museum and the stories recalled by old-timers. The museum guide says the work was hard and dirty and ran into sixty-six-hour workweeks for low pay, but it claims that wasn't out-of-line for rural people already used to hard work. The pace was relatively slow in the early days, and workers took breaks for drinks, snacks, or even a swim in the river. Looking around the town makes it clear the mill houses were never shanties, and old-timers' stories mention improvements such as indoor plumbing and electricity. The museum is open Wednesday through Saturday, 10:00 A.M. to 4:00 P.M., or by appointment. The museum is accessible to people with handicaps. Donations accepted. Phone (336) 284–6040.

Another side trip, to ***Mooresville,*** can be pure fun for kids and exhilarating for racing fans. Like Kannapolis, Mooresville was once a textile town. Today its economic base comes from motorsports. Some forty race teams are based in Mooresville because the town is close to speedways in Charlotte, Wilmington, and Darlington, South Carolina. The town now calls itself Race City U.S.A. To dip into the race and auto culture, check out the ***Dale Earnhardt Inc. Showroom,*** 1675 Coddle Creek Highway (877–334–9663) for displays of Dale Earnhardt Inc. drivers' achievements. Open Monday through Friday 9:00 A.M. to 5:00 P.M., Saturday 10:00 A.M. to 4:00 P.M. At ***5 Off 5 On,*** 156

Remembering the Intimidator

North Carolina is home to forty-six NASCAR (North American stock car racing) teams, more than any other state in the union. The state's focus on NASCAR racing became even stronger after the death of Dale Earnhardt, a Kannapolis native, who died in 2001 in a crash during the Daytona 500, just two months before his fiftieth birthday.

He was a high school dropout who became a racing legend, considered by experts the best ever in the sport.

When the road where Dale Earnhardt drove his 1956 Chevrolet as a teenager was named "Dale Earnhardt Boulevard" in 1993, 8,000 people turned out for the ceremony.

After Earnhardt's death, *Salisbury Post* sportswriter Mike London wrote, "Earnhardt did for racing what Arnold Palmer did for golf and Muhammad Ali for boxing."

Memorials to Dale Earnhardt stand in Cannon Village Park and in the Cannon Village Visitors Center.

Bryers Creek Road, Talbert Pointe (866–563–3566), the specialists who train pit crew personnel explain the science and technology to fans. Call for hours of operation. ***Memory Lane Motorsports and Historic Automotive Museum,*** 769 River Highway (704–892–9853) features exhibits showing the history of both racing and the automobiles. Displays include one-of-a-kind vehicles, race cars, vintage automobiles, motorcycles, toys, and memorabilia. Open Monday through Saturday 10:00 A.M. to 5:00 P.M. The ***North Carolina Auto Racing Hall of Fame,*** 119 Knob Hill Road (704–663–5331; Web site: www.ncarhof.com) has an art gallery of work by motorsports artists, a museum with more than thirty-five cars, a gift shop with all kinds of racing memorabilia, and the Goodyear Mini-Theater, which shows forty-five-minute films about peak moments in racing. The hall of fame is open Monday through Saturday, 9:00 A.M. to 5:00 P.M., Sunday 12:30 to 4:30 P.M. Admission is $5.00 for adults, $3.00 for children and seniors.

The only thing ***Lazy 5 Ranch*** has to do with automobiles is that the owners want you to stay inside yours as you drive around the place looking at exotic animals. The ranch is between Interstates 85 and 77, on State Highway 150 East (704–663–5100). The ranch has about 400 animals from around the world and you drive about 3.5 miles through pastures to see them: camels, Watusi cows from Africa with horn spreads of up to 12 feet, water buffalo, zebras, and so on. Although you have to stay in your car to see these animals, you can get out to enjoy the petting zoo and feed some of the animals there. This place is run with a sense of humor. Rules that make sense in any language are expressed with a grin: "You are not allowed to feed your children to the animals, no matter how bad they are behaving; don't honk your horn or turn on your lights unless you need help because it gives our animals heartburn; when you stop to take photos from your car, pull over to the side. This will allow other cars to drive around. It will also give the animals time to fluff their hair. So you get animal slobber all over your car . . . they're just trying to be friendly. You can wash it off later." Lazy 5 Ranch is open Monday through Saturday from 9:00 A.M. to an hour before sunset, Sunday from 1:00 P.M. until an hour before sunset. Admission: adults $7.50, children and seniors $4.50; wagon rides $3.00, horse-drawn wagon rides by appointment $5.00.

Back in Salisbury once again, you might spend the night at ***Rowan Oak House,*** 208 Fulton Street, which offers Victorian elegance in a 1902 Queen Anne house (704–633–2086). The house is notable for its remarkably intact interior, where the original wallpaper is still in perfect condition.

Another hostelry up the street takes a different approach to the Victorian era. Karen Windate rescued an old Victorian home at 529 South Fulton Street, in the historic district, with a full-scale historic restoration that has won preservation prizes. ***Turn of the Century Victorian Bed and Breakfast*** offers three guest rooms and a two-room suite, all with private baths, decorated and furnished in understated elegance with period antiques. Karen prides herself on serving a different full breakfast, on different china, each morning. Guests who've stayed for several days have sometimes made bets about how long she could go without repeating herself. Phone (704) 642–1660 or (800) 250–5349. Web site: www.turnofthecenturybb.com.

Leaving Salisbury, take US 52 South for an interesting drive that shows you the down-home, not the tourist, version of the Piedmont. In about 6 miles, almost before you've left Salisbury's environs, you come to Granite Quarry, where a big billboard on the left side of the road directs you to ***Kluttz Piano Factory.*** They deliver free, but probably not if you live in Cincinnati. Stop in and look around, even though you probably aren't planning to buy a piano while you're out tracking unbeaten paths. Ray Kluttz Sr., the company patriarch, says they have, in fact, had customers from distant states. He loves it. This place, which advertises more than 500 new and rebuilt pianos, is awesome. The showroom, where you try out new and reconditioned pianos, looks fairly standard, but you'll be dumbfounded by the work area, which seems roughly the size of a football field, filled with pianos—whole pianos and pieces of pianos in every make, model, and size. Ten minutes of just looking will tell you more about what's inside a piano than you've ever dreamed you could know.

Talk about Beating a Path to the Door . . .

Just southeast of Kannapolis, around Concord, stands an example of the burgeoning development in North Carolina. Lowe's Motor Speedway is a kind of mecca of motor sports, especially stock car racing. The speedway features two NASCAR Winston Cup races and two Nascar Busch Series races each year, as well as the big NASCAR all-star Winston. On race weekends signs go up for miles around in all directions welcoming race fans and advertising Goody's headache powders. People in the area who aren't race fans (there are a few) always just avoid I–85 and U.S. Highway 29 on race weekends.

Now another attraction in the same area pulls in a steady stream of another huge class of people—bargain shoppers. Concord Mills calls itself a shopping/entertainment destination. It has more than 200 stores, a huge food court, theme restaurants, a twenty-four-screen movie theater and interactive entertainment in some of the retail stores. And, inevitably, hotels, motels, restaurants, and housing developments are filling what, just a few years ago, was farmland.

If you want to join the crowds for a while, check Web sites: www.concordmills.com and www.lowesmotorspeedway.com. And don't say I didn't warn you.

The people who work here talk as casually about the good and bad traits of grands, uprights, spinets, Yamahas, Wurlitzers, and Baldwins as the rest of us talk about the tomatoes in our gardens.

Outsiders sometimes get a chuckle out of the name Kluttz, but around here, Kluttz is just another family name, belonging not only to the owners of the piano factory but also to architects, contractors, and art shop proprietors. Everybody works hard, even the older Mr. Kluttz, who thinks nothing of being one of two men to haul a grand piano off its legs, out of a truck, and into a house. You'll notice that some of the people wear big gold belt buckles shaped like grand pianos. Ask about the buckles, and the only answer you'll get is, "It means we're special." Some workers get there as early as 4:00 A.M., but regular hours for ordinary mortals are Monday through Friday from 9:00 A.M. to 5:00 P.M. and Saturday from 10:00 A.M. to 2:00 P.M. (704–279–7237).

Continuing on US 52 South, which is really going east at this point, brings you to ***Rockwell,*** which you should pronounce *ROCKwul,* not *RockWELL.* The town bears no relationship to Norman Rockwell, but it should: Flags fly from all the porches on Memorial Day; signs advertise BAIT, CRICKETS, AND NIGHT CRAWLERS; women still appear occasionally with their hair in curlers; neighbors stop each other in the grocery store to ask if the new "granbaby" has arrived yet; pink and blue bows on mailboxes announce when the new grans do come into the world. Stop for some good, authentic barbecue at ***Darrell's Bar-BQ,*** 117 East Main Street. If you call ahead, you can even pick it up at a drive-through window, although then you'll miss the chance to mingle with the local people inside (704–279–6300). Darrell's is open Tuesday through Saturday from 10:00 A.M. to 9:00 P.M. Closed Sunday and Monday.

In a brick building at 111 East Main Street, bearing the sign F. W. KLUTTZ BUILDING, 1921 in gold letters, the ***Rockwell Museum*** serves as a repository for all kinds of old things reflecting life in Rockwell—photographs, apparel, antique retail store display cases, old typewriters and office equipment, all labeled as to who used it, when, and where. A large map with text explains that, in the days when this part of the country was the western frontier, Rockwell was an overnight rest stop because it had a good well. The map shows trails used by early settlers as they migrated. The museum has been a labor of love by the Bost family, who've been active in town government for decades, and they don't keep set hours, but you can arrange to see it by calling (704) 279–8783. The town Web site also has information about the museum: www.rockwellnc.com.

Continuing east on US 52, you'll come to ***Gold Hill.***

Orient yourself so that the Gold Hill Post Office and a convenience store stand on your left. On the right-hand side of the road, a sign carved from wood and set in brick announces GOLD HILL. Turn right through the gate and onto Doby Road. Cross the railroad tracks, turn left onto Old 80, and go a short block to a stop sign. At the sign, turn right onto St. Stephen's Church Road, follow it just a little more than a half mile, and you'll come to a section where green banners welcome you to the ***Historic Village of Gold Hill.*** Gold Hill was once the largest mining district east of the Mississippi— a boomtown in the mid-1800s. But it's been hard to extract ore from the soil here, and the gold rush moved on to other sites, leaving Gold Hill a sparsely populated rural community until recently, when community members began to rejuvenate the place.

The first thing you come to is a park bordered by fieldstone fences, complete with a pavilion shelter, a museum building, an outdoor stage, picnic tables, playground equipment, bike and walking paths, bridges, and information signs explaining the history of mining in Gold Hill, all the work of a community park committee. Across from the park, Gold Hill United Methodist Church, a simple white building with six columns, is a fully active church.

End of an Era

Granite Quarry lost a piece of its heart in 1999, when Carolina Maid, a company that made women's dresses, closed after sixty-four years in business. Unlike many textile mills and other manufacturing plants that have closed in North Carolina—Cone and Burlington Mills, for instance—Carolina Maid was always a strictly local, family-owned and run operation.

The redbrick building of about 6,500 square feet still stands intact by the highway. In its prime the plant produced up to 600 dresses a day, and almost everyone in the area either worked at Carolina Maid at one time or another or has kin who did.

When the plant closed, many of the workers were already well past retirement age. They had stayed on, not just for the income, but because coming to work was a social thing for them. Their coworkers were also their friends and, often, their relatives.

Sam Miller, who worked in the cutting room for forty years, remembered the time a local baker tried to hire him away from Carolina Maid, saying, "As long as there are people, they're going to be eating bread."

Sam replied, "As long as there's women, they're gonna be wearing dresses."

He told the story and shook his head, saying "Boy, was I wrong."

The good news is that Farmers & Merchants, a local bank, has renovated the main part of the building to use as operations headquarters, thus preserving it for the community.

Boardwalks beginning here run the length of the "new" old village, past renovated, reproduced, and imported old buildings. One observer said this section looks like a Western movie set. The people who live in the restored house next to the church are working on one old store, while the ***1840 Mauney Store*** (704–279–1632) already sells antiques, and the restored ***E. H. Montgomery Store*** (704–279–1632) across the street has ice cream, pop, hot dogs, and Moon Pies. At the ***Gold Miner's Daughter*** (704–788–4459), Frankie Harrison runs a floral shop in a reproduction post office, and next door Nancy Atkins operates the ***Gold Hill Mint & Bake Shoppe*** (704–209–3280). A woodwright shop is in the works too. Store hours may vary. Call ahead.

More shops, artists' studios, and a few private homes will come along too. As more businesses open, the hours for any of the establishments could change, so it's a good idea to call ahead. The community is so small that a phone call to any of the numbers will usually yield information about all the businesses if you ask.

Miss Ruby's Restaurant, in the center of the village, owned by Darius and Nina Hedrick and run by Nina, is the big news in Gold Hill and the surrounding area. There really is a Miss Ruby, too. She lives just down the street. The restaurant is in a building that started as a home, was used as a doctor's office, and was later converted into apartments. In its new incarnation, the building, with an addition, houses a restaurant that is part down-home country and part gourmet cuisine, with a definite emphasis on casualness. No two tables are alike in the main dining room, where a collection of church plates decorates one wall, and in the new addition diners sit in oak booths or perch on antique stools along the bar. The dining rooms overlook a pasture where Longhorn steer graze by a lake. A typical lunch offering is the Gold Plate Special, which changes daily. Wednesday, for instance, is meat loaf; Thursday is chicken pie. Dinners include mushrooms stuffed with crabmeat and crab cakes, pasta primavera, and beef tenderloin stuffed with lobster. For Sunday brunch Miss Ruby's serves sourdough French toast, cheese grits with shrimp and ham, and steak and eggs. The chef uses local herbs and baked goods and can tell you the names of the people who made the pies and cakes.

Miss Ruby's Restaurant is open for lunch and dinner Wednesday through Saturday. Open 11:00 A.M. to 3:00 P.M. Sunday. Reservations are recommended. Phone (704) 209–6049.

When you're done in the village, if you drive straight on through, you'll come to Old Beatty Ford Road, which, if you turn left, will take you back to US 52 in a couple of minutes, or you can turn right for an hour's diversion down a different kind of entrepreneurial row.

Turn left onto a road that crosses the railroad tracks and runs past a large quarry operation. You'll drive about 12 miles along this road, past a Soil Conservation Service demonstration farm on the left; a home-based sewing-machine repair shop called Sew and Sew; another home business, "Why Knot Upholstery"; and Miller Farms Racing (a track around grassy fields). Among these little businesses, many yards have for-sale signs offering produce in season, a piece of used farm equipment, a boat, a camper "like new" with tow bar and a pickup (there must be a story in that one), firewood, oil paintings—it all changes with fortune and the seasons. You'll also pass a couple of uncommonly attractive older churches, the kind with their own manicured graveyards in back. Old Concord Road intersects Old Beatty Ford Road after about 12 miles. Turn left. Drive about 3 miles more, passing Roy Cline Road and Irish Potato Road, and turn right immediately onto Goldfish Road. You're at ***Greendale,*** 6465 Goldfish Road, Kannapolis, which from the outside looks like one more sprawling roadside building. Inside you'll find wonder and the ultimate rural entrepreneurial enterprise.

Long rows of beautifully clear, brightly lighted aquariums gleam in the dim room, covering 44,000 square feet of display space. Here in the boonies, where if you tell your mother you're going to the fish store she assumes you're going to buy flounder, you discover gouramis and guppies, oscars, cichlids, corals, and saltwater exotics whose names you don't even know, all apparently thriving. OK, you can't keep goldfish on the road, but just looking beats watching television, and you may find the selection and prices on aquarium equipment appealing enough to tease a traveler's check out of your wallet before you leave.

Greendale started out as a goldfish farm back in 1929, when Rufus Green got laid off by Cannon Mills and decided to make his living raising goldfish in outdoor ponds to sell to dime stores. One of his first sales was to get money to buy a shirt for church. The years passed, Rufus died, and his wife maintained the business as well as she could. Rufus's son, George, returned in 1978 from another war that wasn't called one, with his wife, Gaysorn, a classical dancer from Bangkok. By now hobbyists had turned enthusiastically to exotic tropical fish, so it made sense for Greendale to develop accordingly. The whole story, in a yellowing newspaper clipping, is taped to the front wall.

It's hard to imagine there would be enough customers to keep the business going, but they come from all directions: Concord, Kannapolis, Salisbury, Albemarle. The store is closed on Tuesday, partly because new shipments of plants and fish come then. On Wednesday it's so busy that, as one employee put it, "People just come in and throw money at you." They're all there: Gay and George and local young people who work here and often get themselves hooked on the hobby in the process. You can always find someone to chat with about the troublesome habits of live bearers and how hard it is not to disrupt a gourami's bubble nest. Open Wednesday through Saturday from 10:00 A.M. to 6:00 P.M. and Sunday from 2:00 to 6:00 P.M. Closed Monday and Tuesday. Phone (704) 933–1798.

When you leave, depending on which way you turn, you may see a large block-lettered sign inside a cul-de-sac in front of a mobile home: IF YOU DON'T HAVE BUSINESS HERE, THIS IS A GOOD PLACE FOR YOU TO TURN AROUND. This may be the only guy in the county who *isn't* looking for customers at home. The best way to return to US 52 is the way you came in. Since everything looks different going in the opposite direction, you'll see things you missed the first time and won't feel that you're backtracking.

Coming into Misenhiemer, US 52 runs through the middle of the small ***Pfeiffer College*** campus, where all the classroom buildings, administration buildings, dormitories, and faculty houses are made of red brick. You might think that this is the kind of place, a film director would like to shoot *Who's Afraid of Virginia Woolf?,* although a director would never get approval in this Bible pocket. If it did happen, people would raise a big stink in the *Stanley News and Press.*

Farm Country

From Pfeiffer College it's only a couple of miles to the intersection of US 52 and State Highway 49 at Richfield. Go north on Highway 49 for about as long as you need to take two deep breaths and pull into the parking lot of the ***Motel Restaurant.*** This is the breakfast and lunch spot for many of the local farmers, the people who work in the mobile- home factories and the Perfect Fit textile plant down the road. For breakfast you get two eggs, bacon, grits or hash browns, biscuits or corn bread, and coffee for less than $5.00. Lunch is one meat (meatloaf or fried fish, maybe; the selections are written on a blackboard at the door), two vegetables, and beverage for less than $5.00. Sit at the counter and you can study the ever-lengthening row of imprinted mugs: *Old Age Ain't No Place for Sissies, If God Wanted Me to Cook and Clean My Hands Would've Been Made of Aluminum, My Parents Went to Myrtle Beach and All They Got Me Was This Dumb Mug, God Loves You and I'm Trying.*

The Motel Restaurant waitresses know all the regulars by name, ask "You doin' OK?" as they take your order, and after the first time, remember what it is that you always have. They like a good joke. Did you hear about the prostitute who told her tax consultant that she was a chicken farmer? Well, she said

Old Timers

They still tell the story in Richfield about a bet two of the men once made. Nobody remembers for sure what it was about, though it may have had something to do with whether or not a kid could steal some chickens and then sell them back to the owner, but they do know that the loser had to push the winner to Albemarle, about 10 miles away, in a wheelbarrow.

How long did it take?

Didn't keep time, exactly, but it definitely took most of the day.

. . . Country music plays in the background, and while Willie and Waylon are appreciated, one of the waitresses says she'd really like to marry Garth Brooks, even if she is already married. But Randy Travis, now, he's one of our own, coming from Monroe and all. This is the kind of place where everybody knows everybody, and the local bank manager sits next to the local welder, who calls his regular morning trip to the restaurant "going to the office." When you've had all the coffee or iced tea you can hold, leave a dollar on the counter, pay your bill, and when someone says, "Come back," you say, "I'll do it." Open Monday through Friday from 5:00 A.M. to 2:00 P.M. and Saturday from 5:00 to 11:00 A.M.

From here you could take Highway 49 North through the Uhwarrie Forest back up to Asheboro, or you could go south for an interesting drive to Charlotte. Expect to have to be patient. Much of the road is only one lane in each direction, with few places to pass, and you'll probably spend some time behind a tractor or a slow-moving truck hauling logs. Even going slowly, driving south will take you to Mount Pleasant in ten or fifteen minutes.

Shortly before you come to the crossroads at Mount Pleasant, a sign on the right advertises ***Cline's Country Antiques.*** A big, rusting antique tractor marks

Jazz Great

The saxophonist John Coltrane, considered by many lovers of music to be one of the great musicians of the twentieth century, was born in Hamlet on September 23, 1926. He built his reputation as an innovator in jazz within about ten years. Coltrane died in 1967.

the lane back to the seven long buildings where Don Cline manages an ever-changing stock. He buys and wholesales antiques by the truckload but attends with equal care to your $5.00 purchase of an old advertising sign or kitchen utensil. One of the most fascinating things you can do is ask for a particular kind of antique—an oak washstand or armoire, or a pie safe, for instance—and then watch Don reflect a minute before he directs you, without consulting any kind of inventory list at all, to the precise building and corner in which you'll find what you're looking for. No one's quite sure how he does it, but no matter how often or how fast his inventory changes, Don always knows where everything is.

His appearance reflects the fact that Don detests malls and spending money on glitzy new things; he prides himself on living out of his junk. His britches came from a load the pickers hauled in, his sweater was in a bin of post office surplus that he found at a dumpster, and his Sunday suit was part of the stock he got when he bought all the remaining merchandise of a department store that went out of business several years ago.

If he's not out supervising the coming and going of truckloads, Don will probably be sitting in the old barber chair by the woodstove in the barn, talking with visiting dealers or reading old issues of antiques magazines. Don collaborated with a professional writer on the book *Buying and Selling Antiques*. Across from Don's barber chair, Vichard, his assistant, nailed up a wooden box to hold copies of the book, with a sign above that reads the book and an arrow pointing down to the copies that are for sale.

The idea of Don's writing a book seems surprising when you first encounter his plain-old-country-boy demeanor, but pay attention, ask a few questions, and you'll learn that he has taught economics in a couple of area colleges, has a photographic memory, and is perfectly willing to let you think he's stupid if you're so inclined because it helps business. Not that he's dishonest; he won't sell an imperfect piece without pointing out the flaw, he won't knowingly misrepresent anything, and he charges only a modest markup on his merchandise. Don Cline may be the most scrupulously honest antiques dealer in the business, but he doesn't see any reason to rouse your jousting instincts by flaunting his brain.

Hey Ma, Look What I Found!

The gold nugget Conrad Reed found in 1799 weighed seventeen pounds, but he was only twelve and everybody figured the kid was just hauling a big rock home. The family used it as a doorstop for three years before the boy's father sold it for $3.50.

Actually, in the beginning he wasn't that eager to go into business at all. It's just that he loved auctions and couldn't resist good buys. When he got married, his wife pointed out that unless he started moving stuff out at something close to the speed with which he brought it in, there wasn't going to be room for her. Then, too, there on his father's farm were all those long chicken sheds, empty since the cholesterol scare made producing eggs unprofitable. All the setup really needed was customers, so Don began to let it be known that he had some stuff to sell. The rest, as they say, is history. Cline's Country Antiques (704–436–6824) is open from sometime around 8:00 or 9:00 A.M. to sometime about dark, Wednesday through Saturday. Closed Sunday, Monday, and Tuesday.

If you get to hanging around the Cline place so late that you don't feel like driving anymore, you could stay at the ***Carolina Country Inn*** in Mount Pleasant. This is a simple, clean, quiet motel, with a sign out front pointing out how many long country miles you still have to travel to reach Charlotte or Raleigh and inviting you to stay there instead. A few rooms have refrigerators. Rates are modest. Phone (704) 436–9616.

When you get to where US 601 meets Highway 49, you may decide to make a side trip on US 601 South to State Highway 200 and follow the signs to the ***Reed Gold Mine*** at Stanfield, about 10 miles east of Concord (704–721–4653). This is the site of the first authenticated gold find in the United States. It seems that Conrad Reed found a gold nugget the size of a brick on the family farm, and after that the family sort of lost interest in farming. We tend to associate the gold rushes with Alaska and California, but the fever burned here in North Carolina back in the late 1820s. For a time more people worked at gold mining than any other occupation except farming. Here and there in the state you still find places such as Morning Star Explorations at Richfield, where the search for more gold continues or has begun anew.

At the Reed Gold Mine State Historic Site, you can pan for gold in the spring and summer and tour the mining area year-round. In the visitor center, exhibits and a film explain the history and mining process. Admission is free, but you must pay a modest fee to pan for gold. Open Tuesday through Saturday from 10:00 A.M. to 4:00 P.M. Web site: www.reedmine.com.

Land of the New

Charlotte's an exciting place to visit these days. It's growing so fast that you can find something new almost every day. People seem to exude civic pride. Because they're so pleased about the way things are going, they're incredibly nice to visitors. ***Charlotte*** has reason for pride: the women's professional basketball team, the Charlotte Sting; the Bobcats NFL football team; the Charlotte Knights professional baseball team; the Charlotte Checkers International Hockey League Team; NASCAR racing at Lowes' Motor Speedway; Douglas International Airport, with direct flights to major cities; a Pulitzer Prize–winning newspaper, the *Charlotte Observer;* the highly rated University of North Carolina at Charlotte; a slew of smaller colleges and universities; new skyscrapers; and both a new and an old coliseum.

Until Hurricane Hugo hit in the fall of 1989, Charlotte was famous for its streets lined with huge old oak trees. People called the city "The Shady Lady." Since the 90-mile-per-hour winds, things are a lot more open—including some roofs—but even before the repairs were finished, committees were planting new trees and Charlottians were looking proudly at the neighborliness and cooperation with which they handled the days- and weeks-long power outage and the physical destruction to homes, neighborhoods, and businesses. That fighting spirit, they'll tell you, has always been part of the city's heritage.

The city was named for Queen Charlotte of Mecklenburg, wife of King George III, and it still calls itself "The Queen City," but the city rebelled against England in 1775 and earned from General Cornwallis the complaint that Charlotte was "a hornet's nest."

Charlotte's growth brings traffic, unfortunately, along with the excitement, but it would be too bad to miss some of the city's special features because of traffic. The best advice for a visitor to minimize problems is to study a city map ahead of time and try to avoid the major high-traffic highways—Interstates 85 and 77 and Independence Boulevard—as much as possible. Once you're actually in the city, the traffic isn't bad, except at rush hour; it's the main arteries that clog up. Don't hesitate to ask for directions if you get confused. People seem to be used to it and are good at helping, probably because the ongoing construction everywhere has forced them to figure out new routes.

The Art Is on the Wall

A fresco is a watercolor painting done on a wet plaster wall or ceiling. The colors sink into the plaster and become permanent as it dries.

Artist Ben Long has created much-loved frescoes in various locations across the state, including Charlotte. In the Bank of America Corporate Center lobby, on North Tryon Street, a series of scenes depict workers in North Carolina.

Keeping It on Ice

North Carolina has one National Hockey League team and four minor league hockey teams. The NHL Carolina Hurricanes are based in Raleigh. In the minors, the Asheville Smoke, Charlotte Checkers, Fayetteville Force, and Greensboro Generals all play regular season schedules. For details check the Web sites: www.ashevillesmoke.com; carolinahurricanes.com; www.gocheckers.com; www.fayettevilleforce.com; www.greensborogenerals.com.

You'll find enough special places here to warrant spending a night, so perhaps you'll want to arrange for accommodations first. In addition to plenty of standard hotels and motels, Charlotte has a number of bed-and-breakfast inns.

At the ***Homeplace*** (5901 Sardis Road; 704–365–1936), Frank and Peggy Dearien bought a restored country Victorian home with the requisite heart-of-pine floors, formal parlor, and 10-foot beaded ceilings. The next thing anyone knew, they were operating a bed-and-breakfast inn, serving bountiful breakfasts and, as a bit of lagniappe, evening desserts. The house is decorated in a soothing combination of blue and rose colors. A unique aspect of the decor is the collection of primitive paintings by John Gentry, Peggy's father, with his handwritten stories on the back personalizing each one. This inn has become very popular with business travelers, so it's always busy. You will need to make a reservation well ahead of time to stay here. Web site: www.bbonline.com/nc/homeplace.

The ***Inn Uptown,*** 129 North Poplar Street, in a restored 1890 home, has six guest rooms, some with gas-log fireplaces and some with whirlpool bath, and provides breakfast in the morning. The rooms are elegantly appointed and have such facilities as modem hookup for business travelers, but the inn's greatest attraction is its location within walking distance of many uptown restaurants and activities. Phone (704) 342–2800 or (800) 959–1990. Web site: www.innuptown.com.

The ***Mint Museum of Art,*** at 2730 Randolph Road, has exhibits that celebrate both local history and world culture. The name comes from the building's having been a branch of the United States Mint in the 1800s. That made sense back when the Piedmont was producing most of the country's gold.

In 1988 the museum created a huge stir with the exhibit "Ramses the Great: The Pharaoh and His Time," which featured, among other items, a gold statue of the pharaoh so large the building had to be modified to give him extra headroom. That exhibit is gone now, but a new permanent collection, "Spanish

Colonial Art," is attracting attention. Other permanent collections include American and European paintings, African artifacts, pre-Columbian art, costumes, and gold and currency of the Carolinas.

The Mint Museum Gift Shop specializes in offerings that reflect the museum exhibits. For instance, in connection with the pre-Columbian art exhibit, the shop sells replicas of pre-Columbian gold charms. Artifacts imported directly from African suppliers complement the museum's African displays. As the exhibits change, so do some of the gifts. A standard item in the shop that makes a nice gift is the miniature brass replica of Queen Charlotte's gold crown. A painting in which she wears the original crown hangs in a prominent position. The museum is open Tuesday from 10:00 A.M. to 10:00 P.M.; Wednesday through Saturday from 10:00 A.M. to 5:00 P.M.; and Sunday noon to 5:00 P.M. Closed Monday. Also closed Christmas and New Year's Day. Admission $6.00 adults, $5.00 senior citizens and students, $3.00 children. Includes Mint Museum of Craft and Design. Phone (704) 337–2000. Web site: www.mint museum.org.

The ***Mint Museum of Craft and Design,*** located in center city at 220 North Tryon Street, exhibits collections of ceramics, fiber, glass, metal, and wood, showing the development of handcrafts from the early days of practical use to contemporary studio art. The museum is open the same hours as the Mint Museum. Ticket price is also the same and includes both museums. Phone for both museums (704) 337–2000.

Another museum in the vicinity worth your attention is the ***Hezekiah Alexander Homesite*** and Museum of History, at 3500 Shamrock Drive. The Hezekiah Alexander house is the oldest dwelling still standing in Mecklenburg County. It was built of local quarry stone in 1774 and has been restored. Costumed guides lead tours of the house, log kitchen, barn, and gardens. The history museum displays local crafts and artifacts. Hezekiah was a delegate to the Fifth Provincial Congress and served on the committee that drafted the North Carolina State Constitution and Bill of Rights. The site has a number of fascinating details. The house is known as "The Rockhouse." Its doors are unusually low by today's standards, a feature intended to keep heat inside when people opened the doors. In the master bedroom a rope bed dominates the room. In this kind of bed a latticework of ropes supported the mattress. Every so often the ropes had to be tightened—giving rise to the old phrase, "Sleep tight." Don't even think about the origins of the rest of the phrase, "Don't let the bedbugs bite." The boys' rooms on the back side of the house also served as an army post during the Revolutionary War. And in the re-created spring house behind the house, you can see how milk and butter were cooled in the late 1700s. Open Tuesday through Saturday from 10:00 A.M. to

The Hezekiah Alexander Homesite

5:00 P.M., and Sunday from 1:00 to 5:00 P.M. Admission $6.00 adults, $4.00 senior citizens and students, $2.00 children ages six to twelve. Sundays free. Web site: www.charlottemuseum.org. For tour hours, call (704) 568–1774.

In uptown Charlotte at 301 North Tryon Street, the kids will enjoy ***Discovery Place,*** a hands-on science and technology museum where they can experience some close-up encounters with fish and birds, the natural sciences, and computers. One of the most impressive exhibits is the tropical rain forest, which fills three stories with plants, rocks, waterfalls, and appropriate wildlife. The exhibits related to the human body are interesting, too. One description claims that you learn about characteristics of the human body in a "hands-on manner," which could make you nervous if you didn't know about models and machines. Open Monday through Saturday from 9:00 A.M. to 6:00 P.M., and Sunday from 1:00 to 6:00 P.M. during summer. Closes earlier the rest of the year. Call (704) 372–6261 or (800) 935–0553 for rates to various areas. Web site: www.discoveryplace.org.

When you need nourishment, you have a surprisingly varied choice, especially when you consider that only a decade or so ago your choices were Southern homestyle and Southern homestyle plus a Greek restaurant with food remarkably similar to Southern homestyle. A recent local magazine noted that virtually every national cuisine is represented in Charlotte now, sometimes by several different restaurants. People actually travel to Charlotte just to eat. In the uptown area, ***Carpe Diem,*** 1535 Elizabeth Avenue, offers a variety of "new American" entrees, including vegetarian dishes, reflecting some Middle Eastern and Caribbean influences. The restaurant serves lunch and dinner. Phone (704) 377–7976. The ***Pewter Rose,*** at 1820 South Boulevard, is close to the southeast edge of town and not difficult to reach. Phone (704–332–8149). The restaurant is in a renovated textile mill. You'll feel comfortable here in either informal or business dress, and you'll find menu items ranging from fancy burgers to some outstanding salads and platters. Open every day for lunch and dinner.

Charlotte has a brewpub, ***Southend Brewery and Smokehouse,*** at 2100 South Boulevard, in the Atherton Mill Complex. This is a large establishment with the brewing vessels, enclosed in a glassed-in room, serving as the visual centerpiece of the space. The kitchen is also fully visible. The food is California style but also includes a number of smoked specialties, including ribs and sausages. They serve astonishingly large portions. One of the principals in this operation is said to have "invented" Bud Lite. Phone (704) 358–4677. Open 11:30 A.M. to 9:00 P.M. Sunday and Monday, closes at 10:00 P.M. Tuesday, Wednesday, and Thursday. Closes at 11:00 P.M. Friday and Saturday.

On the north side of Charlotte, on Highway 49, the botanical gardens at the University of North Carolina at Charlotte deserve a lot more attention than they receive. The ***UNC Charlotte Botanical Gardens*** have three parts: the McMillan Greenhouse, the VanLandingham Glen, and the Susie Harwood Garden. The greenhouse has one of the best collections of tropical orchids in the South, with something like 800 species. The tropical rain forest conservatory is a convincing simulation of a real rain forest. Other greenhouse rooms include a cactus room and a cool room. A great variety of carnivorous plants grow in a protected outside area by the greenhouses. The VanLandingham Glen started as a rhododendron garden in 1966 and has expanded to include more than 4,000 rhododendrons, mostly hybrids. Another interesting feature is the 1,000 species of Carolina-native plants growing in the gardens. The Harwood garden, with gravel paths, is more formal and includes exotic plants from around the world. The collection of Japanese maples is noteworthy, as is the winter garden. The greenhouse is open during normal business hours, but you can visit the gardens any time. The best way to find the gardens is to go onto campus through the main gate on Highway 49 and follow the signs to the visitor parking garage and ask for directions from there. For more information call (704) 547–2870.

About 20 miles west of Charlotte, in Gastonia, which you can reach quickly on I–85, the ***Schiele Museum of Natural History and Planetarium,*** at 1500 East Garrison Boulevard, attracts large numbers of visitors, especially schoolchildren, with its collection of North American mammals in habitat settings, a one-hundred-seat planetarium, a restored pioneer site of the 1700s, and a reconstructed Catawba Indian village. Other exhibits deal with everything from forestry to archaeology. A brochure maps out several self-guided tour suggestions for the outside grounds. Don't skip this one because it's popular; it has good reason for being so. Open Monday through Saturday from 9:00 A.M. to 5:00 P.M. and Sunday from 1:00 to 5:00 P.M. Call for planetarium show times, (704) 866–6908. Modest admission fee. To get there, take the New Hope Road exit from I–85 and follow signs. Web site: www.schielemuseum.org.

Places to Stay in the Lower Piedmont

CHARLOTTE

Comfort Inn–UNCC
I–85 Service Road
Charlotte 28269
(704) 598–0007
(888) 763–7733

Fairfield Inn by Marriott
7920 Arrowridge Boulevard
Charlotte 28273
(704) 319–5100
(800) 228–2800

Holiday Inn–Independence
3501 East Independence Boulevard
Charlotte 28205
(704) 537–1010
(800) 465–4329

La Quinta Inn
3100 South I–85 Service Road
Charlotte 28208
(704) 393–5306
(800) 531–5900

Red Roof Inn Coliseum
131 Red Roof Drive
Charlotte 28217
(704) 529–1020
(800) 843–7663

MT. AIRY

Comfort Inn
2136 Rockford Street
Mt. Airy 27030
(336) 789–2000
(800) 672–1667

Hampton Inn
2029 Rockford Street
Mt. Airy 27030
(336) 789–5999
(800) 565–5249

Mayberry Motor Inn
U.S. Bypass 52 North
Mt. Airy 27030
(336) 786–4109

SALISBURY

Days Inn
1810 Lutheran Synod Drive
Salisbury 28144
(704) 633–4211
(800) 329–7466

Hampton Inn
1001 Klumac Road
Salisbury 28144
(704) 637–8000
(800) 426–7866

Holiday Inn
520 South Jake Alexander Boulevard
Salisbury 28144
(704) 637–3100
(800) 465–4329

STATESVILLE

Fairfield Inn by Marriott
1505 East Broad Street
Statesville 28625
(704) 878–2091
(800) 228–2800

Hampton Inn
715 Sullivan Road
Statesville 28677
(704) 878–2721
(800) 426–7866

Holiday Inn I–77
1215 Garner Bagnal Boulevard
Statesville 28677
(704) 878–9691
(800) 465–4329

Places to Eat in the Lower Piedmont

CHARLOTTE

Amalfi's Pasta and Pizza
8542 University City Boulevard
Charlotte 28213
(704) 547–8651

THE LOWER PIEDMONT WEB SITES

Charlotte
www.visitcharlotte.org

Salisbury and Spencer
www.visitsalisburync.com

Lowe's Motor Speedway
www.lowesmotorspeedway.com

Statesville
www.visitstatesville.org

Gus' Sir Beef
4101 Monroe Street
(704) 377–3210
and 324 South Tryon
Charlotte 28205
(704) 347–5741

Providence Cafe
110 Perrin Place
Charlotte 28207
(704) 376–2008

Rheinland Haus
2418 Park Road
Charlotte 28203
(704) 376–3836

Thai Taste
324 East Boulevard
Charlotte 28203
(704) 332–0001

MT. AIRY

Aunt Bea's Barbecue
Highway 52 North
Mount Airy 27030
(336) 789–3050

Michael's Restaurant
1263 North South Street
Mount Airy 27030
(336) 789–5375

Ocie's Restaurant
730 West Lebanon Street
Mount Airy 27030
(336) 789–1211

Wagon Wheel Family Restaurant
845 West Pine Street
Mt. Airy 27030
(336) 789–4653

SALISBURY

Farmhouse Restaurant
1602 Jake Alexander Boulevard
Salisbury 28144
(704) 633–3276

The Wrenn House
115 South Jackson Street
Salisbury 28144
(704) 663–9978

STATESVILLE

The Black Angus Grille
125 North Center Street
Statesville 28625
(704) 872–4200

Carolina Bar-B-Q
213 Salisbury Road
Statesville 28677
(704) 873–5585

Gluttons
1539 East Broad Street
Statesville 28625
(704) 872–6951

Mayo's Italian Restaurant
123 North Center Street
Statesville 28625
(704) 872–5557

Sagebrush Steak House and Saloon
117 Turnersburg Road
Statesville 28625
(704) 873–246

The Mountains

The Western Mountains

Whatever you plan in the North Carolina mountains, allow about twice as much travel time as usual. Narrow roads wind through woodland and countryside, up hills so steep you sometimes feel as though your car will peel off the road backward, from hairpin turns into switchbacks followed by more curves. The squiggles don't all show on the maps, and the maps can't allow for the time it takes if you get behind a big truck with no place to pass for 50 miles. Decide ahead of time not to hurry; relax and absorb the peerless scenery.

One way to enjoy the panoramic views of mountains and valleys is by driving some part of the ***Blue Ridge Parkway.*** It stretches from Shenandoah National Park in Virginia along the Blue Ridge Mountains into the southern part of the Black Mountains, through the Craggies, the Pisgahs, the Balsams, and into the Great Smokies, a total of 469 miles. The maximum speed limit along the parkway is 45 miles per hour, but in reality, traffic is often slower. It doesn't take much arithmetic to figure that it would take a long time to cover the entire length of the parkway at 30 or 40 miles per hour. The best way to plan a trip is to alternate stretches of the parkway with drives on the

THE MOUNTAINS

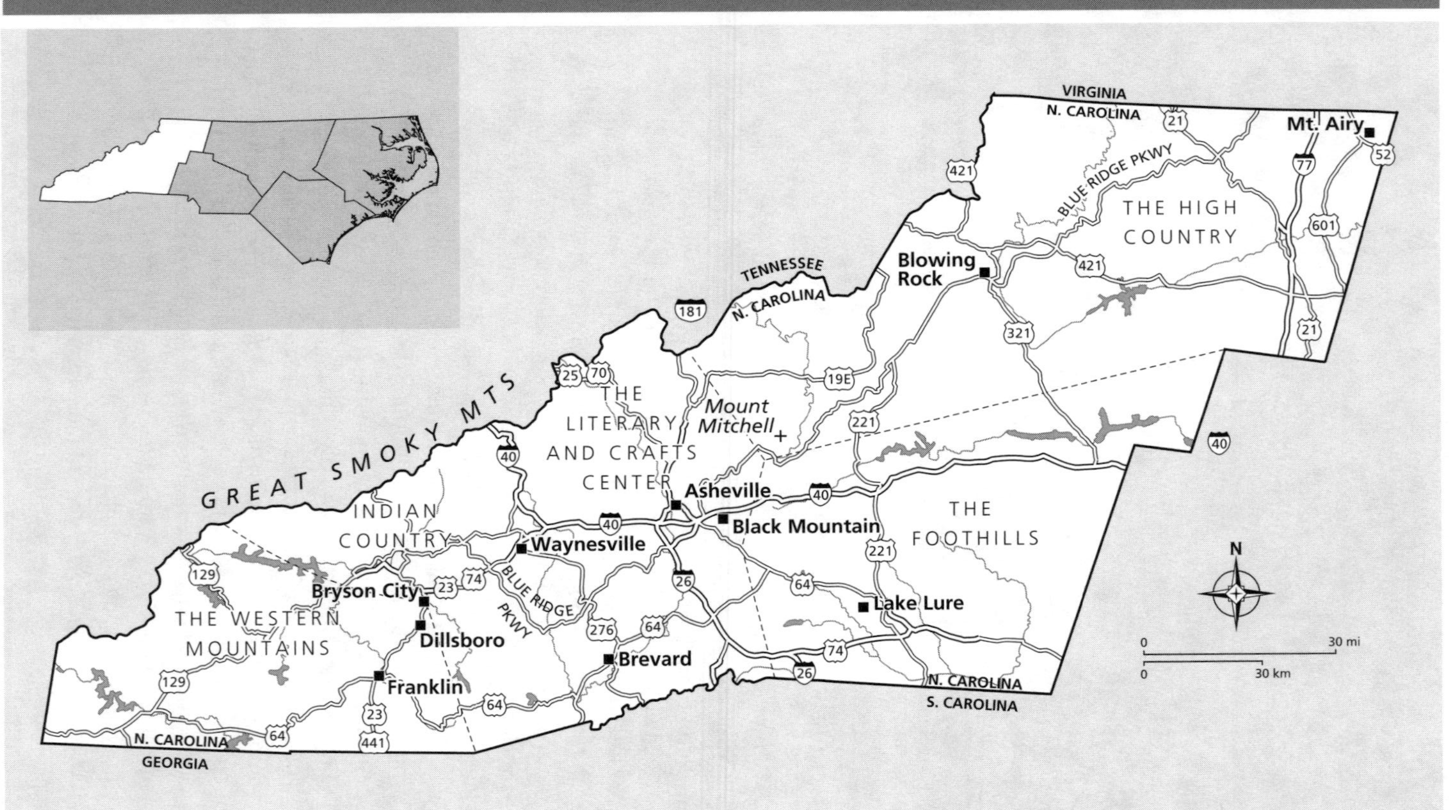

ANNUAL EVENTS IN THE MOUNTAINS

Asheville
Annual Spring Wildflower and Bird Pilgrimage
(early May)
(828) 251–6444

Biltmore Estate's Annual Festival of Flowers
(early May)
(828) 274–6333
or (800) 543–2961

Black Mountain Sourwood Festival
(mid August)
(828) 669–2300
or (800) 669–2301

Blowing Rock Independence Day Festival
July 4
(828) 295–7851

Valle Crucis
Annual Apple Festival
(late October)
(828) 963–4609

roads you can reach by turning off along the way. Crossovers from the parkway are marked with mileposts that are numbered and named.

Before you get on the parkway, spend some time enjoying the Nantahala National Forest, Nantahala Gorge, and Bryson City in the mountains. ***Randolph House,*** 223 Freymont Road, Bryson City, built in 1895 by Amos Frye, is run today by his niece, Ruth Adams, and her husband, Bill, as a homey country inn. As Ruth tells it, Amos once had owned all the timber around, but when the government decided to declare most of the area national forestland, Amos had to sell. He kept the right to lumber out the sold acreage for a limited time; to get his money's worth, he set to building, using wood, of course, as fast as he could. Randolph House was one of the results.

Because the house is furnished with family antiques that have always been there, things don't all match, leaving you with the feeling that if you blink hard you'll see old Amos there in the worn leather chair. The inn's dinners are strictly by reservation because Ruth hates waste, and when you make the reservation, you choose from a list of entrees planned for that night. The cuisine might be called "Southern Gourmet," featuring choices such as Cornish hen in orange sauce and trout in pecan sauce, served perhaps with a classic Southern squash casserole and a dessert of Three Hundred Dollar Chocolate Cake or Mile High Lemon Pie. Bill maintains a nice wine list. Although the Adamses are in their eighties, they continue their hospitality with few changes. The inn is open April through October (828–488–3472 or 800–480–3472). Web site: www.randolphhouse.com.

To take in some of the rugged mountain scenery without driving the winding roads, you might board the ***Great Smoky Mountains Railroad*** at the depot on Depot Street in Bryson City. The tracks were first laid in the 1890s and rail transport made it possible to establish a vigorous logging industry in the mountains. Eventually highways replaced trains and by 1988 the state of North Carolina had taken over the tracks in this region and leased a 53 mile stretch to the Great Smoky Mountains Railroad, which runs a variety of excursion trips through the mountains. Although the main offices and depot are in Dillsboro, you can also board at Bryson City except in winter. All reservations and arrangements go through the Dillsboro facility (see p. 162). Phone (800) 872–4681. Web site: www.gsmr.com.

The ***Scenic Model Railroad Museum,*** 100 Greenlee Street, Bryson City (866–914–5200; Web site: www.smokymtntrains.com), next to the Great Smoky Mountains Railroad Depot, honors the area's railroading history with a 24-by-45-foot model layout, with more than a mile of track on three levels over which six trains run at once. The layout has a working roundtable with roundhouse and a 5-foot waterfall. The model includes a freight yard with at least 400 cars, a dozen animated scenes, and more than sixty buildings made by hand, not assembled from packages. This collection has 7,000 Lionel engines, cars, and accessories. Model railroad enthusiasts travel to Bryson City specifically to visit the museum. A retail store is attached to the museum as well as an activity center for children. This facility is open Monday through Saturday, 8:30 A.M. to 5:30 P.M. In January and February it is open only Fridays and Saturdays. Admission is $8.00 adults, $5.00 children under twelve, free for children under three.

From Bryson City drive 9 miles southwest on U.S. Highway 19 to ***Nantahala Outdoor Center*** at the Nantahala Gorge. The outdoor center attracts the outdoors crowd, especially rafters and hikers. This is a congenial place to hire a guide and all the equipment you need for a white-water rafting trip down the Nantahala River. It's also great for fishing, picnicking, and hiking. Part of the fun is watching the serious rafters, who, as one observer put it, seem to have a continuing contest to see who can show up in the most worn, mismatched, clothes-don't-matter outfit. The ***River's End Restaurant,*** right by the river, has been a popular eating place with hikers and rafters for years. Some of the most popular recipes have been bound into a cookbook, *River Runners Special,* with each recipe listed for difficulty (Class I, II, III, and so on) like the rapids on the river. Vegetarian lentil mushroom soup is Class II; amaretto cream pie is Class IV.

At ***River's End*** you'll feel perfectly comfortable in your mismatched hiking clothes and down vest, sitting at a rustic table looking out over the river while you gobble a hearty serving of spicy beef stew with the restaurant's spe-

It Was Inevitable

In his younger years a good friend of mine spent most of his free time at the Nantahala Outdoor Center (they call it NOC). Several of his brothers were river guides over the years, and they finally convinced their mother, a good-natured Pittsburgh lady, to venture onto the river on a raft. She listened to the lecture about keeping her feet pointed downstream if she fell off, but she didn't take it very seriously. And she buckled into her life vest without protest but didn't take *it* very seriously either. She listened to the paddling instructions without getting especially serious. But she did know what to do if the raft dumped her off.

It did. And that nice lady ended up floating rapidly in icy water, with her feet pointed downsteam, bouyed by her flotation vest, shouting to her sons at the top of her lungs, "I'll never forgive you for this."

cial herb bread. Just across the river, ***Joe's Riverside Café*** is the place for quick meals and snacks. ***Relia's Garden,*** near the center of the property, caters to private groups and people taking NOC instruction. With a view of the mountains rather than the river, this restaurant sits in a field on the hill across from the garden, landscaped with terraced gardens of herbs, unusual vegetables, and exotic plants. A walk through the gardens crushes fragrant bits of mint and thyme underfoot.

Staff members of the Nantahala Outdoor Center, from guides to cooks, tend to return year after year, as do visitors. The Appalachian Trail, crossing right through the center, brings many serious hikers. Moreover, the presence of the family that started the center is still much in evidence. Relia's Garden, for instance, is named for Arelia, wife of the founder and for many years director of food service. Her plants fill the terrace gardens. Spending time here feels like being part of an extended family or a close community. It is special. The center, its lodging, restaurants, and programs operate from roughly mid-March to November 1, depending on the weather. For information about operating hours when you plan to be here, call (800) 232–7238 for all attractions at NOC. Web site: www.noc.com.

Just a few miles (a long walk or a short ride) beyond the outdoor center on US 19, ***Nantahala Village*** offers a less strenuous and very agreeable alternative approach to the river, the gorge, and the forest. Built before the whitewater craze as a rustic resort in the woods, Nantahala Village has simple rooms in the inn and a variety of cozy cabins built of logs or native stone, with knotty-pine interiors. The cabins have kitchens; some have fireplaces. The original inn burned down in 1997, but it has been replaced by a new structure with classic architecture.

AUTHOR'S FAVORITE PLACES IN THE MOUNTAINS

- Nantahala Outdoor Center
- Folk Art Center
- New River State Park
- Hot Springs
- Carl Sandburg Home National Historic Site
- Mt. Mitchell State Park
- North Carolina Mining Museum
- Sylva
- Chimney Rock Park
- Waynesville

The dining room in the inn serves an interesting combination of traditional foods—chicken, beef, and so on—popular entrees lower in fat and emphasizing the flavors of fresh herbs. The owners are committed to keeping the original atmosphere and setting but wanted to update the dining room menu to include vegetarian and lighter fare. They offer these options along with the traditional southern mountain favorites. They're also committed to getting people into appropriate accommodations. For instance, they wouldn't put a family with tiny children into a cabin that has a deck jutting out over a cliff or an elderly person into a room that requires a lot of walking to reach. Nantahala Village is usually open from mid-March to January 1, but weather could change this. It's a good idea to call ahead (828–488–2826, or outside North Carolina 800–438–1507). Web site: www.nvrc.com.

Indian Country

Picking up the Blue Ridge Parkway at Cherokee brings you to some decisions about the kind of tourist you mean to be. The town, in the ***Qualla Boundary Cherokee Indian Reservation*** where U.S. Highways 441 and 19 meet, maintains several features dedicated to preserving and explaining the history of the Cherokee nation, which was nearly wiped out by the infamous "Trail of Tears" forced walk in 1838, when the U.S. government tried to relocate all Indians to west of the Mississippi River. Some of the Cherokees escaped the march by hiding in the hills.

Eventually they were able to return to this area, where they were once the powerful Cherokee nation. Their story is told in ***Unto These Hills,*** an outdoor drama played by a cast of 130 people, beginning between 8:00 and 9:00 P.M.

nightly, except Sunday, from mid-June through late August, in an outdoor theater that seats 2,800 people. The program is presented by the Cherokee Historical Association with support from the Theatre Arts Section of the North Carolina Arts Council and funds appropriated by the North Carolina General Assembly. The story begins with Spanish explorer Hernando DeSoto's arrival in 1540 and climaxes with the Trail of Tears exodus. Many of the players are descendants of the Cherokee who lived the story. Moderately high admission fee. Box office (828–497–2111) open from 9:00 A.M. to 10:00 P.M. during the summer season and from 9:00 A.M. to 4:30 P.M. in the off-season. The story and performances are frankly moving; it's not uncommon to see people in the audience cry. Web site: www.untothesehills.com.

Unfortunately, activities of this caliber are surrounded by the tourist-tacky pseudo-Indian concessions that seem to plague the areas around Indian populations across the country. The matter is further complicated by the addition of ***Harrah's Cherokee Casino*** (800–427–7247; Web site: www.Harrahs.com) several years ago. The casino, which has 60,000 square feet of electronic gambling area with 2,800 video machines, three restaurants, and a 1,500-seat theater, attracts people by the busload. The area now has at least one hundred motels, hotels, cabins, and campgrounds, all pretty much one right next to another. Harrah's is an enterprise of the Cherokee tribe. Trying to sort out the authentic from the merely exploitative can be depressing. You can count on quality at the ***Oconaluftee Indian Village,*** sponsored by the Cherokee Historical Association. The village is on the Cherokee Indian Reservation. It is a living replication of a 1750s Cherokee village and shows you Indians practicing their historical crafts of basket making, pottery, canoe building, food preparations, and weaponry and, perhaps even more important, explains the culture within which these activities proceeded. Tours begin every fifteen minutes, but you are not locked into them, and there is plenty of time for exploring, photographing, and questioning. Open from 9:00 A.M. to 5:30 P.M., May through October. Moderately high admission charge (828–497–2111). Web site: www.oconalufteevillage.com.

Qualla Arts and Crafts Mutual, Inc., the most successful Indian-owned and -operated craft cooperative in the country, representing 350 Cherokee crafters, at the entrance of the *Unto These Hills* theater on US 441, offers you an opportunity to buy genuine Indian beadwork, baskets, wood carvings, pots, masks, and the like. Cherokee work is displayed in separate rooms from that of other tribes. Open daily 8:00 A.M. to 4:30 P.M. These hours may vary slightly seasonally. It's a good idea to call ahead (828–497–3103).

Finally, the ***Museum of the Cherokee Indian*** displays traditional arts and crafts and offers a video on the history of the nation, along with displays of tools and various accounts of the Trail of Tears journey. Computer-generated images and holographic imaging bring scenes to life. Open daily from 9:00 A.M. to 5:30 P.M., later during the summer. Moderate admission charged. Closed Thanksgiving, Christmas, and New Year's Day. For full information about attractions call (828) 497–3481.

The Cherokee Visitor Center on the reservation is a good source of information about the village, crafts co-op, and museum. Phone (800) 438–1601. Web site: www.cherokee-nc.com.

Cherokee is considered the gateway to the Great Smoky Mountains, and it seems important to mention, however briefly, the ***Great Smoky Mountains National Park,*** established in 1934 partly with money donated by John D. Rockefeller. The park merits a full book in itself: Elevations climb as you move along the northeast; plant life, wildlife, and scenery invite superlatives; the bears and the weather are unpredictable. About half the park falls in Tennessee, but North Carolinians, figuring there's plenty for all, forgive that. Staying on the North Carolina side, you'll find enough hiking, fishing, and camping to last most of your life without being repetitious. There are several visitor centers in the park. For information, call (616) 436–5615. It's a Tennessee number, but it's also park headquarters and the best place to start when you need advance information. The park is said to have attracted more than ten million visitors annually in recent years, mostly in the summer, although with about 500,000 acres to explore, there'd seem to be enough room for everyone. You'll probably enjoy your visit more if you avoid the peak summer season.

Southeast of Cherokee and Bryson City, where US 23/74 and US 441 come together, the little town of ***Dillsboro*** stretches along the banks of the Tuckasegee River. This community, with a population of only a couple hundred residents, is working actively to develop awareness of its history and to offer visitors local arts and crafts. More than fifty shops sell pottery, handmade jewelry, unusual gifts with a regional theme, wood carvings, metal works, and paintings.

This is also the ***Great Smoky Mountains Railroad*** main depot, ticket office, and boarding center. The excursion line, with both steam and diesel engines, began running in 1988, on what had been the Murphy Branch Line, dating back to 1891. The trains travel through 53 miles of track in the Western North Carolina mountains, going through two tunnels and crossing twenty-five bridges.

You Ought to Be in Pictures

The Great Smoky Mountains Railroad trains have been used in several movies, including *The Fugitive, My Fellow Americans, Digging to China, Paradise Falls,* and *Forces of Nature.*

The Wolf Chooses You

During one Gourmet Dinner Train trip, a couple celebrating their anniversary requested boxes to pack up the remains of generous servings of duck they were too full to finish. The woman said she would take it home to feed her wolves. She kept a dozen in a fenced field behind the house, she said. These were wolves that had sprung from dog–wolf unions. As other guests in the car began contributing their leftovers to Operation Wolf Feed, the woman went on to explain that she didn't go out to acquire wolves, they came to her house. "You don't choose the wolf," she said. "The wolf chooses you."

Great Smoky Mountains Railroad schedules a tremendous variety of trips, ranging from the Gourmet Dinner Train and Mystery Theatre Dinner Train to autumn scenic excursions and a Rapid Transit experience with Nantahala Outdoor Center, which offers a combination of a white-water raft trip and a 30-mile scenic train ride to explore the Nantahala River. In December a Santa Express Train geared to children welcomes the Christmas season. Schedules and offerings change each year. For specifics, call (800) 872–4681. Web site: www.gsmr.com.

Right next to the railroad depot, at the ***Applegate Inn,*** 163 Hemlock Street (800–353–0377; Web site: www.applegatebed-breakfast.com), Andree and John Faulk offer twelve really unusual guest rooms, each with private bath, some with whirlpool, refrigerator, microwave, big-screen TV, and fireplace. From the outside, all you see is a series of single-story buildings and a screened gazebo on the creek. Inside, the rooms range from the John Deere Room to the Stationmaster's Room. In the John Deere Room you find a collection of pictures and memorabilia related to the John Deere tractor, with green the dominant color. Even the guest robes hanging in the bathroom are green. And you can check the accuracy of the colors against the real, rebuilt John Deere tractor standing out front that John Faulk uses to take people on old-fashioned hayrides in the evening. The Stationmaster's room is filled with train memorabilia. The largest rooms have private entrances; the smaller ones cluster around a living room, with a fireplace, TV, and some of Andree's personal collections, including a slew of miniature clocks. The Faulks say they offer guests a sense of what living in the area was like in earlier and simpler times. A bountiful breakfast on the gazebo is part of that offering.

People go to the ***Jarrett House,*** 100 Haywood Street (800–972–5623; Web site: www.jarretthouse.com), to eat, but the old inn also has eighteen guest rooms, each with private bath. Jarrett House is famous for its food, which includes huge servings of country ham or fried chicken, your choice, accompanied by unlimited amounts of old Southern classics—green beans, slaw, pickled beets, baked apples, potatoes—and heaps of little light biscuits. The proprietors, Jim and Jean Hartbarger, and Jim and Jean's sons, Scott and Buzz, with their wives, Mary and Sharon, work actively in the community to revitalize a sense of history and continue the inn's tradition of hospitality. Jarrett House, standing on the corner in the center of town, has been an inn since back in the 1800s. The inn opened at the Mount Beulah Hotel in 1884 and was a stopping place for trains of the Western North Carolina Railroad traveling between Asheville and Murphy. The inn's name came from Frank Jarrett, who bought the place in 1894, when tourists began coming to the area to get away from summer heat in the lowlands. The Hartbargers have kept the place fastidiously clean, white on the outside, with such antiques as old sewing machines and oak pieces in the halls upstairs. In the downstairs Victorian parlor, an old Bacon & Raven piano that belonged to Jim's grandmother holds pride of place in one corner. The inn is open May through December; the dining room is open April through December.

Just fifteen or twenty minutes farther east via US 23/74, the town of ***Sylva,*** which once would've been only a quick stop on the way to other attractions, has become the kind of community where people wish they could live, and it's full of quirky and interesting spots, beginning with the historic downtown area, which has been in the process of revitalization since about 1998. On Main Street, a variety of thriving shops—outfitters, bookstores, music stores, and specialty shops—attract both local and tourist traffic. When you get into the downtown area, park. Traffic tends to be slow because the streets are narrow, and you can walk the town easily, to see more with less aggravation.

Two old structures hold special interest, and you'll have no trouble seeing either one. First is the ***Hooper House,*** 773 West Main Street (828–586–2155; Web site: www.mountainlovers.com), where offices of the Jackson County Chamber of Commerce, the Jackson County Travel and Tourism Authority, Sylva Partners in Renewal, and the ***Jackson County Museum*** are headquartered. The building is open daily Monday through Saturday from 9:30 A.M. to 5:30 P.M. and 1:00 to 4:00 P.M. on Sunday. This Queen Anne Victorian structure was designed from plans that came from Sears, Roebuck & Company. Completed in 1906, the building became the home of Dr. Delos Dexter Hooper, one of the first medical doctors in Jackson County .

It had fallen into disrepair and was scheduled for demolition when a group of local citizens in 1999 began a drive to raise money for its restoration, which cost more than $347,000. Much of the passion for the project came from Julie Spiro, the chamber's director and a great-niece of the doctor. She not only worked on fund-raising but also did much of the physical work on the build-

The Jackson County Courthouse

ing herself. Renovation involved scraping away fourteen layers of old paint, analyzing and duplicating the colors of the original coats, and removing more than 800 nails from the walls.

On a hill above Main Street, the ***Jackson County Courthouse*** attracts photographers and fitness nuts. It's a 1913 neoclassic revival building that sits so high above the town it appears on a foggy day to be floating. If you want to climb from the street to the entrance, you've got 107 steps to negotiate. Locals say this is the most photographed court house in North Carolina.

Should all that climbing steps and walking along Main Street work up your appetite, Sylva has a number of good places to eat. ***Lulu's Café*** at 612 West Main Street (828–586–9096) has attracted not only local diners but also those from nearby towns with an offbeat menu the owners call "eclectic." They emphasize fresh ingredients and offer everything from black bean vegetarian chili to grilled salmon with mustard and sour cream sauce on saffron couscous. Sandwiches include a white albacore (dolphin free) tuna salad and a huge ground chuck burger on a French bun. A children's menu offers peanut butter and jelly on whole wheat bread from Annie's Bakery and pasta dishes. Lulu's maintains an extensive wine and beer list. The restaurant serves lunch and dinner, Monday through Saturday, beginning at 11:30 A.M. By the way, there's no Lulu. Never was.

Walking a block up the hill from Main Street, on Spring Street, you'll come to ***Spring St. Café,*** 3 East Jackson Street (828–586–1800), a restaurant tucked into the bottom floor of the building that houses City Lights Book Store. It features organic produce, locally raised trout, hormone-free meats, and fresh seafood. The menu here is also widely varied, with such choices as Indonesian Gado-Gado, roast turkey sandwich, and jumbo shrimp on a rosemary skewer. The cafe serves locally roasted coffees, bakes its own desserts, and has good beer and wine lists. It has two entrances, one from the sidewalk on the hill, where there's a small outdoor serving area for nice weather, and another down the stairs from the bookstore above. Work by local artists lines the stairway and walls in the restaurant. Spring St. Café is open for lunch and dinner 11:00 A.M. to 9:30 P.M., Tuesday through Saturday, Sunday brunch 10:30 A.M. to 2:30 P.M.

In contrast to the relative sophistication of Spring St. Café and Lulu's, the ***Coffee Shop,*** 385 West Main Street (828–586–2013), almost at the edge of town, is one of those places where working people eat, day after day. Men meet in small groups early in the morning or at lunch for a little gossip to break up the work day, and old-timers come in knowing a waitress has started getting their regular order ready as soon as she sees them park. The restaurant has been in operation since 1927 and probably doesn't look much different now than it did then, with red booth seating and round stools at the counter, which stands in front of the grill and stove burners. This is a meat-and-three place, specializing in such meals as meatloaf with green beans, mashed potatoes, and slaw. You can get a sandwich here and a slice of homemade pie. The restaurant serves breakfast, lunch, and dinner from 6:00 A.M. to 8:00 P.M. Monday through Friday, until 4:00 P.M. Saturday. Closed Sunday.

Both Lulu's and Spring St. Café, as well as more than thirty other restaurants and stores in North Carolina and Georgia, sell baked goods from ***Annie's Naturally,*** 506 West Main Street (828–586–9096). This bakery produces its goodies in a large, commercial French stone-hearth oven in the basement of the building. At street level customers come in steadily to buy coffee, croissants, cookies, breads, pies, and cakes. All the products are made with organic

The Usual

"He's coming now," a Coffee Shop waitress called to a cook behind the counter. The cook began frying a couple of eggs, sunny side up, poured a mug of coffee, popped two slices of bread into the toaster, and spooned applesauce into a side dish. By the time an elderly man in a plaid flannel shirt got inside the door, his breakfast was set up for him in front of the end stool at the counter.

and natural ingredients, with no artificial sweeteners, fats, or preservatives. One of the most popular items is a multigrain bread. Other choices include an authentic French baguette, focaccia, Jewish Challah bread, and a huge assortment of pastries. The retail shop is open Tuesday through Saturday from 8:00 A.M. to 3:00 P.M. and sells lunch sandwiches as well as the baked items.

Culturally, this area is influenced by the Tuckasegee River, which runs through it. It is popular for trout fishing, rafting, kayaking, and canoeing and has the advantage of being gentle enough, at least in areas, to be appropriate for young children and beginners who'd like to try rafting. The main fish in the river are rainbow and brown trout, which are stocked, as well as catfish and small mouth bass near the dam at Dillsboro.

In addition to a number of standard motels, ***Mountain Brook Fireplace Cottages,*** 208 Mountain Brook Road (828–586–4329; Web site: www.mountainbrook.com) has twelve cottages, each with fully equipped electric kitchen, private bath, and fireplace; some with whirlpool and sauna. The proprietors of Mountain Brook have pulled off an unusual accomplishment. They've taken a group of cottages built in the woods in the 1930s and renovated them without losing the rural feel of the original buildings. No two are alike. They're built variously of log, stone, brick, and frame. The cottages called "Romancers" have a whirlpool-sauna area and a bedroom from which you can see the fireplace in the living room. Guests in all cottages may use the whirlpool spa and cedar sauna in a separate building surrounded by mountain laurel and rhododendron. In another building, the game room includes a pool table, pinball machine, some sports equipment, board games and a lending library. Other amenities on the property include a picnic area, charcoal grills, nature trails, and a stocked trout pond. You don't need a license to fish here. The Mountain Brook folks provide bait and tackle, charge a nominal sum for each fish you catch, and expect you to keep the fish, not throw them back. Rates include wood for the fireplace.

Just south of Sylva, on State Highway 107, Western Carolina University is another significant influence on the area. For visitors, a stop at ***Mountain Heritage Center,*** on the university's campus, provides a detailed and graphic glimpse of the region's history. A permanent exhibit depicts the migration of the Scottish and English migrants whose descendants came from Northern Ireland to settle in Western North Carolina. Other exhibits are built around such themes as early mountain skills and culture, mountain trout, and Appalachian handicrafts. A collection of thousands of western North Carolina artifacts from mountain families illustrates old mountain life. The center also publishes books, tapes, and shorter printed material about mountain culture based on academic research. On the last Saturday in September, 35,000 visitors congregate in ***Cullowhee*** for

Mountain Heritage Day, a celebration of music, storytelling, food, and crafts. The center is open, free of charge, Monday through Friday, 8:00 A.M. to 5:00 P.M., Sunday 2:00 to 5:00 P.M., from June through October. The center operates on the university's holiday schedule. Call (828) 227–7129 for specifics.

At Cullowhee, the ***River Lodge Bed and Breakfast,*** 619 Roy Tritt Road (828–293–5431), sits at a bend in the river, with views of the Blue Ridge Mountains on all sides. The lodge was built from one-hundred-year-old hand hewn logs found in old barns and cabins around the area. In addition to six guest rooms, it has a large greatroom dominated by a stone fireplace and decorated with antiques and native American artifacts. It's filled with books and art and games such as chess and billiards. Each of the guest rooms is decorated according to a mountain theme, such as mallards in flight and the trout and creel. A hideaway suite with a private entrance has a whirlpool for two and a cathedral ceiling. But the real pleasure of this place comes with the innkeepers, Cathy and Anthony Sgambato, a couple of Italians originally from the Bronx who intended to open an inn in the Adirondacks and ended up here instead. They love to laugh and tell stories, and their breakfasts go beyond the ubiquitous grits and sausage to include such treats as lox and bagels, sugar waffles, fresh fruits, and ham.

And almost directly across the road at the ***Tuckaseigee Valley Vacation Cabins,*** at 897 Roy Tritt Road (828–293–5131 or 888–906–7409; Web site: www.tuckaseigeevalleycabins.com. Each of the cottages is decorated thematically, in a Western motif or Native American, for instance, and has a fully equipped kitchen, lots of sleeping space, a fireplace, and a television. These are fairly new structures, designed to look rustic. The property is hilly, with lots of grass and fruit trees that were once used by the family on the homestead.

A Mystery Carved in Stone

Lying in a grassy field about 7 miles from Cullowhee, a big gray soapstone boulder known as the Judaculla Rock mystifies locals and visitors alike. It is covered with markings that people have variously identified as stick figures, pictographs, and hieroglyphics. The rock is named after a giant Cherokee monster, and one popular legend is that he made the marks when he jumped off a mountain. Others speculate that the rock marks the location of a hidden treasure, that it is a space aliens' map, or that it was an ancient community bulletin board. To find the rock, drive about 4 miles south from Cullowhee on US 107. Turn left at State Highway 1737, Caney Fork Road, and follow the signs about 3 miles more, through a farm where the rock is protected by an open shed. A wooden observation deck is in place as well.

Although the river for which the cabins are named is the Tuckasegee, the owner of the cabins has retained the Cherokee spelling, "Tuckaseigee." It can mean "long man" or "slow turtle." Other accommodations in the area include an old inn outside the little community of Balsam, which isn't much more than a dot on the map. ***Balsam Mountain Inn*** (800–224–9498; Web site: www.balsaminn.com), just off US 23/74, has 50 guests rooms in an old frame inn. Since 1908 the three-story frame building has stood at 3,500 feet on a ridge above Balsam Gap, just off the Blue Ridge Parkway. Early in the 1990s, Merrily Teasley rescued it from gradual deterioration. Teasley followed guidelines for restoring historic buildings, preserved the beaded board walls, and restored the hardwood floors. (The inn is designated a National Historic Place.) But she took care to include modern essentials such as a good elevator, efficient plumbing, private baths with showers or claw-foot tubs, and quality beds. The inn is decorated throughout with strong colors—lots of maroon and purple, large-print flowered fabrics—with eclectic displays of art, sculpture, and crafts in the halls. Teasley's daughter, Noel, who has had broad experience in restaurants, serves as inn chef, producing the kinds of appetizers, entrees, and desserts that prompt diners to share tastes around the table. Mountain trout stuffed with shitake mushrooms is a good example of a simple but flavorful treatment. Some Saturday nights include live performances from Songwriters in the Round, small groups of both well-known writers and newcomers. Wine and beer are available both with meals and at the front desk for sipping at one of the two fireplaces in the parlor or in a rocker on the long porches. Early risers will find coffee available in the library, which has more than 2,000 volumes, mostly from Teasley's personal collection. Balsam Mountain Inn is a short drive from Sylva, Dillsboro, and Waynesville.

Almost in the inn's backyard, though you can't see or hear it because it's at a lower elevation, ***Moonshine Creek Campground,*** 7 Moonshine Creek Trail (828–586–6666), offers RV sites, tent sites, and camping cabins. The RV sites have water, electricity, and sewer. Tent sites have water and electricity. The first thing you notice is how quite everything is. Moonshine Creek Campground is tucked into a wooded cove off a rural road that winds up and down several hills and around curves from US 441, between Sylva and Waynesville. The facility includes a sparkling clean bathhouse and laundry facilities, as well as a children's playground, camp store, and walking trails. The sites are level and well maintained, with woodland growth providing an unusual degree of privacy between sites. The tent sites are clustered in a grassy creekside area a bit apart from the RV sites. One RV site, more secluded than the others, sits on a rise next to a waterfall with its stream running down to the creek, so you hear the continuous sound of flowing water. The creek is good for fishing. The camping cabins are simple wood shelters with doors, windows, and beds, but no other facilities inside. The campground also offers a few furnished rentals with bathrooms and kitchens. It is open April 1 to November 1.

From this area it's a drive of approximately 30 miles down Highway 107 to ***Cashiers,*** a community of fewer than 2,000 people at an elevation of nearly 3,500 feet. The drive will seem longer because the road is narrow, steep, and twisting. But it's also beautiful, as is Cashiers itself, with scenic views of even higher mountains, the Blue Ridge Parkway, waterfalls, and multifingered Lake Glenville. This is the home of many waterfalls, including ***Whitewater Falls,*** which has a total drop of 800 feet. Kevin Adams, author of *North Carolina Waterfalls—Where to Find Them, How to Photograph Them,* calls Whitewater Falls "the most spectacular cascade east of the Rockies." The Whitewater Falls Scenic Area turns of State Highway 281. This is also home of the smallest U.S. post office, still standing on Whiteside Cove Road. It was in operation from 1903 to 1953.

Just north of Cashiers, off Highway 107, you'll find a bed-and-breakfast as different from standard motels as it could be, and as unlikely for the area as well. ***Innisfree Victorian Inn and Garden House*** (write to P.O. Box 469, Glenville 28736; 828–743–2946) has five rooms in the main house and four in the garden house, each with private bath, some with Jacuzzi or garden tubs for two, some with fireplace. The garden house rooms have wet bar, private phone, and TV with VCR.

This is not a place where you expect to find an old Victorian structure. In fact, although Innisfree is the perfect representation of old Victorian mansions, it is actually a new building. Henry Hoche bought the land in 1981, had the inn built there, and opened for guests in 1990.

Innisfree is not at all about the comforts of home. Home was never like this. Innisfree is a place of luxury, romance, and exotic furnishings, a special-occasion place. Depending on your room, you have window or veranda views of the mountains and valleys, elaborate bed and window treatments, fine art, and Victorian-period furnishings. In the Garden House you can look out over the green landscape from the showers and tubs. All these rooms carry the names of Victorian writers, and their books are included in each room, so that, for instance, you can lounge in Lord Tennyson's suite and read his work. Breakfast at the inn is served by candlelight, on fine china, accented by antique silver pieces in the room. The inn's common rooms are filled with collections of crystal, silver, and Victiorian-esque decor. Innisfree overlooks Lake Glenville, in the Blue Ridge Mountains—the highest lake east of the Rockies. The place seems isolated but is close to the attractions of Cashiers, as well as places for hiking, horseback riding, waterfalls and boating. The landscape in this area is filled with Christmas tree farms, which have replaced the many fields of cabbage that used to be found here.

Even though it is away from major highways, in a remote mountain setting, Cashiers has its share of local crafts and specialty shops and tourist attractions. During the peak season, May through October, the area is very, very popular, which means lots of people.

In the off-season, some of the businesses won't be open, but your experience will be much more off the beaten path.

High Hampton Inn and Country Club, on Highway 107 South in Cashiers (800–334–2551 or 828–743–2411), has been known as *the* mountain getaway in this area for three generations. In its beginnings, the place was where Wade Hampton, a South Carolinian from the days of the Civil War and then governor of South Carolina, came to escape the heat of Columbia, South Carolina. In the early 1920s, the McKee family bought the property from the Hampton family and opened it as an inn. A third generation of McKees continues the operation. High Hampton Inn is known for rustic decor, massive buffets that include fried chicken and trout, good golf and tennis, and myriad outdoor activities such as hiking and swimming. Accommodations include more than one hundred rooms and cottages. Most of them are quite simple, and the family boast about not changing what has been attracting faithful guests for years. Something else that hasn't changed: Guests are assigned a table which is their spot for the duration of the stay, and men must wear coats and ties for dinner.

From here you can drive to ***Brevard*** on US 64. The town's big claims to fame are its proximity to the Pisgah National Forest, the many waterfalls in the area, and the Brevard Music Center. ***Brevard Music Center,*** 1000 Probart Street (888–384–8682 or 828–884–2011; Web site: www.brevardmusic.org), holds a festival each summer from late June through mid-August during which almost nightly concerts, from opera to chamber music to jazz, are offered. At the center, which has been operating since 1936, 400 students, ages fourteen to post-college, study and play with professional musicians each summer. The

No Shades of Gray

Watch for the Belgian white squirrels scampering up trees and across roofs around town. This area is noted for these squirrels, which are not albinos—they have normal eyes—and don't seem interested in other kinds of squirrels.

oh tannenbaum

Around Christmas time each year, the Aluminum Tree and Aesthetically Challenged Ornament Museum and Research Center invites visitors to see their collection of aluminum Christmas trees. The trees come in all sizes and colors, including pink, and some are thematically decorated: the Elvis tree, the bathroom tree, the Jim and Tammy Faye Baker tree, for instance. The collection has more than sixty trees and keeps growing as people find old oddities in the attic. The museum doesn't have a permanent home, but you can find out how to see the collection by calling curator and founder Stephen Paul Jackson at (828) 884–5304.

main auditorium, Whittington-Pfohl Auditorium, is an open structure that seats 1,800 people, with additional seating on the lawn on both sides of the building. In good weather, audience members are invited to bring a bottle of wine and a picnic basket to enjoy on the lawn. Concerts are held also in several smaller auditoriums in the grounds.

On Main Street, Brevard's center, you'll find a variety of specialty shops, an antiques mall, a variety of eating places, and a fine arts co-op. The co-op, ***Number 7 Arts,*** run by the ***Transylvania County Arts Council,*** has showrooms at 7 East Main Street (828–883–2294; Web site: www.number7arts.com). The work of the artisans includes pottery, jewelry, wood, and fabrics, often reflecting a western North Carolina mountain influence. The shop is open Monday through Saturday, 10:00 A.M. to 5:00 P.M.

Brevard Antique Mall, 57 East Main Street (828–885–2744), has more than 20,000 square feet of shopping space in a former department store. Booths have a great variety of antique furnishings, china, maps, magazines, and vinyl recordings. The mall is open 9:30 A.M. to 5:30 P.M. every day but Sunday, when it is open 1:00 to 5:00 P.M.

Of the possibilities for eating, ***Jason's Main Street Grill,*** 48 East Main Street (828–883–4447), serves breakfast, lunch, and dinner every day, beginning at 7:00 A.M. You can get everything from a burger to macadamia crusted trout here. For a more old-timey experience, ***Rocky's,*** 36 South Broad Street (828–862–4700), claims to be Brevard's original lunch counter and serves up soups, sandwiches, shakes, sundaes, and homemade ice cream. Rocky's is open Monday through Saturday, 10:00 A.M. to 6:00 P.M., Sunday 11:30 A.M. to 5:00 P.M.

Among the various motels and bed-and breakfast accommodations in the area, ***Womble Inn*** is a longtime, well-established favorite in a residential area (301 West Main Street; 828–884–4770). Guest rooms in the large brick New Orleans-style house are filled with real home furnishings, even a spinet piano in one room. A cabin next door has a fully equipped kitchen. In addition to giving guests breakfast, Womble Inn has a cafe in the areas that once would have been the dining room and living room, where you can have lunch. The schedule varies with the time of year. The Wombles cater too, with a list of cakes and sweets that makes you long for a special occasion. They have their own line of little cheese biscuits in tins and a spicy apple chutney in glass jars. You can arrange to have a picnic basket prepared for a hike or concert.

As you might expect in an area so full of forests and parks and lakes and rivers and waterfalls, the services of all kinds of outfitters and guides are available, as are maps for hiking and touring. Check with the Transylvania tourism offices and Brevard Chamber of Commerce (35 West Main Street; 800–648–4523; Web site: www.visitwaterfalls.com; www.brevardncchamber.org) for brochures and details.

When you are ready to head north, to Waynesville, allow enough time to make the drive up U.S. Highway 276. It's winding and slow but also a lot of fun, and what you see going up this route, except for a of couple sites, is authentic, not gentrified, mountain country. The ***Sliding Rock Recreation Area*** in the Pisgah National Forest is just north of Brevard, about 7½ miles from the junction of US 64 and 276. This is nature's version of a commercial waterslide. It is a slippery rock slide of about 60 feet that drops you into a 6-foot-deep pool. Wood steps, places to sit, and a small park office make the spot a little more comfortable, but pictures of injuries that can happen in such a slide and bulletins about how to treat hypothermia make it clear that rock sliding is not without risk. The rushing water in here is beautiful, though, and you don't need to get into it at all to enjoy it.

Continuing north on US 276, you'll come to the entrance to the ***Cradle of Forestry in America National Site*** (800–660–0671; Web site: www.cradleofforestry.com). The first forestry school in America was founded here in the early 1900s, and the National Historic Site stands today as a commemoration of the importance of forests in the North Carolina mountains. Paved trails take you down to old cabins and a logging train. In the Forest Discovery Center, hands-on exhibits and an eighteen-minute film explain early forestry in detail. From spring through autumn, the center has a variety of tours, programs, and crafters on site. Open in season 9:00 A.M. to 5:00 P.M. daily. Hours may change. Admission is $5.00 for adults, $2.50 for children four to seventeen, and free for children three and younger.

After this, you'll pass an entrance to the Blue Ridge Parkway, the Big East Fork Trailhead into the Pisgah National Forest, and some spots for camping and fishing. Further north, churches, a trout farm, and some accumulations of junk on private properties dot the roadside. At the community of Cruso, a handmade sign tells you this is, "9 MILES OF FRIENDLY PEOPLE, PLUS 1 OLD CRAB."

Following U.S. Highway 23 East from Sylva brings you quickly to ***Waynesville,*** a town of Scotch-Irish and English founding, at an altitude of 3,000 feet. It is doing an outstanding job of revitalizing its downtown with art galleries and shops selling the work of local crafters, as well as a bookstore, the popular Mast General Store, a high-quality cooking store, a wine shop, and a number of good restaurants and bakeries. In addition, the town holds an ever-increasing number of street fairs, dances, and celebrations, including the ***International Folkmoot USA*** in July. This international festival of dance and music brings groups from more than ten countries each year to perform in their national costumes. Call (828) 452–2997 for performance dates. Web site: www.folkmoot.com.

Waynesville is the home of the annual ***Ramps Festival.*** The ramp is a rank, onionlike, wild plant of no particular virtue, except that every summer the American Legion throws a big party to cook it all the ways they can think of: steamed ramps, braised ramps, ramps a la king, ramps fritters. Presumably, folks eats the results, but that is not as conspicuous as the cooking, which leaves a garlicky odor heavy on the town all day. For some reason it's a popular time and place for politicians to appear. The festival is always held on the first Sunday in May, at the American Legion Park, 171 Legion Drive. A ramp-eating contest is the high point of the day, unless you're one of the contestants, in which case it may be the beginning of a big bellyache for the rest of the day. For more information call (828) 456–3517. Other ramp festivals are held in nearby counties, but an American Legion representative says, "Ours was the first one, and it's the real one. The others aren't like ours."

Here's a place to stay and dine that you probably wouldn't find unless you were specifically looking for it. The ***Old Stone Inn*** (109 Dolan Road; 828–456–3333 or 800–432–8499), owned and operated by Cindy and Robert Zinser, was known in earlier years as Heath Lodge. It's a larger operation, technically an inn rather than a bed-and-breakfast, tucked under lots of shady foliage and rhododendron on top of a hill at the edge of Waynesville.

The Zinsers have upgraded the inn in many ways since they bought it, improving the rooms, making the dining room more attractive, and best of all, moving from old-style Southern all-you-can-eat meals served at huge round tables to more sophisticated and very good food served at tables appropriate for the size of your party. Robert has made a hobby of learning about wine and maintains a sophisticated wine list. The shady site, comfortable rooms, and good food make this a great rejuvenating spot. This isn't a place to make new friends around a breakfast table so much as one for retreating from a noisy life for a while. Web site: www.oldstoneinn.com.

For the smaller bed-and-breakfast experience where you mingle with other guests, try ***Herren House,*** 94 East Street (800–284–1932 or 828–452–7897), run by Jackie and Frank Blevins. This beautifully restored Victorian used to be a boardinghouse. As a bed-and-breakfast, it has six guest rooms. The house has wraparound porches and a gazebo in the perennial gardens, both good places for socializing, as is the dining room, where guests eat breakfast and later can help themselves to homemade baked goods on the sideboard. Saturday night a five-course candlelight dinner is available in the dining room by reservation. The house is in a quiet residential neighborhood just a block from downtown.

Another place to eat in Waynesville is ***Maggie's Galley III*** (828–456–8945) at 22 Howell Mill Road. The building housing the restaurant was made from primitive log cabins. An earlier owner had an antiques business here, and as his need for space grew, he just kept tacking on additional old cabins. He used five cabins to make the building as it is today. Each of the cabins has a story and a bit of history attached. The restaurant has a flier with all the information. The food at the restaurant includes fresh seafood, steaks, and a good selection of sandwiches. The atmosphere is zany, and a meal here, in addition to being good, is a lot of fun. Open for lunch and dinner. Sometimes closed on Monday.

Lomo Grill, 44 Church Street (828–452–5222; Web site: lomogrill.com), has been going full steam since 1995. Ricardo and Suzanne Fernandez have earned a reputation for serving interesting and unusual Argentine food with Italian and Spanish influences, much of it cooked on an open-flame grill. Ricardo, a master gardener, grows the herbs he uses. In addition to the grill, a formal restaurant for dinner, the operation has expanded to include a sidewalk cafe for lunch, a European-style bakery, and an espresso and wine bar. Hours vary seasonally.

Close to Waynesville, off US 74, the community of ***Clyde*** is a place in the mountains for which guide books typically list no attractions. However, it is the home of ***Wind Dancers Lodge and Llama Treks*** (1966 Martins Creek Road; 877–627–3330; Web site: www.winddancersnc.com), a complex of nine rooms in three contemporary log buildings, each with private bath, soaking tub for two, fireplaces, and VCRs.

Getting to Wind Dancers means a careful 2-mile drive up a gravel road, taking you to an elevation of more than 3,000 feet. The Livengood family bought this 270 acres, which once were a mountain farm, and erected the new log buildings to accommodate couples on a getaway in the inn rooms, as well as families with children in the lodges, all out of each other's way. In this appropriately high mountain setting, the Livengoods maintain a herd of llamas and take guests on treks into the woods. Some treks are just part of the day, with lunch; others include overnight camping. The views are simply stunning, and if you sign on for a lunch llama trek you'll go on about 400 feet higher, while an overnight trek, with dinner, will take you up 1,200 feet more. All the llamas have names and distinct personalities. If you don't want to deal with them up close, you can sit on the porch of the lodge and watch them move along the side of the mountain as the mist rises in the morning or settles in the evening.

One spot in the area that has a Waynesville address, but is actually out of town and 5,000 feet up, offers fine food, rustic lodging, hiking trails, and an entry to the Great Smoky Mountains National Park. The ***Swag,*** 2300 Swag Road, comprises a collection of pioneer buildings that were hauled up the mountain about thirty years ago. Innkeeper Deener Matthews has managed to combine rustic elements such as the rough wood interior walls of the rooms with luxurious amenities, including handmade covers on the beds, coffee grinders, coffeemakers,, hair dryers, and terry-cloth robes in the rooms. She's managed something similar in the dining room, where guests sit around handmade tables to enjoy first-rate food professionally prepared and served.

And although the other recreational facilities are tucked unobtrusively into the property, you can find everything from a racquetball court and sauna to a library. For more details call (828) 926–0430 or (800) 789–7672. Web site: www .theswag.com.

All that is up on the mountain. Down in the valley you'll find some other interesting attractions. ***Maggie Valley*** is a year-round resort town between Cherokee and Waynesville. On both sides of US 19, or Soco Road, which runs through the valley, you'll see one motel after another, every kind of eating place, and souvenir shops galore—generally not the kind of places an off-the-beaten-path traveler wants to visit at all. But you'll also find a place worth the drive because it began as a labor of love.

The ***Stomping Ground*** is a huge building on US 19 with a massive dance floor and seating for 2,000 people. Kyle Edwards hopes to make it the world center for clogging. The Edwards are a clogging family, but they've always thought of it as "mountain dancing." Kyle thinks the word *clogging* came into use in 1935, in Chattanooga, Tennessee. His mother and his uncle performed with a Maggie Valley team in the 1920s that performed in the White House for President Franklin D. Roosevelt and the Queen of England. Kyle and his wife, Mary Sue, also danced on teams. Their son, Burton, was a world champion clogger in 1981, when he was eighteen. (He is running the operation now.) And their daughter, Becky, had won two championships by the time she was thirteen. It doesn't take a rocket scientist to figure out that if you go to the Stomping Ground, you're either going to clog or watch clogging. Dances and shows are held every night from April through November. A number of large display cases related to clogging give you a lot of information about the his-

Let's Get Lost

Being able to walk through the backyard of the Swag and right into the forest of the Great Smoky Mountains National Park was an opportunity too good to ignore. The hiking trails were all there, well marked and shown on a large map on the grounds. Sorry to say, I forgot to look at it. But figuring that all the trails would loop, I just got onto one and started walking. After walking a couple of hours, I was on a road I had never heard of, with no money in my pocket and no place to spend it anyway.

I asked an old man in a pickup truck where I was. He told me, but I was still disoriented. He gave me a ride to a campground where he introduced me to some friends with a trailer. Within minutes, I was sitting at a picnic table, digging into hot roast beef sandwiches, sliced fresh tomatoes, and mashed potatoes. We were all laughing and chatting so much, it was like a party.

Eventually, the idea of getting back where I belonged came up. Everyone knew right where the Swag was, because a swag is a dip in the mountains. It was about 30 miles away by road, a substantial drive for a stranger to make for another stranger.

The old man not only drove me, he had fun doing it, telling me all about his family, life in this area, secrets you can learn on back roads, and who lives on them. When we got back to the Swag, he got out of the truck to look around. "Always wanted to see the view from up here," he said. Then we hugged and he was gone.

That's why I love North Carolina.

tory, contests, and fun of the dance. Call (828) 926–7767 or (828) 926–1288 for details about times, shows, and admission fees. Don't hang up if you get what sounds like a private home instead of a business, with a recorded message telling you that you've reached 926–1288. The telephone rings at the Stomping Ground, in Mary Sue's beauty shop, and in the family's residence. Just leave a message. They'll get back to you.

The Literary and Crafts Center

It's only 25 miles from Waynesville to Asheville. ***Asheville*** is crammed with arts, crafts, antiques, literary and musical people, and a healthy assortment of free spirits deeply involved in the unique Appalachian culture. The best place to see and buy a variety of area crafts is the ***Folk Art Center,*** just east of town at milepost 382 on the Blue Ridge Parkway, about a half mile north of US 70. It has been operated by the Southern Highland Handicraft Guild since 1980 and houses permanent and traveling exhibits and the Allanstand Craft Shop, where you can buy items similar to those in the exhibits. Crafts represented include weaving, pottery, basketry, quilting, jewelry, wood carving, stitchery, and musical instruments. Admission is free; donations are welcome. Open every day except Thanksgiving, Christmas, and New Year's Day from 9:00 A.M. to 5:00 P.M., except that it stays open until 6:00 P.M. April through December. Closed occasionally for inventory and changing exhibitions. Phone (828) 298–7928. Web site: www.southernhighlandguild.org.

At the edge of town, two well-known attractions have become almost obligatory stops for anyone who wants to claim to have seen the area: Grove Park Inn and Biltmore Estate. Both nearly defy description. As newspaper writer Jean Thwaite once said of ***Grove Park Inn,*** 290 Macon Avenue, "It would almost be ugly, were it not so interesting." The building, of a size that seems to dwarf pyramids, is built of red boulders hauled from Sunset Mountain, on which it's located, in 1913. William Grove did well, to understate matters, in pharmaceuticals in St. Louis. He liked Asheville, so he bought a lot of it, including Sunset Mountain. Then, eschewing architects, who didn't understand him, he got his son-in-law to design and build (without a contractor) the massive hotel. The inn is 500 feet long, with a flagstone-floored lobby 80 feet wide and almost half the length of a football field. The fireplaces at each end are so big they burn 12-foot logs, and when there's no fire, children can walk into them upright to play.

George Washington didn't sleep here, but practically everyone else of importance did: Thomas Edison, Henry Ford, Enrico Caruso, the Roosevelts, Dwight Eisenhower, even F. Scott Fitzgerald. Today the inn is popular with people looking for a place to celebrate a special occasion and with companies and organizations that want somewhere extra nice to gather their members.

After recent additions the inn has more than 500 rooms. Facilities include restaurants, cocktail lounges, indoor and outdoor swimming pools, golf, tennis, racquetball, and a fitness center with an aerobics room, weight room, Nautilus equipment, whirlpools, saunas, and a luxurious spa. The accommodations are luxurious; rates are correspondingly high, although they drop considerably in the off-season, when a variety of special packages are available. Phone (828) 252–2711 or (800) 438–5800. Web site: www.groveparkinn.com.

Many of the packages include a tour of the ***Biltmore Estate,*** which seems appropriate because it operates on the same grand scale. Like Mr. Grove, George Vanderbilt liked Asheville, and he, too, had a little money. He bought a lot of Asheville, too, about 125,000 acres, and had a 250-room private home built on the property. (Today only 7,500 acres belong to the estate. The rest is part of the Blue Ridge Parkway or Mount Pisgah National Forest.) The home was famous from the beginning for the beauty of its design and workmanship.

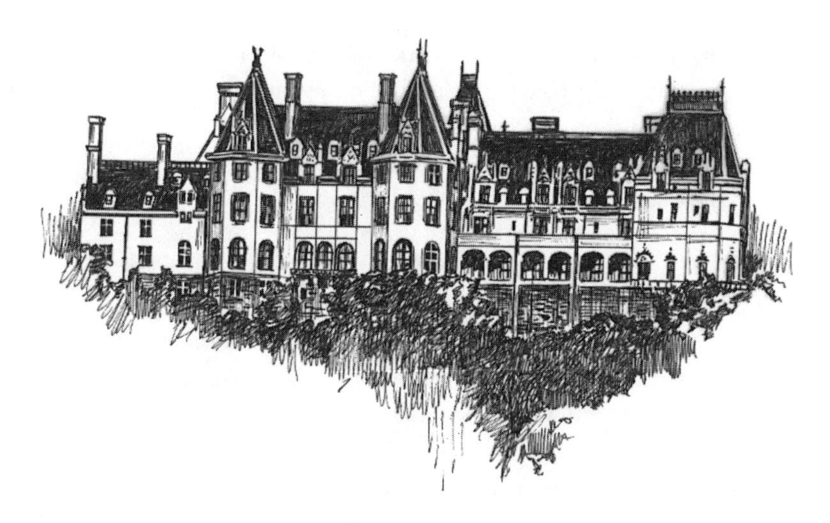

Biltmore Estate

The master builders were brought from Europe. The home was also famous for being ahead of its time in its modern conveniences, having early forerunners of washing machines and driers. Art in the mansion includes originals by Boldini, Ming dynasty china, and antiques that belonged to Napoleon.

It will take you the better part of a day to see the place properly, especially if you go beyond the mansion to explore the gardens and visit the winery. Although the ***Biltmore Estate Winery*** is still relatively young, some oenophiles say the wines—red, white, rosé, and champagne—are developing nicely. They are for sale, priced in the moderate range. Admission fees to the Biltmore Estate are high. The estate is open daily from 9:00 A.M. to 5:00 P.M. Phone (828) 274–6333 or (888) 804–8258. Web site: www.biltmore.com.

If you're not overwhelmed by the grandeur of Biltmore Estate, you're a rare bird. A nice way to decompress and get things back in perspective again is to spend a night at ***Cedar Crest,*** 674 Biltmore Avenue (828–252–1389 or 800–252–0310). This bed-and-breakfast inn has ten rooms in the main house and a guest cottage. There is a two-bedroom suite with a parlor and fireplace and a single-bedroom suite with a parlor. This is an 1890 Queen Anne–style Victorian mansion in which the work was purportedly done by the same craftsmen who worked on the Biltmore mansion. Apparently, once they were in this country and established in the little village built for them to work on Biltmore, they decided to hang around afterward and pick up a few odd jobs. Like the Biltmore Estate, Cedar Crest is so full of wonderful features that you can't take them all in at once, but the scale is more human and easier to relate to. The elaborate, first-generation oak woodwork differs in every room, with such subtle distinctions as being heavy and masculine in the library, but delicate and ornate in the dining room, which was considered ladies' territory. Other special features in the house include a corner fireplace with fluted columns, a gilded cherub, and splendid stained-glass windows. There's a secret closet where silverware used to be hidden in troubled times. And the house has what may be the longest (6 feet) and smallest (4 feet) bathtubs in North Carolina. Web site: www.cedarcrestvictorianinn.com.

Another place in Asheville worth a stop is the ***Richmond Hill Inn,*** 87 Richmond Hill Drive (828–252–7313 or 888–742–4553), even if you aren't looking for overnight lodging. This is a luxurious inn with a heroic saved-from-the-wrecking-ball story. The century-old mansion was the home of a former congressman and diplomat, Richmond Pearson, and his wife, Gabrielle. It was one of the most innovative and elegant homes of its time. But it outlasted the people who wanted to live that way and could afford it. Toward the end, the Pearsons' daughter, Marjorie, then an elderly woman, lived there alone, using just one room.

In subsequent sales and maneuvering, the building was scheduled to be torn down and then reprieved several times. Many community organizations, including the Preservation Society, campaigned and raised money to try to save the mansion. They also found the Michel family, which was willing to buy and restore it. It was moved, *all in one piece,* to its current spot on the hill. You can begin your stay here by watching a videotape showing the tense moving process.

The building was preserved where possible and restored or re-created where necessary, with fidelity to the mansion's original state. Much work was done by hand as it would originally have been, rather than with electric tools. Now listed on the National Register of Historic Places, it is considered one of the best examples of a Queen Anne–style mansion in North Carolina. It's a must-see if you are interested in architecture and preservation.

Because of the fine woodwork, soaring ceilings, and generously sized rooms, the mansion makes a fine inn. Some guest rooms are named for Pearson family members who once lived in them, others for important guests, and, on the third floor, for Asheville-connected writers, such as Carl Sandburg. Each writer's room has a picture of the writer and a collection of his or her books.

Also re-creating the past, several hundred of Mr. Pearson's own books have been recovered and placed in the inn library along with books about North Carolina and those by North Carolina authors.

The restaurant is open to the public for dinner. It reflects the mansion's history in being named "Gabrielle's," after Mrs. Pearson. The food, however, is clearly a product of modern times. Considered American and nouvelle cuisine, it features lighter sauces and more healthful preparation than earlier haute cuisine.

Finding the place is tricky the first time. From Interstate 240 take the 19/23 Weaverville exit. Continue on 19/23 and take exit 251 (UNC–Asheville). Turn left at the bottom of the ramp. At the first stoplight, turn left again onto Riverside Drive. Turn right on Pearson Bridge Road and cross the bridge. At the sharp curve, turn right on Richmond Hill Drive. The mansion is at the top of the hill. Web site: www.richmondhillinn.com.

For more homey accommodations, try ***Flint Street Inns,*** 100 and 116 Flint Street (800–234–8172; Web site: flintstreetinns.com). The innkeepers, Rick and Lynne Vogel, have eight rooms in two houses connected by gardens and walking paths. Each room has private bath, TV, and computer hookup; phones are available on request. These inns have retained the homey feel and casual atmosphere of the early bed-and-breakfast days, and the Vogels have been innkeepers in the same location for more than two decades, a record in North Carolina. This is in Asheville's oldest neighborhood, within easy walking distance of downtown restaurants and attractions. Both houses are filled with comfortable turn-of-the-century antiques, the well-used kind, not the don't-break-me kind. A number of working fireplaces add atmosphere as well as warmth. Beds in the guest rooms are covered with quilts Rick's late mother, Marion, made. Lynne was baking cookies for guests before the idea ever occurred to the keepers of boutique hotels, and she does all the inn's other baking, except for croissants, so the aroma of something good in the oven often fills the air.

And just 4 miles north of downtown Asheville, ***Old Reynolds Mansion,*** 100 Reynold Heights (828–254–0496 or 800–709–0496; Web site: www.oldreyn oldsmansion.com), a bed-and-breakfast in a brick antebellum mansion on a high ridge, may be a testimony to the strength of people from Minnesota. Fred and Helen Faber bought the place in 1977 and moved here from Minnesota to restore it in 1981. It was in sad shape, and the operative word is "restore," not "cause to be restored." The Fabers did virtually everything, including the gardening and construction work, with their own hands. The place has become consistently better and better. It stands in the middle of an expanse of gardens, grass, and pines atop a ridge with a magnificent view, seeming secluded and rural. The rooms are furnished with comfortable antiques. Children over six are welcome during the week, over twelve on weekends. In warm weather the 25-by-62-foot cement swimming pool, the courtyard, and the gardens appeal to adults as well as children. And in cold weather, the fireplace in the great room is a popular attraction. Since Fred Faber passed away, Helen, with friends and family, continues to maintain their hands-on innkeeping tradition.

Camping is another popular option around Asheville. At ***Campfire Lodgings,*** 7 Appalachian Village Road (800–933–8012; Web site: www.camp firelodgings.com), on a wooded mountaintop, elevation 2,270 feet, you can camp in anything from a an RV or simple tent to a luxury cabin or an exotic yurt, just 6 miles north of downtown Asheville and 10 miles from the Blue Ridge Parkway. The facility includes a bathhouse with laundry facilities and private bathrooms with showers—an unusual feature in a campground. Beyond that, it all depends on what you want. Pets are welcome here; a courtesy phone/modem hookup is available; and the 120 acres includes hiking trails, a private fishing pond, and meditation spots. Some of the RV sites have phone/modem hookups, and all the RV sites have water, sewer, electric, and cable.

The yurt is a large, round, domed tent of insulated canvas set up on a large wooden deck. The screened walls and dome can be opened in good weather or closed against rain. Inside a bed is made up with luxurious bedding. The yurt has cable TV and a small kitchen. The deck is large enough to put up a tent for families with children. Guests in the yurt use the bathhouse. The luxury cabins, which sleep seven, have two bathrooms, a gas log fireplace, a fully equipped kitchen, air-conditioning, a washer and dryer, a telephone, cable TV, and linen service. Not exactly roughing it. The views from this campground are stunning, and the wooded sites are large enough to afford considerable privacy.

One thing you might not expect to find in a mountain city is the ***Botanical Gardens at Asheville,*** located on a ten-acre site next to the campus of the University of North Carolina at Asheville. The gardens were begun in 1960 by the Asheville Garden Club and designed by Doan Ogden, a landscape architect of repute. The gardens are open all year, and no matter when you visit, you'll find something in bloom, bud, or fruit.

The Botany Center is open from March to December. Other parts of the gardens include a library and gift shop. You can arrange for garden tours or use a map to explore on your own. Special places in the property include a spring house, a garden for the blind, a rock garden, an azalea garden, and an herb garden. For more detailed information about the gardens, call the Botany Center at (828) 252–5190. Web site: www.ashevillebotanicalgardens.org.

Here's the unexpected kind of place you can find in Asheville. ***Blue Moon Bakery,*** 60 Biltmore Avenue (828–252–6063), specializes in European-style breads and a variety of specialty breads. The bakery is owned by its workers, which means they are especially dedicated to doing a good job.

Your choices here range from old-fashioned European-style baguettes to slow-rising sourdoughs to soft crusted breads. The bakery also has a cafe that serves soups, salads, sandwiches, and desserts. It seats about eighty in an informal atmosphere dominated by a mural depicting bakers and bread. European prints on the walls add to the French feel. Open 7:30 A.M. to 4:00 P.M. Monday through Wednesday, 7:00 A.M. to noon Thursday through Sunday.

Downtown in Asheville, at 40 Wall Street, ***Laughing Seed Cafe*** serves vegetarian and vegan meals in an atmosphere that calls to mind the days of tie-dyed shirts and Volkswagon vans. But don't be fooled by the funky atmosphere. This is a sophisticated restaurant that offers creative entrees and wine and beer to go with them. If you call the restaurant's phone number (828–252–3445), you can choose a menu option that lets you listen to a description of the day's specials, complete with an explanation of which are vegan—no dairy products or eggs—and which are simply vegetarian. For instance, the Seven Sisters soup with barley and many different vegetables is not vegan because it contains some dairy. Laughing Seed also prepares a variety of smoothies using soy milk and organic fruits. The restaurant is open Monday through Thursday (closed Tuesday) from 11:30 A.M. to 9:00 P.M., Friday and Saturday until 10:00 P.M. Sunday brunch is served from 10:00 A.M. to 2:00 P.M., with the regular menu in place the rest of the day until 9:00 P.M.

Downtown Asheville continues to develop and renovate its historical center. The best way to take it in is to park your car in one of the parking garages and walk, because the streets are narrow, on-street parking is scarce, and traffic tends to back up. One massive undertaking you can't miss, ***Grove Arcade Public Market,*** 1 Page Avenue (828–252–7799; Web site: www.grovearcade.com), a structure with 269,000 square feet of floor space, is Western North

BETTER-KNOWN ATTRACTIONS IN THE MOUNTAINS

Asheville
Biltmore Estate
(828) 274–6333
(888) 804–8258

Blue Ridge Parkway
(828) 298–0398

Blowing Rock
The Blowing Rock
(828) 295–7111

Cherokee
Cherokee Indian Reservation
(828) 497–9195
(800) 438–1601

Harrah's Cherokee Casino
(828) 497–7777
(800) 427–7247

Chimney Rock
Chimney Rock Park
(828) 625–9611
(800) 277–9611

Carolina's largest commercial building. It was built in 1929, housing shops on the ground floor and offices above. The arcade was one of the first indoor public markets in the country, and it thrived as the center of Asheville commercial activity until 1942, when the U.S. government took it over to use for activities related to World War II, displacing 74 shops and 127 offices in a single month. Later the building began to fall into disrepair, and the space was too big and expensive for a commercial investor to take on the project, although local opinion increasingly demanded restoring the building to its original appearance and use. In 2002, with funding and direction from a foundation, the renovation was completed, and the building's cream glaze terracotta facing gleams again. Shops selling everything from antiques and art to bread and meat, ice cream and candy have been moving in. It will probably be a while before all the available space is rented to businesses and offices stable enough to stay there, but there will be plenty to see and do anytime you visit. Outside the building, bordering on Battery Park Square, artisans and farmers in outdoor market stalls open 10:00 A.M. to 6:00 P.M. every day sell directly to the public.

Also in this part of town, the ***Basilica of St. Lawrence,*** at 97 Haywood Street, has the largest unsupported tile dome in North America. It was designed by Rafael Guastavino in 1909. The downtown Asheville Historic District has an interesting assortment of early-twentieth-century architecture, much of it being restored or renovated and filled by specialty shops, galleries, and restaurants. Walking the district, you encounter a rich mix of old and young hippies, artists, entrepreneurs, intellectuals, shopkeepers, businesspeople, tourists, and just folks.

If you're feeling literary, visit the ***Thomas Wolfe Memorial,*** 52 Market Street. This is the novelist's boyhood home, described in his novel, *Look Homeward, Angel,* as "Dixieland." In real life it was called "The Old Kentucky Home." Wolfe's mother, Julia, ran a boardinghouse in the rambling Victorian house, and its various rooms and furnishings, along with local people, were all incorporated into Wolfe's novel, mostly in unflattering terms. The people of Asheville didn't like that one bit, which led to Wolfe's second novel, *You Can't Go Home Again.* After Wolfe died, the townspeople relented, as they often do when a troublesome celebrity stops being troublesome and remains merely famous, and bought the house to turn into a memorial for him. It is now a North Carolina State Historic Site. Visiting the house, which has been kept the same as it was when the Wolfes lived in it and has descriptions from Wolfe's writing in appropriate places so you can compare the words with the reality, goes a long way toward explaining the often gloomy tone of his writing. Nominal admission fee. The Wolfe house was damaged by fire a few years ago but has been restored and reopened. Open Tuesday through Saturday 10:00 A.M. to 4:00 P.M., Sunday 1:00 to 4:00 P.M. in winter. Summer hours are 9:00 A.M. to 5:00 P.M. Tuesday through Saturday, 1:00 to 5:00 P.M. Sunday. Closed Monday. Call (828) 253–8304 for rate details. Web site: www.wolfememorial.com.

Just about 10 miles outside Asheville, near Weaverville on Reems Creek Road off U.S. Highway 25 North, is another state historic site, the ***Zebulon B. Vance Birthplace.*** Vance was a Civil War officer, a U.S. senator, and governor of North Carolina. In fascinating contrast to the splendor of the Biltmore Estate, this restored pioneer farmstead has only a five-room log house and some outbuildings. The log house was reconstructed around the original chimneys. The outbuildings, including a loom house, springhouse, toolshed, smokehouse, corncrib, and slave cabin, are furnished as they would have been between 1795 and 1840. Displays instruct you further in life of the times. Admission by donation. Hours of operation vary because of budget constraints, so call ahead (828–645–6706).

Also outside the city, the ***North Carolina Arboretum,*** at milepost 393 (off State Highway 191), features southern Appalachian landscape plants on a 426-acre site, as well as hiking and nature trails. The arboretum also has a state-of-the-art greenhouse complex. Call (828) 665–2492. Web site: www.nc arboretum.org.

Asheville makes a good center from which to go in several different directions. Following the parkway takes you to ***New River State Park.*** A drive of about 20 miles down Interstate 26 takes you into the southern mountains, where Flat Rock, Hendersonville, and Saluda offer many rural pleasures and some interesting crafts and antiques shops. Driving northeast from Asheville along the Blue Ridge Parkway takes you higher into the mountains to Blowing Rock and environs. And a scenic ride east along I–40 and Highway 226 to Polkville brings you back into the lower elevations of the Piedmont.

If you follow the parkway almost to the Virginia border, getting off to drive north on U.S. Highway 221, you come to the oldest river in North America and the second oldest (the Nile is older) in the world. It's the only major river in the country that runs south to north. Paradoxically called New River, it meanders peacefully through more than 100 miles of northwestern North Carolina. The name was the result of surveyors' surprise when they finally chanced upon the river they hadn't known about in this remote part of the state in 1749.

You'll enjoy good access to the river from New River State Park (336–982–2587), an area of breathtakingly lovely mountains, valleys, woods, and fields, 8 miles southeast of Jefferson off State Highway 88 on State Road 1588. Compared to other state parks, New River shows up infrequently in travel books and articles, probably because it is in a remote part of the state and because the facilities are primitive. This is the river to find if you like placid canoeing rather than wild races through white water and want fishing spots not bothered by heavy powerboat traffic. There are canoe landings and campgrounds. The woods are great for hiking and are full of spots that cry out for a simple picnic.

Behind the peaceful scene lies the story of a dramatic struggle that isn't anywhere near being over. It started in the 1960s, when the Appalachian Power Company planned to build a dam there, eliciting tremendous public objection. In protective response Congress designated the area a National Wild and Scenic River in 1976, effectively stopping the power company.

But little funding was ever forthcoming to actually buy and protect the land, and a new force is changing the scene along the river: subdivision and development. New houses, roads, and lots are appearing on what was farmland or woodland. Although none of it is in the state park, of course, people who like their countryside bucolic and unspoiled are getting nervous, whereas those who value economic development for the area are digging in their heels and sending out the bulldozers.

Given the usual inclination of those who can afford to build in the prettiest places—high on mountain summits, on beaches and islands, and along rivers—it's hard to say what will happen along the New River in the coming decade. The good news is that the state park is, as locals like to call the river, "a national treasure" and should remain a special place to visit for a long time to come. It has four access sites, three for camping and one with a canoe launch for day use.

About thirty-five minutes north of Asheville, in Madison County, you'll find an interesting cluster of places near the ***French Broad River.*** This river is a step above the Nantahala River in difficulty for white-water rafting, but the water is warmer and far fewer users come into the area, so your experience will be considerably more off-the-beaten-path than it is on the Nantahala. The greater part of Madison County is part of Pisgah National Forest, and the Appalachian Trail passes through the county, offering short segments of trail for day hikers. In the little town of ***Hot Springs,*** you can soak in outdoor tubs along the banks of the river. Hot mineral water, flowing constantly from natural springs at a temperature of about one hundred degrees, has often been considered therapeutic and is certainly relaxing, the more so if you indulge in a massage while you are there. Spa rates are figured by the hour and vary depending on the time of day. Massage rates are calculated by the half-hour and become proportionately slightly less expensive per half-hour the longer the time you reserve. For information about the hot springs and massages, call (828) 622–7676 or (800) 462–0933. For information about white-water rafting tours and hiking, contact the Visitors Information Center at (828) 680–9031 or (877) 262–3476.

On the drive down I–26, one of the most interesting stops is the ***Carl Sandburg Home National Historic Site,*** a 240-acre farm called ***Connemara,*** a bit south of Hendersonville in Flat Rock. Sandburg spent the last twenty-two years of his life here, mostly writing, while his wife and daughter managed the place as a goat farm. His collection of poems, Honey and Salt, was written here when he was eighty-five. The poems contrast with such earlier works as "Chicago," reflecting not only the work of an older man, but also of one living in different surroundings. For instance, in the poem "Cahokia," Sandburg writes about an Indian watching a butterfly rise from a cocoon, flowers sprouting in spring, and the sun moving. The Indian, Sandburg writes, doesn't worship the sun but dances and sings to the "makers and movers of the sun." It takes on added significance when you know that Flat Rock was named for a large granite plateau that had once been a Cherokee sacred ground. Sandburg's life here was influenced not only by the early cycles of nature but also by Cherokee Indian lore. Similarly, looking across the mountains, it's easy to understand how Sandburg might have arrived at his poem "Shadows Fall Blue on the Mountains."

enoughofagood thing

North Carolina has nearly 600 golf courses scattered across the state. For a free copy of the Official North Carolina Golf Guide, call (900) VISIT–NC, or check the Web site: www.nc.com/golf.

When you visit Sandburg's study at Connemara, both the man and his poetry seem alive. The study is said to be exactly as he left it, with a shawl tossed over the back of his desk chair, a clunky manual typewriter standing on an upended crate, and stacks of paper and disorderly piles of books everywhere. A fascinating aspect of the entire home is the simplicity of its furnishings. To say the interior is plain puts it mildly. The furniture resembles what you find in a summer camp, functional but not decorative. Also fascinating is the fact that every room is crammed with books, all of which appear to have been well used. Similarly, the rooms where Helga kept records about breeding her goats are functional and were apparently furnished with no thought to decoration. What you find outside seems more carefully designed. You may also walk along trails on the grounds, where you'll see the kinds of plants and wildlife from which Sandburg must have drawn many of his images. Nominal admission is charged. Open daily except Christmas from 9:00 A.M. to 5:00 P.M. Tours begin at 9:30 A.M. and last tour departs at 4:30 P.M. Tours $3.00, free for children under sixteen. Inquire about some special seasonal activities (828–693–4178). Web site: www.nps.gov/carl.

The town's ***Historic Flat Rock District*** is on the National Register of Historic Places. It began about 150 years ago as summer estates for wealthy people from Charleston, South Carolina. Web site: www.historicflatrock.org. Flat Rock has a wonderful place to enjoy a good dinner and spend the night. ***Highland Lake Inn,*** on Highland Lake Drive, is a complex with inn rooms, cabins, and cottages scattered on a wooded property that also has a lake, a swimming pool, and one hundred acres of walking trails. The Lindsey family's objective was to create a self-sufficient compound, and although they didn't manage that entirely, they came close. They've sold the property to Jack Grup, who continues in the same spirit. The restaurant, ***Seasons,*** serves vegetables and herbs organically grown on the property and provided by local gardeners. The food is simply wonderful. Offerings range from an herb-stuffed free-range chicken breast to some elaborate pasta and seafood dishes, as well as vegetarian dishes. Every bite you take bursts with flavor. Seasons offers a good wine list and full bar service. If you are traveling with children, this is a place where you can take them to see vegetables growing in a garden, look at honey bee hives, and watch a goat being milked. Phone (828) 693–6812 or (800) 762–1376. Web site: www.hlinn.com.

nina'ssecret

The jazz/soul singer and piano player Nina Simone was born February 21, 1933, in Tryon. She was one of eight children, four boys and four girls. Simone was playing the piano and singing before she reached the age of five and developed her talent in the early years singing in the local church with her sisters. She left home for Philadelphia when she was seventeen and later studied at Juilliard in New York. Some of her earliest gigs were in a piano bar in Philadelphia, a job she kept secret from her church-going family in North Carolina.

From Flat Rock you can head over onto U.S. Highway 176, driving about 12 miles to ***Saluda,*** a little town of less than 1,000 people, with a notable concentration of antiques and artisans. Walking around in the little town itself, you'll find several shops selling local crafts and antiques and a general store run by a pair of women reminiscent of the sisters on *The Waltons* television show, except, of course, they aren't offering Mason jars full of the "recipe"—as far as anyone knows.

The town is at the crest of the steepest mainline railroad in the country. The business district is on the National Register of Historic Places.

Saluda has two overnight possibilities, quite different from each other. At the top of a steep hill, overlooking Saluda's main street, Dottie Eargle's ***Woods***

House, at Henderson and Church Streets, has six rooms, including one in a separate cottage. The place is furnished throughout with Victorian and turn-of-the-twentieth-century antiques, highlighted by an outstanding collection of old needlework displayed throughout the inn. Dorothy worked in an antiques shop for many years, and she has the ability to put together a room as only those intimate with antiques and their earlier uses can. The inn (828–749–9562) is open May through October. Web site: www.woodshousebandb.com.

Like Asheville, Saluda has a bakery that comes as a surprise. Debi Thomas started out catering for *Mother Earth News,* whose facilities are in the country nearby. In her own ***Wildflour Bakery and Café on Main Street,*** Thomas still concentrates on flavor and nutrition. She and her friends have created all the recipes, including a variety of vegetarian soups, salads, and sandwiches. All her recipes use stone-ground flour, ground fresh as needed from untreated wheat. Ingredients are measured and mixed mostly by hand.

Wildflour offers a variety of loaves, ranging from the regular oatmeal bread and the nutritious Boogie Bread (seven grains) to gourmet choices such as roasted walnut and English cheddar bread. In addition to earning a living, Thomas says her reward is older people who say, "I remember good bread like this." Open Wednesday through Saturday, 8:00 A.M. to 3:00 P.M. Sunday brunch 10:00 A.M. to 2:00 P.M. during summer months. Phone (828) 749–9224.

A few miles into the country, in a totally different mood, the ***Orchard Inn,*** on US 176, sits atop the Saluda rise on eighteen wooded acres at an elevation of 2,500 feet. The inn comprises nine rooms in the main house plus four cottage suites, each with private bath, some with fireplace and whirlpool tub. Cottages have telephones. Kathy and Bob Thompson are the innkeepers. Kathy is one smart lady. She says some people come to the inn for a private getaway and others for a social experience as part of the inn. She and Bob took over Orchard Inn after ten years of visits as guests in the main house, but she understands why some people prefer the cottages. "Our job is to create a place for people to come and be together differently than they do in the real world," she says. The inn removes you from the real world with its quiet atmosphere and its mix of good art, antiques, and books. Orchard Inn serves a four-course dinner Tuesday through Saturday, with white linens, fresh flowers, and candlelight, on a glassed-in porch.

The inn has a good wine cellar and serves wine and beer. Jackets are suggested for men at dinner, furthering the sense of escaping the real world. Phone (828) 749–5471 or (800) 581–3800. Website: www.orchardinn.com.

A stop suggested by several readers of this book is ***Pearson's Falls,*** on Pearson Falls Road. This nature and wildlife preserve is a gift to the public owned and maintained by the Tryon Garden Club since 1929. It includes the 90-

foot falls, which you get to by a short trail of less than a half mile. The area is ideal for a picnic, a photo session, and a little walk. A nominal admission fee is charged. From March 1 to November 1, the preserve is open Tuesday through Saturday from 10:00 A.M. to 5:15 P.M., Sunday noon to 5:15 P.M., gates locked at 6:00 P.M. During the winter months the preserve is closed Monday and Tuesday, open Wednesday through Saturday 10:00 A.M. to 4:15 P.M., gates locked at 5:00 P.M. The preserve is closed completely from January 1 through January 14. No pets are allowed in the preserve. To get to the falls from Saluda, head toward Tryon on US 176. Just a couple miles past Orchard Inn, as you head down the mountain, you'll see a giant sign identifying Pearson's Falls Road and Pearson's Falls. Turn right. The entrance to the preserve is a mile farther in.

The 10-mile stretch of road from Saluda to ***Tryon*** is the ***Pacolet River Scenic Byway,*** which gives you glimpses of the Pacolet River, wonderful vistas, and historic sites as well as more waterfalls. Tryon is known as an equestrian center. The ***Foothills Equestrian Nature Center,*** 3381 Hunting Country Road (828–859–9021; Web site: www.fence.org) is a nature education and recreation center with 5 miles of trails for hiking and riding, horse stables, and family-oriented nature education programs and outdoor concerts. The programs are often seasonal, such as a kite-flying day and a Mother's Day celebration, and most are free.

Not far from the center, ***Pine Crest Inn,*** 200 Pine Crest Lane (828–859–9135 or 800–633–3001; Web site: www.pinecrestinn.com), has thirty-five rooms in a variety of buildings including the main inn, as well as a restaurant and business meeting rooms. The overall theme here is the English Country Hunt, probably due at least in part to the influence of earlier owners who were British. The restaurant serves new American-style cuisine, and all spirits are available at the Fox and Hounds bar. All rooms have private bath, television, telephone, and VCR players. Some have fireplaces and whirlpool baths.

Downtown Tryon is filled with quaint stores and antiques shops, many of them also reflecting the local interest in horses.

The High Country

The next drive you might make from Asheville continues north on the Blue Ridge Parkway to ***Mount Mitchell State Park,*** elevation 6,684 feet, the highest point in the eastern United States. You'll leave the parkway at milepost 355.4 to take State Highway 128 to the 1,500-acre wilderness park. It's a 5-mile drive to the peak, but it will feel a lot longer. The park has hiking trails, picnic areas, a visitor center with maps, camping areas, and a lookout tower from which you can see what must be the most stunning mountain views east of the

Mississippi. There are also a restaurant and a refreshment stand. Be careful while you're here. Mount Mitchell is named for Dr. Elisha Mitchell, who fell off the summit and died. Your falling off too probably wouldn't lead to getting the mountain renamed in your honor. Park hours vary depending on the weather and time of year. You can call ahead (828–675–4611).

The next step you might try along the parkway is at milepost 331, where State Highway 226 and State Road 1100 take you to Emerald Village near Little Switzerland. At Emerald Village, established on the site of the Old McKinney and Bon Ami mines, you can visit the ***North Carolina Mining Museum,*** which displays the tools used at the height of gem mining in the area. Outdoor displays and a printed trail guide explain the entire mining process, and you'll have the opportunity to look for your own emeralds, rubies, aquamarines, and the like. More vigorous tours through mines not previously open to the public, including a hot dog lunch, are available at scheduled times. If your gem hunting doesn't go well, you can pick up something at the shop or have a rough gem cut, polished, and set into a piece of jewelry. Other attractions include a fluorescent mineral display, railroad items, and a craft shop. Open from 9:00 A.M. to 5:00 P.M., April to November. Modest fee for mining tour. Phone (828) 765–6463. Web site: www.emeraldvillage.com.

From here you could return to the parkway or go north on US 221 to get to ***Linville Caverns*** and ***Linville Falls,*** just beyond the caverns. If you're back on the parkway, exit at milepost 317.4 and turn left on US 221. Linville Caverns lie under Humpback Mountain and were believed to be have been forgotten by the white race until about one hundred years ago, when fish that seemed to be swimming out of the mountains caught the attention of explorers. During the Civil War, deserters from troops on both sides hid in the caverns. Today the caverns are lit electrically, showing stalactites and stalagmites and trout that, having always swum in the dark, can't see. Guides lead the tours 2,000 feet underground, pointing out important features and answering questions. Admission $5.00 for adults, $4.00 for senior citizens, $3.00 for children ages five through twelve, free under five. Open June 1 through Labor Day from 9:00 A.M. to 6:00 P.M. Closed at 5:00 P.M. in April, May, September, and October and 4:30 P.M. in March and November. Open weekends only 9:00 A.M. to 4:30 P.M., January and February; closed Thanksgiving and Christmas. Phone (828) 756–4171.

Linville Falls comprises two waterfalls at Linville Gorge and a primeval canyon in the sizable wilderness area given to the Blue Ridge Parkway by John D. Rockefeller. The gorge is the deepest cut east of the Grand Canyon. There are hiking trails and picnic spots.

At a convenient spot where the Blue Ridge Parkway and US 221 meet, ***Parkview Lodge*** (Blue Ridge Parkway and US 221; 800–849–4452; Web site:

www.parkviewlodge.com) is a most un-chain-like place to stay. This is the full-time home of innkeepers Cindy and David Peters. Parkview Lodge consists of a series of knotty-pine paneled rooms in a long stone building and three cabins in the woods, all furnished with locally purchased pieces, old family items, and bed heads David built by hand. The atmosphere fits with the inn's Blue Ridge Parkway mountain location while offering more comfort than a tent or camper. Some of the lodge accommodations are especially designed for private, romantic getaways. Other rooms are basic, with recognizably old heaters and close quarters. But they're not boring. Rates include breakfast: homemade quiche made from eggs gathered at the Peters' hen house, which is open for children to see, and coffee made with beans ground on the premises. The lodge's main room, where breakfast is served, also has a wine shop, a cooler with forty brands of cold beer, and local arts and crafts.

Across the highway and back a gravel road into the woods, ***Linville Falls Trailer Lodge and Campground*** (Gurney Franklin Road; 828–765–2681; Web site: www.linvillefalls.com), has nice sites for RVs of all sizes as well as a section for tent sites. The bathhouses are clean, with plenty of hot water, and laundry facilities are available at the small campground store and office. In warm months, each campsite is marked with a hanging basket of blooming flowers.

A little jog off US 221, onto State Highway 194 leads into the little community of ***Crossnore,*** with a population of just a few hundred friendly people. This is not a place that generally makes it into guide books, because it is not tourist-oriented, but it is known for the ***Weaving Room and Gallery*** (100 D. A. R. Drive; 828–733–4660), a handweaving center with a gift shop featuring Appalachian crafts as well as woven goods. The operation was founded in 1920 as a way to raise money for the Crossnore School. This school was run by several committed women as a way to educate children in Appalachia, for whom few opportunities existed. The school had a boarding section as well as classrooms. In addition to weaving, the sale of old clothes was a source of revenue for the school. Today sales from the weaving room and a large thrift shop still benefit Crossnore School students.

Still moving north along the parkway, you'll come to ***Grandfather Mountain,*** where, if you've got the nerve for it, you can walk across the ***Mile-High Swinging Bridge,*** a 218-foot suspension bridge between two peaks that sways in the wind. Should you quite sensibly prefer to put your feet on something more solid, Grandfather Mountain has lots of hiking trails. You'll need to pick up a moderately priced permit and a trail map at the entrance. This is the area where the ***Scottish Highland Games,*** open to the public, are held the second weekend in July every year. It is also a spot that attracts hang gliders. Open from 8:00 A.M. to dusk summers; closed at 5:00 P.M. in winter. Admission is $12.00 for adults, $6.00 for children aged four to twelve. Phone (828) 733–4337 or (800) 468–7325. Web site: www.grandfather.com.

A few minutes farther brings you to U.S. Highway 321 and the ***Blowing Rock,*** a cliff 4,090 feet above sea level that overhangs Johns River Gorge, 3,000 feet below, at the town of Blowing Rock. Because of the way the gorge is shaped and overhung, air blows upward, making snow appear to fall upside down and throwing upward light objects tossed over the edge. According to the legend of Blowing Rock, a Cherokee brave leaped to his death here to keep his tribe from making him return to the plains, leaving his Chickasaw wife behind. She prayed to the Great Spirit until the sky turned red and the wind blew her brave back up onto the rock. A wind has blown up from the valley ever since. A moderate admission is charged. Hours vary with the season and the weather. For details call (828) 295–7111. Web site: www.theblowingrock.com.

By the time you get to Blowing Rock, the children will probably have heard of ***Tweetsie Railroad,*** a family theme park that has been operating in North Carolina since 1956. It's touristy but kind of fun. Coal-fired steam engines pull the train of open cars through 3 miles of staged events: a train robbery, an Indian raid, and so on. Also, a chairlift carries you up to Mouse Mountain, where you can pan for gold and walk through the petting farm. Another section of the park duplicates a country fair of the early 1900s, right down to the cotton candy. Among other features are an ice-cream parlor, a jail, and a fire-

Tweetsie Railroad

house. Moderately high admission is charged. Open daily from Memorial Day through October from 9:00 A.M. to 6:00 P.M., with shorter hours and some features closed weekdays after Labor Day. The days and hours of operation here can, as one employee put it, "change at any time," so do call ahead (828–264–9061 or 800–526–5740). Web site: www.tweetsie.com.

A luxury-class place to stay right in Blowing Rock is the ***Inn at Ragged Gardens,*** 203 Sunset Drive (828–295–9703; Web site: http://ragged-gardens.com). The original stone structure was built in the late 1890s as a summer cottage. In later years it operated as a boarding house, then a bed-and-breakfast lodge. In 1996, the place was renovated and opened as a small inn. Successive renovations and expansion have turned it into a first-class inn with eleven rooms, each with private bath and fireplace, some with Jacuzzi, some with sitting rooms, some with balconies. The inn has a fine restaurant, Heirlooms. Offerings from the professional culinary team and a knowledgeable wine steward rise above the norm for this area. Rates include full gourmet breakfast, refreshments, wine, and hors d'oeuvre hour.

Just outside of town, ***Cliff Dwellers Inn,*** 116 Lakeview Terrace (800–322–7380; Web site: www.cliffdwellers.com), offers some of the best vistas in an area known for great mountain views. The inn is just a mile south of the Blue Ridge Parkway, off US 321. But this place has none of the closed-in feel of many mountain cabins. The inn has twenty rooms, each with private bath, TV, telephone, and refrigerator, plus three suites, all with gas log fireplaces. Two suites have whirlpools. The guest rooms are unusually spacious, with large windows to take advantage of the mountain views, and airy, cheerful furnishings that emphasize the light. Balconies with rocking chairs run the length of the building. Look down from the sundeck onto the rock garden; from various other perches see Lake Chetola and the outlet Shoppes on the Parkway, across US 321. From here it's a quick drive to Tweetsie Railroad and the town of Blowing Rock. You are also just 8 miles south of Boone, a commercial resort area where you'll find lots of motels, which, though out of spirit with the off-the-beaten-path traveler, are easy and comfortable when you're tired and just need to sleep.

A fun stop at 175 Mystery Hill Lane in Blowing Rock is the ***Appalachian Heritage Museum,*** in what used to be the home of the Dougherteys, who founded Appalachian State University. This is on US 321/21 North. The home is decorated authentically in turn-of-the-century furnishings and shows how mountain families lived in the early 1900s. Sometimes the museum holds demonstrations of mountain crafts or cooking. There's a separate exhibit of Native American artifacts on a lower level in the building. The museum is open every day from 8:00 A.M. to 8:00 P.M. from May through September, from 9:00

A.M. to 5:00 P.M. other months. Museum admission by donation, a modest fee for the Native American exhibit. For a schedule of demonstrations call (828) 264–4726 or (828) 264–2792.

Breakfast in downtown Blowing Rock, at ***Sonny's Grill,*** is an intensely local experience. The area has more popular tourist restaurants, but Sonny's, on Main Street in the center of town, is where you're most likely to find the folks who actually live in Blowing Rock. You'll find Sonny's in a small cinderblock building painted gray with no visible street address. Inside, diners sit at Formica tables or, if alone, at the counter, from where they can watch the bacon frying and the eggs flipping. This is the kind of place where people gossip about local events, talk about who went to Cherokee to play the slot machines over the weekend, and joke among themselves. And they welcome strangers, at least those who come in smiling. Sonny's starts serving breakfast early in the morning—an exact time isn't posted—and continues into lunch. One of the cooks says he flips burgers until about 2:00 P.M. Call (828) 295–7577.

When you have more energy, save it to drive on up into ***Valle Crucis,*** close to Boone but totally unlike it in nature. Although the little town sees hundreds and hundreds of visitors, it manages to continue operating and looking like a small town. Its history dates back to 1780, when Samuel Hix, the first known white settler in Valle Crucis, staked a claim to 1,000 acres. Later he traded the land for a gun, a dog, and a sheepskin. Eventually it became an Episcopal mission, named Valle Crucis because three creeks came together in the shape of a cross. Today the mission serves as a retreat for many church denominations.

notinkansas anymore,toto

The Land of Oz Theme Park, in the Beech Mountain ski area, west of Boone on US 321, was popular several decades ago but has since fallen out of fashion and closed, except for the first weekend in October, when visitors come into the park to mingle with Tin Man and Dorothy and the other Oz characters wandering along the Yellow Brick Road, investigating the old Kansas farmhouse that still has remnants of its 1930s decor, and indulging in quirky nostalgia. For details call (828) 884–5304.

People stop most often at the ***Mast Store,*** on State Highway 112/194, an authentic general store listed on the National Register of Historic Places, which still sells penny candy, seeds, leather boots, Woolrich sweaters, flannel shirts, long johns, and about everything else you can think of, mostly stacked, not too neatly, along wooden shelves. The store sends out a mail-order catalog reminiscent of early L. L. Bean. The Mast General Store has a couple of other locations, but this is the original 1883 landmark, listed on the National Register of Historic Places as one of the best remaining examples of an old country store. Call (828) 963–6511. Web site: www.mastgeneralstore.com.

The ***Mast Farm Inn,*** not associated with the store, is just outside the village on State Road 1112 (828–963–5857 or 888–963–5857). It's one of the most pleasant places in the area to stay, and a night's accommodation includes breakfast. Dinner is served at small tables suited to the size of your party, and the menu is a la carte, by reservation. The owners call the food "southern gourmet." It includes sautéed shrimp, trout prepared in various ways, and such favorites as grits with sautéed shrimp and white cheddar. Many vegetables and herbs come from organic gardens on the property. Of the desserts, fruit cobblers are the most popular. Mast Farm is also on the National Register of Historic Places as a restored, mountain homestead, comprising a springhouse, icehouse, washhouse, barn, blacksmith shop, gazebo, and cabin, in addition to the inn. Sleeping here is quiet and comfortable. The antiques are sparingly arranged to avoid a sense of clutter. Web site: www.mastfarminn.com.

The Foothills

Instead of heading north from Asheville, you may choose to start east toward the foothills and the Piedmont. A drive of about forty minutes on US 74, heading southeast from Asheville, takes you to the little vacation community of ***Lake Lure.*** Everything centers on the 1,500-acre lake, which has 27 miles of shoreline. The area is surrounded by the Blue Ridge Mountains. It's in the heart of the thermal belt, where the climate is almost always a bit milder than the extremes of heat and cold in the rest of North Carolina. The temperate climate makes Lake Lure excellent for boating, fishing, hiking, and horseback riding year-round. Lake Lure, Chimney rock, and Bat Cave, three tourist towns, run together one after another along the narrow mountain road.

Because of the temperate climate, the lake, and the views, this area has several places to stay that are destinations in themselves, away from the downtown shops.

Lodge on Lake Lure, 361 Charlotte Drive (800–733–2785; Web site: www.lodgeonlakelure.com), has a long history as a place for casual retreat, conducive to meeting new people and relaxing near the water. The building first served as a retreat for North Carolina highway patrolmen in the late 1920s, then as a vacation spot for members of the U.S. Army Air Corps, before becoming a bed-and-breakfast inn. The lodge has wormy chestnut paneling, a massive stone fireplace in the great room, a sun porch where breakfast is served, and fine views of the lake and mountains. In recent years a new owner bought the property and put a lot of money into refurbishing, upgrading, and expanding the place, putting in new, modern bathrooms, enlarging guest rooms and soundproofing the walls. Each of the sixteen rooms has a private bath, TV/VCR, telephone, and dataport; some have a large tub or Jacuzzi, some a fireplace, some a balcony or deck. Four of the rooms are in a contemporary style house next door and offer greater privacy. Dinner is available at the lodge weekend nights. The cuisine is upscale American. The wine list features South African wines.

A sister inn owned by the same people offers an entirely different ambience. ***Ivivi Lake and Mountain Lodge,*** 161 Waterside Drive (866–224–7740; Web site: www.ivivilodge.com), Ivivi overlooks Lake Lure, the Blue Ridge Mountains, and golf courses. The building has floor-to-ceiling windows letting in light and framing views in every direction. "Ivivi" is a South African word meaning "first light of day," a moment when the Zulu warriors believe magic happens and the world is in perfect balance. The lodge tries to create that moment and keep it going all day, every day, with its panoramic views, contemporary, mostly windows architecture, and interior decor. Everything in the inn comes from South Africa, where the owner lives: art, furniture, dishes, firm mattresses and silk bedspreads, even bathroom fixtures. Each of the seven guest rooms is named for a South African animal and has a picture with a short description of that animal on the wall. In common areas, portraits of Nelson Mandela and pictures of South African street scenes mingle with African artifacts and sculpture. A large stone fireplace dominating the living room is flanked by long, soft couches and pillows in shades of gold, orange, and cream, reflecting the colors in an ornament above the firebox. The result is exotic, a little unusual to the American eye, and luxuriously comfortable. Ivivi offers a variety of package activities, including golf and massage.

Nearby, ***Hickory Nut Gap Inn,*** US 64, Chimney Rock Road, Bat Cave (828–625–9108; Web site: www.hickorynutgapinn.com), sits on a mountaintop, elevation 2,200 feet, in a spot where you can look out over mountains in all directions and not see another manmade structure. The inn was built in the 1950s as a wealthy man's mountain retreat. Later it served as a gathering place for the rock group Lynrd Skynrd, and memorabilia from their activities are still on the walls in one hallway. It's been an inn open to the public for more than two decades. The inn has six guest rooms, each with private bath, and a long great room dominated by a cathedral ceiling and stone fireplace. The wood paneling throughout the inn celebrates the diversity of trees that have grown in the North Carolina mountains and was cut on the property. Each room is finished in a different wood: maple, cherry, poplar, black walnut, and red and white oak, as well as cedar in the closets. A screened porch running the length of the building makes a fine place to sit and watch hummingbirds. Breakfast is served on a glassed-in porch that looks over the perennial gardens and into the woods. Hickory Nut Gap Inn is closed during some winter months.

For hiking you have your choice of hundreds of trails. Organized hikes leave from ***Chimney Rock Park*** (828–625–9611 or 800–277–9611), located on US 64/74 in Chimney Rock, a private park with hiking trails, easier paths, and even an elevator to the top. From the top you can look down and see Lake Lure and mountains in all directions. Hickory Nut Falls, one of the highest waterfalls in the East, is on the grounds. The park is open daily from 8:30 A.M. to 5:30 P.M. during summer months, closes at 4:30 P.M. as days grow shorter. In bad weather the park closes. Rates vary seasonally. For simpler hiking you can ask almost any local person to recommend a favorite trail. These personal favorites are loosely kept secrets because no one wants them to become overrun with lookey-loos and littered with aluminum cans, but locals gladly share the information with anyone who cares enough to ask personally. Many climactic scenes of the film the *Last of the Mohicans,* starring Daniel Day-Lewis, were filmed at Chimney Rock. Web site: www.chimneyrockpark.com.

The town marina, on the lake and right next to US 64/74A, has boats for rent, and ***Lake Lure Tours*** runs hourly tours and twilight and dinner cruises. Phone (877) 386–4255 or (828) 625–1373. Web site: www.lakelure.com.

From here it's an easy drive up either US 74A or State Road 9 to I–40, where you'll find ***Black Mountain,*** an interesting village that was once a Cherokee Indian center and now is a thriving community specializing in all kinds of top-quality arts and crafts. The town has taken to calling itself "the front porch of western North Carolina," a name that seems to suit the peaceful but interesting atmosphere of the community.

In May and October Black Mountain sponsors the Mountain Music Festival, during which musicians play the old mountain music on dulcimers, fiddles, bagpipes, and mandolins. In August the Sourwood Festival features more music and dancing and a large arts and crafts show. These events are fun; they're also well attended, so if you have any notion of being in Black Mountain when they occur, you will need to arrange for lodging well ahead of time.

The ***Black Mountain Inn,*** 718 Old Highway 70 (800–735–6128 or 828–669–6528; Web site: www.blackmountaininn.com), has seven guest rooms and a suite. The building was once a studio and retreat where artists and writers such as Norman Rockwell and John Steinbeck spent time. The decor is casual country; the breakfasts are buffet-style, with home-baked breads and homemade granola.

The ***Red Rocker Inn,*** 136 North Dougherty Street (888–669–5991 or 828–669–5991; Web site: www.redrockerinn.com), is a long-established, seventeen-room inn long known for its food, served in portions that leave guests needing a walk after dinner. The rooms all have private baths and in cool weather a fire in the great room. The proprietors take special pride in the long row of red rocking chairs on the porch and go so far as repainting them regularly to keep them looking bright and shiny.

When the Red Rocker Inn is full, the folks there recommend the ***Inn Around the Corner,*** 109 Church Street (800–393–6005 or 828–669–6005; Web site: www.innaroundthecorner.com). This is a more recently established bed-and-breakfast operation in a residential part of town, in the same block as a church. The restored 1915 Victorian inn has five rooms and two luxury suites, all with private bath, as well as sleeping space on the upstairs porches. This place is ideally set up for families. It has a full kitchen available for guests, and the restaurants and shops of downtown are a quick walk away. Rates include an ample breakfast.

Visiting the ***Song of the Wood,*** at 203 West State Street, a workshop and salesroom devoted to dulcimers and unusual string instruments and their music, leaves you feeling exhilarated and refreshed. Jerry Read Smith makes hammered dulcimers and the even more unusual bowed psaltery, a small triangular instrument played with a violin-type bow, similar to a medieval bowed harp. JoAnn, Jerry's sister, manages the showroom. Everything about the shop is devoted to keeping the old music alive, producing fine-quality handmade instruments, and surrounding you with music.

You'll first be attracted by the music coming through outside speakers. When you get inside, they'll play lots more music for you. You may hear the music from their independent record albums, *The Strayaway Child, Homecoming, One Wintry Night,* and *Heartdance.* The shop sells a highly personal selection of other tapes and albums, mainly hammered dulcimer music, piano music, and Celtic music. The shop is light and airy, with instruments on the walls, a fuel-efficient wood-burning stove, and a mountain rocker. You're invited to sit down and try any of the instruments or listen to the recorded music. If you're interested and ask, you can almost always manage to be shown through the design studio and workshop in a building about twenty minutes away and have the whole process explained to you. Open from 10:00 A.M. to 5:00 P.M. Monday through Saturday. Phone (828) 669–7675. Web site: www.songofthewood.com.

As for shopping, the streets are lined with crafts shops, antiques shops and antiques malls, and a craft co-op. For instance, on Cherry Street, the ***Seven Sisters Gallery and Shop*** (828–669–5107) is notable for its fine selection of pottery, jewelry, fiber art, wood crafts, and glass art. This shop is open from

10:00 A.M. to 5:00 P.M. Monday through Saturday and until 7:00 P.M. in summer; 1:00 to 5:00 P.M. Sunday. And on Sutton Avenue the ***Old Depot*** (828–669–6583), a nonprofit arts and crafts center of the Swannanoa Valley, is located in the old Southern Railway Depot. The building, constructed in 1893, was turned into a crafts center in 1976. Classes, demonstrations, and crafts sales are all held here. The center is not open in winter, and hours in spring, summer, and fall may vary, so call ahead.

In the old Black Mountain Fire Department building, the ***Swannanoa Valley Museum,*** 223 West State Street (828–669–9566; Web site: www.swannanoavalleymuseum.org), focuses intensely on local history from the Stone Age to the present. For instance, exhibits depict the lives of Native Americans, early settlers, the coming of the railroad, and Billy Graham and other famous valley personalities. One of the museum's most popular programs is a series of hikes to points of historical interest in the valley. To participate in a hike, call for details. The museum isn't open in winter because it's too costly to heat the big building. It is open April through October, Tuesday through Saturday, 10:00 A.M. to 5:00 P.M., Sunday 1:00 to 5:00 P.M.

Immediately after Black Mountain, you come to ***Old Fort,*** an area that was still considered Cherokee Indian land for some time after white pioneers began pushing in during the mid-1770s. At the beginning of the American Revolution, General Griffith Rutherford assembled 2,500 troops to attack the Cherokees, who seemed to be siding with the British. Afterward the Indians conceded a huge portion of land, a pattern that was repeated often up to the time of the Trail of Tears in 1838. In subsequent years the Western North Carolina Railroad became important here. The ***Mountain Gateway Museum,*** in the 100 block of Water Street, tells the story, as do the Stepp and Morgan cabins that were moved here later. The site is a branch of the North Carolina Museum of History. It's not a big, splashy place and deserves your attention for that very reason. Admission is free. Open daily from 9:00 A.M. to 5:00 P.M. except opens at noon on Mondays; Sunday from 2:00 to 5:00 P.M. (828–668–9259). Web site: www.ncmuseumofhistory.org.

An outdoor treat in the same area is the ***Catawba Falls Trail,*** a special place that Eleanor Brawler wrote about for the Charlotte Observer. The main falls are the headwaters of the Catawba River. You'll find Catawba River Road at the Old Fort exit off I–40. Follow the road through 3 miles of farmland, where you'll come to a small bridge and a private road at a tree farm. Cross the street to the right bank, walk past an old dam about a mile on, and when the path ends, cross the stream again, to the left bank. Here you should be able to hear the falls, and you'll come to a trail and then a clearing, where you'll find the waterfalls, falling from 220 feet above you. If you're hesitant about hiking into unfamiliar territory, ask in town for advice. Local people know the area.

Brawler suggests a second, shorter hike in the Falls Branch area, to see falls so little known they aren't even named. At Marion go north from I–40 on US 221/Highway 226, crossing the Catawba River and passing the River Breeze Restaurant. Drive 5.5 miles after crossing the river. Turn left at the Woodlawn Motel and continue on 0.8 mile. The paved road ends. Bear left at the fork on a dirt road far enough to park. At the little bridge you'll find a trail to the right that wanders through the rhododendrons beside a mountain stream. At the next fork bear left again to see the falls. The area is also rich in wildflowers.

After these adventures return to I–40 and drive on to where Highway 226 intersects I–40 at Glenwood. From here, you can enjoy a beautifully scenic drive to ***Polkville*** while you also enjoy a good brisk sit. This is one of the prettiest drives in the state.

From Polkville you might want to take a quick drive north on State Highway 10 into the little village of ***Casar***—pronounced *KAYser,* population about 340. It's a place you'd never know about unless someone told you. Elizabeth Sturgeon, a woman who was raised here, remembers every quaint detail. The people who founded the town meant to call it "Caesar," but somehow they got the spelling wrong, and it's been Casar ever since. Until recently, all the major roads were dirt; even today they are not all paved. When the roads came into the center of this little spot, a stop sign stood—most of the time. Every Saturday night one old gentleman who didn't navigate too well when he was in his cups (homemade 'shine—it was a dry area) ran into it and knocked it down. Every Monday morning, someone put it up again.

Even into our high-tech age, Casar has been a place where electricity, telephones, and indoor plumbing were frills, luxuries nobody wanted. Hamburgers and hot dogs were unknown. Today, Elizabeth estimates, most people have power and plumbing. You still could have trouble over the hamburgers and hot dogs with the older folks.

In the center of town you can see what used to be Tom Hoyle's grocery store, where he accepted eggs and chickens in payment for flour and other merchandise.

The school used to serve grades one through twelve and have a phenomenal basketball team. School started early in the season and closed for six weeks during cotton-picking time because all the children, generally ten to twelve to a family, were needed to work in the fields you see around the school. Elizabeth still has her cotton-picking sack. If you look behind the school, you can find the place on the bank where the kids ran down to the store to buy penny suckers with coconut in them.

Elizabeth doesn't live in Casar any more, but she goes back often and finds it only a little changed—more modern in its technology, but the same warm little place as far as its people go. Park your car and walk around awhile. Elizabeth says, "You might get looked at, but somebody will come to see if you need help."

Places to Stay in the Mountains

ASHEVILLE

Biltmore Village Inn
119 Dodge Street
Asheville 28803
(866) 274–8779

Cedar Crest Victorian Inn
674 Biltmore Avenue
Asheville 28003
(800) 252–0310

Flint Street Inns
116 Flint Street
Asheville 28801
(800) 234–8172

Old Reynolds Mansion
100 Reynolds Heights
Asheville 28804
(800) 709–0496

Richmond Hill Inn
87 Richmond Hill Drive
Asheville 28806
(888) 742–4553

BALSAM

Balsam Mountain Inn
68 Seven Springs Drive
Balsam 28707
(800) 224–9498

BLACK MOUNTAIN

The Inn Around the Corner
109 Church Street
Black Mountain 28711
(800) 735–6128

Red Rocker Inn
136 North Dougherty Street
Black Mountain 28711
(888) 669–5991

BLOWING ROCK

Cliff Dwellers Inn
116 Lakeview Terrace
Blowing Rock 28605
(800) 322–7380

The Inn at Ragged Gardens
203 Sunset Drive
Blowing Rock 28605
(828) 295–9703

BOONE

High Country Inn
1785 Highway 105
Boone 28607
(800) 334–5605

Maple Lodge Bed and Breakfast Inn
152 Sunset Drive
Boone 28605
(828) 295–3331

BREVARD

Womble Inn
301 West Main Street
Brevard 28712
(888) 884–4770

BRYSON CITY

Nantahala Village Mountain Resort
9400 Highway 19 West
Bryson City 28712
(800) 438–1507

CULLOWEE

The River Lodge Bed and Breakfast
619 Roy Tritt Road
Cullowee 28723
(877) 384–4400

DILLSBORO

Applegate Inn Bed and Breakfast
163 Hemlock Street 28725
(800) 353–0377

FLAT ROCK

Highland Lake Inn
Highland Lake Road
Flat Rock 28731
(800) 762–1376

LAKE LURE

Lodge on Lake Lure
361 Charlotte Drive
Lake Lure 28746
(800) 733–2785

LINVILLE FALLS

Parkview Lodge
US 221 and Blue Ridge Parkway
Linville Falls 28647
(800) 849–4452

SALUDA

The Orchard Inn
Highway 176
Saluda 28773
(800) 581–3800

WAYNESVILLE

Herren House
94 East Street
Waynesville 28786
(800) 284–1932

Old Stone Inn
109 Dolan road
Waynesville 28786
(800) 432–8499

Places to Eat in the Mountains

ASHEVILLE

Blue Moon Bakery
60 Biltmore Avenue
Asheville 28801
(828) 252–6063

Gabrielle's at Richmond Hill
87 Richmond Hill Drive
Asheville 28806
(828) 252–7313

Laughing Seed Café
40 Wall Street
Asheville 28801
(828) 252–3445

BLOWING ROCK

Blowing Rock Cafe
Highway 321 at Sunset Drive
Blowing Rock 28605
(828) 295–9474

Sonny's Grill
Main Street
Blowing Rock 28605
(828) 295–7577

BREVARD

Jason's Main Street Grill
48 East Main Street
Brevard 28712
(828) 883–4447

Rocky's
36 South Broad Street
Brevard 28712
(828) 862–4700

Womble Inn
301 West Main Street
Brevard 28712
(888) 884–4770

DILLSBORO

Jarrett House
100 Haywood Road
Dillsboro 28725
(800) 972–5623

FLAT ROCK

Highland Lake Inn
Highland Lake Road
Flat Rock 28731
(800) 762–1376

LAKE LURE

Point of View Restaurant
Highway 64/74A
Lake Lure 28746
(828) 625–4380

SALUDA

Wildflour Bakery and Café
21 Main Street
Saluda 28773
(828) 749–9224

TRYON

Pine Crest Inn Dining Room
200 Pine Crest Lane
Tryon 28782
(828) 859–9135

WAYNESVILLE

Lomo Grill
44 Church Street
Waynesville 28786
(828) 452–1515

Maggie's Galley III
22 Howell Mill Road
Waynesville 28786
(828) 456–8945

Old Stone Inn
109 Dolan Road
Waynesville 28786
(800) 432–8499

THE MOUNTAIN WEB SITES

Cherokee History
www.cherokee-nc.com

Great Smoky Mountains
www.visitsmokies.org

List of Movies Shot in North Carolina Mountains
www.ncfilm.com

Official North Carolina Web Site
www.visitnc.com

Transylvania Waterfalls
www.visitwaterfalls.com/travel

Indexes

Entries for Inns, Bed-and-Breakfasts, Potteries, and Botanical Gardens and Arboretums appear in the special indexes on page 213 and 214.

GENERAL INDEX

INNS, BED-AND-BREAKFASTS

POTTERIES

BOTANICAL GARDENS AND ARBORETUMS

About the Author

Sara Pitzer has been writing about people, places, and food in the South since 1983. She is a newspaper columnist.

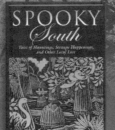

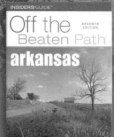

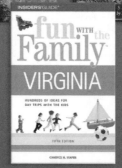

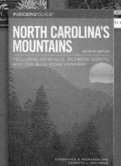